Online Learning Futures

Bloomsbury Higher Education Research

Series Editor: Simon Marginson

The Bloomsbury Higher Education Research series provides the evidence-based academic output of the world's leading research centre on higher education, the ESRC/RE Centre for Global Higher Education (CGHE) in the UK. The core focus of CGHE's work and of The Bloomsbury Higher Education Research series is higher education, especially the future of higher education in the changing global landscape. The emergence of CGHE reflects the remarkable growth in the role and importance of universities and other higher education institutions, and research and science, across the world. Corresponding to CGHE's projects, monographs in the series will consist of social science research on global, international, national and local aspects of higher education, drawing on methodologies in education, learning theory, sociology, economics, political science and policy studies. Monographs will be prepared so as to maximise worldwide readership and selected on the basis of their relevance to one or more of higher education policy, management, practice and theory. Topics will range from teaching and learning and technologies, to research and research impact in industry, national system design, the public good role of universities, social stratification and equity, institutional governance and management, and the cross-border mobility of people, institutions, programmes, ideas and knowledge. The Bloomsbury Higher Education Research series is at the cutting edge of world research on higher education.

Advisory Board:

Paul Blackmore, King's College London, UK; Brendan Cantwell, Michigan State University, USA; Gwilym Croucher, University of Melbourne, Australia; Carolina Guzman-Valenzuela, University of Chile, Chile; Glen Jones, University of Toronto, Canada; Barbara Kehm, University of Glasgow, UK; Jenny Lee, University of Arizona, USA; Ye Liu, King's College London, UK; Christine Musselin, Sciences Po, France; Alis Oancea, University of Oxford, UK; Imanol Ordorika, Universidad Nacional Autónoma de México, Mexico; Laura Perna, University of Pennsylvania, USA; Gary Rhoades, University of Arizona, USA; Susan Robertson, University of Cambridge, UK; Yang Rui, University of Hong Kong, Hong Kong; Pedro Teixeira, University of Porto, Portugal; Jussi Valimaa, University of Jyvaskyla, Finland; N.V. Varghese,

National University of Educational Planning and Administration, India; Marijk van der Wende, University of Utrecht, The Netherlands; Po Yang, Peking University, China; Akiyoshi Yonezawa, Tohoku University, Japan

Also available in the series:
The Governance of British Higher Education: The Impact of Governmental, Financial and Market Pressures, Michael Shattock and Aniko Horvath
Changing Higher Education in India, edited by Saumen Chattopadhyay, Simon Marginson and N.V. Varghese
Changing Higher Education for a Changing World, edited by Claire Callender, William Locke, and Simon Marginson
Changing Higher Education in East Asia, Simon Marginson and Xin Xu
Higher Education, State and Society, Lili Yang
The Governance of European Higher Education, Michael Shattock and Aniko Horvath
Challenging Approaches to Academic Career-Making, Celia Whitchurch, William Locke and Giulio Marini
Universities and Regions, Michael Shattock and Aniko Horvath

Online Learning Futures

An Evidence-Based Vision for Global Professional Collaboration on Sustainability

Eileen Kennedy and Diana Laurillard

BLOOMSBURY ACADEMIC
LONDON • NEW YORK • OXFORD • NEW DELHI • SYDNEY

BLOOMSBURY ACADEMIC
Bloomsbury Publishing Plc
50 Bedford Square, London, WC1B 3DP, UK
1385 Broadway, New York, NY 10018, USA
29 Earlsfort Terrace, Dublin 2, Ireland

BLOOMSBURY, BLOOMSBURY ACADEMIC and the Diana logo
are trademarks of Bloomsbury Publishing Plc

First published in Great Britain 2024

Copyright © Eileen Kennedy and Diana Laurillard, 2024

Eileen Kennedy and Diana Laurillard have asserted their right under the Copyright, Designs and Patents Act, 1988, to be identified as Author of this work.

For legal purposes the Acknowledgements on pp. xvii–xviii constitute an extension of this copyright page.

Series design by Adriana Brioso
Cover image © Setthasith Wansuksri/EyeEm/Getty Images

All rights reserved. No part of this publication may be reproduced or transmitted in any form or by any means, electronic or mechanical, including photocopying, recording, or any information storage or retrieval system, without prior permission in writing from the publishers.

Bloomsbury Publishing Plc does not have any control over, or responsibility for, any third-party websites referred to or in this book. All internet addresses given in this book were correct at the time of going to press. The author and publisher regret any inconvenience caused if addresses have changed or sites have ceased to exist, but can accept no responsibility for any such changes.

A catalogue record for this book is available from the British Library.

A catalog record for this book is available from the Library of Congress.

ISBN: HB: 978-1-3503-2423-7
        ePDF: 978-1-3503-2424-4
        eBook: 978-1-3503-2425-1

Series: Bloomsbury Higher Education Research

Typeset by Integra Software Services Pvt. Ltd.

 Online resources to accompany this book are available at bloomsbury.pub/online-learning-futures. If you experience any problems, please contact Bloomsbury at: onlineresources@bloomsbury.com

To find out more about our authors and books visit www.bloomsbury.com and sign up for our newsletters.

Contents

List of figures		xi
List of tables		xii
Series editor's foreword		xiii
Acknowledgements		xvii

1	Online Learning Futures: Quality, Scale, Equity and Sustainability	1
	Introduction	1
	Why the focus on professional collaboration?	2
	Why global?	5
	The principles guiding our work	7
	The evidence-based approach	7
	How do we do 'collaborative professional development'?	10
	What is the narrative line of the book?	10
	Summary	13
2	What Is Quality Online Learning?	15
	Introduction	15
	What counts as a high-quality learning experience?	15
	The different levels of quality in the move to online learning	20
	Using a learning design tool to improve quality	24
	A quality process for improving the learning experience	28
	Making the move to online	35
	Questions and activities	35
3	What Can We Learn from the Rapid Shift Online During the COVID-19 Pandemic?	37
	A vision for digital tertiary education	37
	The transition to online learning after the COVID-19 pandemic	40
	Staff experiences of the rapid move to teaching online	42
	Learners' experiences: A need for communication and compassion	53
	Support for teachers to teach online	55

	Conclusions	57
	Questions and activities	58
4	How Well Does Online Learning Work at Scale?	59
	Introduction	59
	Interviews using the repertory grid technique	61
	Deep learning	64
	Applied learning	67
	Social learning	69
	Digital engagement as inclusive interactive learning	73
	Learning design	77
	Design implications	79
	Questions and activities	81
5	Balancing Learning Benefits and Teacher Workload for Quality Online Learning	83
	Introduction	83
	Tracking the learning benefits	84
	Problems with the current costing models for teaching	85
	Features of a useful costing model for teaching	89
	Future modelling	102
	Concluding points	105
	Questions and activities	106
6	Co-designing Collaborative Open Online Learning for Professional Communities	107
	Introduction	107
	The non-negotiable features of scaling up open, online professional development	108
	The learning needs of professionals in emergency situations	110
	The importance of co-design	113
	Social and collaborative learning design	114
	Evaluating social and collaborative learning features	121
	Scaling online community knowledge building with the CoMOOC model	127
	Questions and activities	129

7	The Evidence of Impact for Co-designed Massive Open Online Collaborations on the Sustainable Development Goals	131
	Introduction	131
	The UN SDGs as a framework for professional development: A critique	133
	Collaborative knowledge building for the teaching community	138
	How CoMOOCs can improve professional practices	140
	Evaluating impact on knowledge and practice	144
	Future leadership	148
	Questions and activities	150
8	Transformative Online Education in Challenging Contexts	151
	Introduction	151
	Transforming the role of the university to deliver on the SDGs	152
	Digital support for teaching in challenging environments	154
	Co-designing 'Transforming Education in Challenging Environments'	157
	Transformative education with technology in crisis contexts	168
	Elevating the teacher in challenging environments	172
	Conclusion	176
	Questions and activities	177
9	Planning for an Evidence-Based Approach to Co-designed Massive Open Online Collaborations (CoMOOCs)	179
	Introduction	179
	An evaluation framework for online learning	180
	Using a Theory of Change for accountable impact	184
	Building community knowledge	195
	Conclusions	200
	Questions and activities	201
10	Harnessing the Potential of Online Learning to Democratize Knowledge Exchange	203
	Introduction	203
	Knowledge exchange and the future of tertiary education	203
	What makes a CoMOOC an important model for the UN SDGs?	206
	A more equitable future for CoMOOCs	207

Roles and responsibilities for tertiary education in a
    global digital world 208
  Are CoMOOCs sustainable? 210
  Over to you 212
  Questions and activities 213

Appendices 215
  Appendix A: CoMOOCs referred to in this book 215
  Appendix B: Definitions of 'learning types' in terms of
    typical technologies used 216
  Appendix C: Rubric for evaluating a learning design 217
  Appendix D: Learning designs for understanding [the Topic] 219
Notes 225
References 229
Index 243

Figures

1.1 Cycles of CoMOOC Design-Based Research showing cycles of design and redesign within and between each CoMOOC — 9
2.1 The Conversational Framework representing the teaching-learning process in action (with numbered cycles as below) — 16
2.2 Comparing (a) an original generic design with (b) a specific adaptation to a finance topic, showing: similar guidance text; the same digital tool; changing an individual Practice step to a Collaboration among four students; changing an investigate step to a Practice of the presentation; and adding a Discussion — 32
4.1 A completed repertory grid — 63
5.1 Shows (a) the overall proportion of learning types for the f2f session and (b) the overall proportion when converted to online, increasing the proportion of active learning through Practice, Discussion, and Collaboration and reducing Acquisition — 92
5.2 Both learning designs show the same proportion of acquisition learning but there is one hour more of supported learning for the blended design; (a) and (b) show the distributions of types of learning, with additional collaboration possible in the blended design — 95–96
5.3 Comparing teaching time and learning benefits for a lecture given on campus and online, where the total supported learning time and the proportion of active learning is much higher for the latter — 99
6.1 An activity in Transforming Education for Challenging Environments CoMOOC — 119
9.1 The contrast in value between (a) a top-down hierarchy with no internal feedback and (b) a hierarchical network of two-way communication in which the top of the hierarchy can learn from the lower levels — 187
9.2 An iterative co-design theory of change for TPD — 189
9.3 Roadmap of activities for integrating citizen science into SDG reporting. Upper box, global activities. Lower box, national activities — 198
D.1 Representation of the learning experience (f2f) — 221
D.2 Representation of the learning experience (online) — 224

Tables

2.1	The main screens of the Learning Designer	27
5.1	Comparing the main parameters of teaching cost against student fee	86
5.2	Comparing campus and online estimates of teacher time and learning time, for 3 runs. Teacher time increases 7% for online with a 50% increase in supported learning time	100
9.1	The Value Creation Framework as a guide to learning designs for a CoMOOC	181
9.2	From conventional to open methods of TPD and how to achieve them	186

Series editor's foreword

Online Learning Futures is the 9th book to be published in the Bloomsbury Higher Education Research book series. This series brings to the public, government and universities across the world the new ideas and research evidence being generated by researchers from the ESRC/OFSRE Centre for Global Higher Education*. The Centre for Global Higher Education (CGHE), a partnership of researchers from 11 UK and international universities, is the world's largest concentration of expertise in relation to higher education and its social contributions. The core focus of CGHE's work, and of the Bloomsbury Higher Education Research Series, is higher education, especially the future of higher education in the changing global landscape. Each year this mega-topic of 'higher education' seems to take on greater importance for governments, business, civil organisations, students, families and the public at large. In higher education much is at stake. The role and impact of the sector is growing everywhere. More than 235 million students enrol at tertiary level across the world, four fifths of them in degree programmes. Over 40 per cent of school leavers now enter some kind of tertiary education each year, though resources and quality vary significantly. In North America and Europe that ratio rises to four young people in every five. Universities and colleges are seen as the primary medium for personal opportunity, social mobility and the development of whole communities. About 2.5 million new science papers are published worldwide each year, and the role of research in industry and government continues to expand everywhere. In short, there is much at stake in higher education. It has become central to social, economic, cultural and political life. One reason is that even while serving local society and national policy, the higher education and research sectors are especially globalised in character. Each year six million students change countries in order to enrol in their chosen study programme, and a quarter of all published research papers involve joint authorship across national borders. In some countries fee-based international education is a major source of export revenues; while some other countries are losing talent in net terms each year. Routine cross-border movements of students, academics and researchers, knowledge, information and money help to shape not only nations but the international order itself. At the same time, the global higher education landscape is changing with compelling speed, reflecting larger economic, political and cultural shifts in the geo-strategic setting. Though research universities in the United States (especially) and UK remain strong in comparative terms, the worldwide map of power in higher education is becoming more plural. A larger range of higher education practices, including models of teaching/learning, delivery, institutional organisation and system, will shape higher education in future. Anglo-American (and Western) norms and models will be less dominant, and will themselves evolve. Rising universities and science in East Asia and Singapore are already reshaping the flow of knowledge and higher education. Latin America, South East Asia, India, Central Asia and the Arab nations have a growing global importance. The trajectories of education and research in Sub-Saharan Africa are crucial to state-building and community development. All of this has led to a more intensive focus on how higher education systems and institutions function and their value, performance, effectiveness, openness and sustainability. This in turn has made research on higher education more significant – both because it provides us with insights into one important facet of the human condition, and because it informs evidenced-based government policies and professional practices. CGHE opened in late 2015 and is currently funded until October 2023. The Centre investigates higher education using a range of social science disciplines including economics, sociology, political science and policy studies, psychology and anthropology, and uses a portfolio of quantitative, qualitative and synthetic-historical research techniques. It currently maintains 10 research projects, variously of between 18 months and eight years' duration, as well as smaller projects, and involves about 40 active affiliated individual researchers. Over its eight year span it is financed by about £10 million in funding from the UK Economic and Social Research Council, partner universities and other sources. Its UK researchers are drawn from the Universities of Oxford, Lancaster, Surrey, Bath and University College London. The headquarters of the centre are located at Oxford, and there are large concentrations of researchers at both Oxford and UCL. The current affiliated international researchers are from Hiroshima University in Japan, Shanghai Jiao Tong University in China, Lingnan University in Hong Kong, Cape Town University in South Africa, Virginia Tech in the United States and Technological University Dublin. CGHE also collaborates with researchers from many other universities across the world, in seminars, conferences and exchange of papers. It runs an active programme of global webinars. The Centre has a full agenda. The unprecedented growth of mass higher education, the striving for excellence and innovation in the research university sector and the changing global landscape pose many researchable questions for governments, societies and higher education institutions themselves. Some of these questions already figure in CGHE research projects. For example: What are the formative effects on societies and economies of the now much wider distribution of advanced levels of learning? How does it change individual graduates as people – and what does it mean when half or more of the workforce is higher educated and much more mobile; and when confident human agency has become widely distributed across civil and political society in nations with little state tradition, or where the main experience has been colonial or authoritarian rule? What does it mean when many more people are becoming steeped in the sciences, many others understand the world through the lenses of the social sciences or humanities, and a third group are engaged in neither? What happens to those parts of the population left outside the formative effects of higher education? What is the larger public role and contribution of higher education, as distinct from the private benefits for and private effects on individual graduates? What does it mean when large and growing higher education institutions have become the major employers in many locations and help to sustain community and cultural life, almost like branches of local government while also being linked to global cities across the world? And what is the contribution of higher education, beyond helping to form the attributes of individual graduates, to the development of the emerging global society? Likewise, the many practical problems associated with building higher education and science take on greater importance. How can scarce public budgets provide for the public role of higher education institutions, for a socially equitable system of individual access and for research excellence, all at the same time? What is the role for and limits of family financing and tuition loans systems? What is the potential contribution of private institutions, including for-profit colleges? In national systems, what is the best balance between research intensive and primarily teaching institutions, and between academic and vocational education? What are the potentials for technological delivery in extending access? What is happening in graduate labour markets, where returns to degrees are becoming more dispersed between families with differing levels of income, different kinds of universities and different fields of study? Do larger education systems provide better for social mobility and income equality? How does the internationalisation of universities contribute to national policy and local societies? Does mobile international education expand opportunity or further stratify societies? What are the implications of new populist tensions between national and global goals, as manifest for example in the tensions over Brexit in the UK and the politics of the Trump era in the United

States, for higher education and research? And always, what can national systems of higher education and science learn from each other, and how can they build stronger common ground? In tackling these research challenges and bringing the research to all, we are very grateful to have the opportunity to work with such a high-quality publisher as Bloomsbury. In the book series monographs are selected on the basis of their relevance to one or more of higher education policy, management, practice and theory. Topics range from teaching and learning and technologies, to research and its organisation, the design parameters of national higher education systems, the public good role of higher education, social stratification and equity, institutional governance and management, and the cross-border mobility of people, programmes and ideas. Much of CGHE's work is global and comparative in scale, drawing lessons from higher education in many different countries, and the centre's cross-country and multi-project structure allows it to tap into the more plural higher education and research landscape that has emerged. The book series draws on authors from across the world and is prepared for relevance across the world. CGHE places special emphasis on the relevance of its research, on communicating its findings and on maximising the usefulness and impacts of those findings in higher education policy and practice. CGHE has a relatively high public profile for an academic research centre and reaches out to engage higher education stakeholders, national and international organisations, policymakers, regulators and the broader public, in the UK and across the world. These objectives are also central to the book series. Recognising that the translation from research outputs to high-quality scholarly monographs is not always straightforward – while achieving impact in both academic and policy/practice circles is crucial – monographs in the Book Series are scrutinised critically before publication, for readability as well as quality. Texts are carefully written and edited to ensure that they have achieved the right combination of, on one hand intellectual depth and originality, on the other hand full accessibility for public, higher education and policy circles across the world.

Simon Marginson
Professor of Higher Education, University of Oxford, UK
Director, ESRC/OFSRE Centre for Global Higher Education

Acknowledgements

This book is the culmination of over ten years of collaborative work with many people around the world. We would like to acknowledge and thank everyone who has contributed to the ideas we are presenting here. We have been working with two research centres: the Centre for Global Higher Education (CGHE) and RELIEF, both funded by the Economic and Social Research Council (ESRC). Specifically, the research was supported by a series of grants: ES/M010082/1 Future of HE: Centre for Engaged Global Higher Education; ES/T014768/1 Centre for Global Higher Education 2020–2023; ESRC ES/P008003/1 RELIEF and ES/W007835/1 RELIEF II. This funding has been integral to getting this far.

Our colleagues at CGHE and RELIEF have given us their time, skill, ideas and support. We would like to thank the leadership of Prof Henrietta Moore (for RELIEF) and Prof Simon Marginson (for CGHE) and Prof Claire Callender (for CGHE at IOE). In addition, our colleagues at UCL Knowledge Lab have inspired us, listened to us and given us encouragement and constructive feedback, which has been critical to doing this research.

The CoMOOCs that we discuss in this book were created as part of our work in both Centres, and all were the result of collaborative effort. We would like to thank all the teaching colleagues who supported the development of our CoMOOC on teacher professional development for CGHE, and our co-researchers in the Future Education strand for RELIEF: Dr Mai Abu Moghli, Prof Elaine Chase, Rym El Moussaoui, Prof Tejendra Pherali and Prof Maha Shuayb. We would also like to thank all our collaborators in Lebanon. Despite the serious challenges facing Lebanon, we rarely encounter more generosity than from our Lebanese colleagues. We cannot name them all, but special mention goes to Prof Samar Zeitoun, the late Dr Rima Malek, our much missed colleague, both from Lebanese University, A/Prof Bahous and A/Prof Barbar Akle from Lebanese American University, Suha Tutnji, Jusoor, Dr Fadi Halabi, MAPs and Grace Sawan, CERD, all of whom have made significant contributions to supporting our work. We were also supported by many NGOs conducting vital work with refugee communities in Lebanon, particularly Multi-aid Programs (MAPs) and Jusoor.

Particular thanks to Dr Fadi Al Halabi (MAPs) and Suha Tujunji (Jusoor) for showing us how teachers-as-researchers can make such a difference in challenging environments, and to Grace Sawan (CERD) for her encouragement and endorsement.

Our research depended crucially on the two online learning platforms, FutureLearn (UK) and Edraak (Jordan), whose staff were always responsive and helped us to optimize the functionalities and overcome the technical barriers.

Finally, thanks to everyone who has participated in this research, and given us the gift of their time and thoughts. Without the contributions of everyone who has taken part in an interview, completed a survey, participated in a CoMOOC or went on to become a mentor, we would not have the research that is the bedrock of this book.

1

Online Learning Futures: Quality, Scale, Equity and Sustainability

Introduction

The possible futures for online learning received a remarkable uplift from the global tragedy of the COVID-19 pandemic. Universities, colleges and schools across the world had been experimenting with the new technologies throughout the first two decades of the twenty-first century, with occasional ambitious rhetoric but rather limp financial support from their governments. There was a general sense of potential, but not enough focus on making it work well to overcome the inevitable challenges and the ignorant myths that were being perpetrated about its value. In those twenty years online learning failed to become mainstream, and yet in the space of a few months, that was all there was. Online was the only safe space when the physical space was so dangerous.

When the potential became real teachers and students had no choice but to make it work as well as they could. The striking result was the professionalism of the teaching community, utterly committed to their students, achieved enough in their pivot to online to discover its merits as well as the obvious drawbacks. Within just a year or so many of the myths had been dispelled, and both teachers and students were saying they wanted more hybrid learning – both online and in-person – as the norm.

The possible futures for online learning have now been super-charged. The time is right to exploit its powers as a force for good. But where to prioritize?

For the United Nations Sustainable Development Goals (UN SDGs) the pandemic was a disaster. The UN's latest report on progress on all the SDGs documents how the gains of the previous few years have been reversed.[1] That in itself is an argument for where we prioritize the powers of online learning. Much of the natural and social science that underpins the actions to achieve all the SDGs comes from university research. Accelerating the changes in professional practices that could help to meet the 2030 goals must now be an imperative for universities, and yet professional development courses are not what we do. Very little of the professional development that would improve and develop new professional practices is carried out by universities – we could do more.

This defines the threads that run through the book. The priority is the professionals, because they can contribute a lot from their own experience and expertise, and they are in the right position on organizations to reach those who most need support in developing the new sustainability practices needed for the UN SDG framework: their own students, communities, employees or colleagues. No profession escapes this umbrella for urgent global action. In this chapter we present our overall argument.

Why the focus on professional collaboration?

The focus on professionals follows from our priorities above and derives from the need to support them in continuing to learn post-university. The tertiary education sector[2] knows that part of their function is to prepare students for the workplaces they will move into, but there is also the expectation that this responsibility does not end with graduation. There was a clear political focus on this around the turn of the century, as politicians argued that lifelong learning and higher education are indispensable to economic progress (Taylor & Watson, 1998). In rapidly developing national and global systems, learning must continue throughout the modern career. The term 'lifelong learning' has become a political aspiration in recent years, now enshrined in the 2016 UN SDG 4 to: *Ensure inclusive and quality education for all and promote lifelong learning.*[3] The term ranges widely across all forms of adult education (London, 2020), but for universities lifelong learning means especially: 'opening up to wider participation rather than fixing admission to level of qualification, allowing alternative models of access to a degree education throughout life, and supporting professional and community learning' (Yang, Schneller, & Roche, 2015). Our focus is the latter, which means that our target is professional learning for those who are in the kind of post, in any type of industry or organization, where they can expect to contribute to developing new knowledge and practices in response to the most challenging social, economic and environmental contexts. Could universities offer online courses to support them in this by updating their knowledge and practices based on current research findings?

When the learning is being done by professionals, we must acknowledge that they are already experienced and knowledgeable. The conventional modes of education are not appropriate because teachers do not expect to learn very much from their students. In the context of universities updating professionals on the current research in their field of work, it would be ill-advised for any course to ignore that knowledge. The mode of education must be more collaborative, enabling the 'teacher' to learn from the 'students' – so the orientation of both types of actor is different. The focus on professional collaboration is about the *co-development* of professional knowledge and practice.

In studies of continuing professional development (CPD) the language used from the employer side is often about human capital, employee development or company training, casting the learners as creatures of the organizations they work for, rather than as independent professionals, who might be managing their own career development. As employees, we are all subject to the organization's mission and strategy, and must adapt to the needs of current policy and practice. But the Human Resources (HR) responsibility now is to make sure that both sides of the employment interface understand and work to each other's needs (Mikołajczyk, 2022). Sometimes the employees are ahead of the HR demands. For example, teachers have been equipping themselves with IT skills well beyond those required by their university or college; the quality control manager may be well aware of the need to implement energy-saving techniques that the company strategy does not cover; the frontline health staff will be more aware of how the latest medication fails than is the departmental administrator. These are the committed professionals who not only grasp any offer of CPD, but will also seek it for themselves. They are valuable collaborators for a university researcher who wishes to gain impact for their research and feedback on the value of their findings. For this reason, we look for ways of offering CPD that are more about collaboration than knowledge transfer.

Twenty years into the twenty-first century the pressure of workload has increased for the majority of professionals and online communications reach into what used to be leisure time or family time. The trend towards hybrid working online and in work will continue, but we have yet to discern the overall effect on working hours. The expectation is that professionals will always have little time to spare for their own development and short courses will still be very short, often less than 20 hours, unlike normal academic courses, and therefore difficult to fit into accreditation frameworks. However, certification without assessment is the norm for short professional development courses run by either commercial providers or universities, and progress is being made to establish the concept of stackable micro-credentials into university practice (OECD, 2021). Micro-credentialing short learning experiences could offer credits which could be combined over time to obtain a qualification.

However, the first major barrier to promoting the idea of universities delivering large-scale professional development is that universities offer rather few courses that lie beyond traditional award-bearing qualifications. Many professionals are not interested in or have no time for award-bearing courses, especially if they require labour-intensive evaluation of the learner. In the UK the entire system (213 universities) offers only around four million days of CPD per year, and charges around £325 per day on average.[4] For some the fees are higher and it is a worthwhile income, but the average £3m per year of income is a very small proportion of an institution's total income. It is clearly not a strategic priority seen as critical to their growth and sustainability.

On the other hand, university researchers are committed to demonstrating research impact, on which future funding depends. Undergraduate courses that derive from research are critical to the nation's future, and a well-attended short course for the end-users of research outcomes is strong evidence of immediate impact if they are enabled to improve their practice as a result. In the UK only nine of the top-ranked universities are in the top forty of providers of CPD courses, according to the Higher Education Statistics Agency (HESA) data quoted above. The great majority of universities focus on teaching more than research, so the research universities have a responsibility to handle the professional development that derives from research.

The second major barrier to a focus on professional development and collaboration could be the reaction of employers who do not value external support as much as their own internally targeted interventions. There is a clear trend now towards more employee-driven ways of developing 'human capital', where the organization acts as a supportive partner with their employees, creating opportunities to develop through, for example, constructing knowledge sharing systems, making valuable content accessible and facilitating employee growth (Dachner, Ellingson, Noe, & Saxton, 2021). There is recognition in the field that more urgent action is needed, and a recent conference on 'Sustainability and organizational development' set out to address the reality that 'Companies and organizations face … large and fundamental changes in their way of operating if we are to meet the goals of 2030' (Stegeager & Thomassen, 2021, p. 150). One approach combined research on organizational learning and corporate entrepreneurship in an iterative process model for reflection and knowledge sharing with feedback to develop sustainability practices. The model gives strong representation to the employee voice (Brandi & Thomassen, 2021).

If organizations were to face up to the challenges of preparing their employees for meeting the SDGs in time, then this type of partnership between employer and employee for the benefit of both would be a significant driver of progress.

Employer take-up will depend to some extent on an organization's willingness to invest in professional development, and support for sustainability development will depend very much on their organizational strategy. The most likely to invest tend to be larger organizations, sensitive to the sustainability 'brand', with higher competence levels, prepared to follow external frameworks, and which have boards with more younger and female members (Rosati & Faria, 2018).

We can establish the need in terms of the UNSDG framework across all disciplines; there is demand from professionals anxious to update; there is the imperative of research impact; there is the value of engagement with professionals; and there are some precedents for this type of course. Our aim is to establish the evidence that a new model of professional collaboration on the large scale can work.

Why global?

The scale of the need for the collaborative professional development of new knowledge and practices is clear from the UNSDGs, whose scope is global. That is the moral imperative. For universities experiencing uncertain futures in many countries now, there is a clear economic imperative as well. Governments expect universities to deliver a highly skilled and world-competitive workforce through their teaching, and research outcomes that will contribute to the nation's greater prosperity. In the twenty-first century every country expects an economic return on their investment in higher education (Taylor & Watson, 1998).

Universities see themselves as having a key role to play in contributing to solving the grand challenges the twenty-first-century world has accumulated, as their mission statements imply (see Chapter 7). However, only two of the twenty THS top-ranked universities in the world[5] appear in the THS Impact rankings: University of Toronto at 90th and MIT at between 101 and 200th, out of the 1,406 that responded.[6] The rankings assess universities in terms of sustainability comparisons across research, stewardship, outreach and teaching. It is telling evidence that we are in the very early stages of matching our actions to our mission statements in this area. And these rankings are based on our strong point that university teaching dominates in providing the higher education that professionals will need if they are to master sustainability practices. As we saw above, the in-service professional development we provide makes a rather nugatory contribution in comparison with what we could do.

Universities across the world surely have the collective power to make a significantly larger-scale contribution to the lifelong education of the professional workforce in the innovative concepts and practices that derive from our research. In the social and natural sciences knowledge development is already global, Western-dominated at present, but that is changing rapidly (Marginson, 2021a). Global challenges seem to be accelerating beyond our means to cope with them. Tackling them will need universities to deliver the quality and reach they exemplified in responding to the 2020 pandemic. But not just in doing the science. It must be communicated as well and translated into practice by end-user professionals. For example, in the health sector alone, professionals number in the hundreds of millions. The global climate crisis affects professionals in the full range of companies and organizations – no-one is exempt. Those who need to understand and implement the new techniques and practices of sustainability number in the billions.

Universities have a special role in this global collaboration because in most countries they are close to the nation state and yet maintain a degree of independence that allows new knowledge to develop without undue influence. They are also practised at international collaboration, have developed the means to do it well and are committed to the values of openly shared knowledge and practice. Now we need the means to do this well on the very large scale.

We do have the technology. Massive open online courses (MOOCs) have been developed and promoted by many of the world's top universities over the last decade or so. They are short learning experiences that run on online platforms capable of serving 100,000s of learners on one course, and are open to all, in almost every country. Because they are massive, and free, or with low-cost premium versions, and therefore do not return funds to the universities that create them, they cannot support students, who need labour-intensive, and therefore expensive, personal nurturing. For professionals who have completed their basic higher education, and do not need personalized learning, they are an ideal format for postgraduation updating. However, employer take-up of MOOCs is very slow. A recent study of 28,000 learners in 127 countries sought to understand why so many (then 95 per cent) had no support from their companies to use MOOCs for their work-based development even though 'employees who enjoy organizational support for MOOCs are much less likely to want to use what they've learned to look for jobs at other companies', and are motivated by wanting to do a better job (Hamori, 2018). This is in spite of the fact that in-house training is much more costly, at on average US$1200 per annum per employee, than the low-cost large-scale MOOC (Rosendale & Wilkie, 2021).

There is clearly an opportunity here. We have a set of global challenges that require a massive response from the institutions that are primarily responsible for developing and curating the world's current knowledge, and we have the means of contributing to meeting those challenges. Can we match the two successfully?

The principles guiding our work

The book is based on the research we have been doing over some ten years or so, in different contexts, with different types of funding, in the broad post-16 education sector. The principles guiding the choice of projects and methods are important to articulate, and of course they have changed over time and with experience, but have been stable for some years now. They are summarized here as the criteria every project and initiative must meet:

> Quality – it must work, we do not have time to waste, so it must be truly effective in ways that everyone accepts as effective.
>
> Scale – within the framework of the SDGs the scale is massive because they are genuinely fully inclusive, and we must face up to how we deal with those issues at that scale.
>
> Equity – this is an ethical imperative; it must be 'for all' or it will not work in the longer run; and to work at all it must collaborate with stakeholders and users from the start.
>
> Sustainability – this is at the core of the UNSDGs and is the other main ethical focus because there is no point in aiming for anything less than the long-term sustainable improvement of what we do; it must take a holistic approach to the context of any professional work, to understand the wider impact and avoid its negative effects.

We return to these principles throughout the book.

The evidence-based approach

The research evidence presented in this book results from a number of research projects that we have conducted over the last ten years. These include a learning design project and two multi-year research projects with two research centres, all funded by the UK Economic and Social Research Council (ESRC): Centre for Global Higher Education (CGHE) and the RELIEF Centre.[7] With CGHE we have been researching, first, the potential of MOOCs for transforming higher education, and then, ways of realizing that potential. This research dovetails very helpfully with research we have simultaneously been conducting with the RELIEF Centre, a multidisciplinary research centre funded initially through the Global Challenge Research Fund, with an objective to conduct innovative social science research to speed up the sustainability transitions that the world critically requires in the context of large-scale movement of peoples. The RELIEF Centre research is based in Lebanon, a country with the highest per capita number of refugees in the world, which has experienced multiple, complex crises in recent years. Within CGHE we were able to undertake research with MOOC participants and formulate and test our ideas for how MOOCs could help address the UNSDGs by focusing on professional development. With the RELIEF Centre, we were able to put the ideas into practice through design-based research (DBR) and further refine this vision, leading to the development of the Co-designed Massive Open Online Collaboration (CoMOOC) concept which is at the heart of this book.

The DBR project we undertook for both projects developed and evaluated MOOCs codesigned with communities in the UK and Lebanon. These projects were conducted according to the BERA ethical guidelines for educational research.[8] The quotes throughout the book are either pseudonyms or real names where we have permission.

The research aim was to create a new model of professional learning by gradually testing and improving the MOOCs in the light of feedback from stakeholders and participants. The context fits the main requirements for a design-based research project (Anderson & Shattuck, 2012), being a real educational context, where the focus is to design and test the intervention, using mixed methods, over several iterations, as a collaboration between researchers and participants, in the sense that participant feedback and performance guide the redesign. Figure 1.1 shows the cycles of DBR we have conducted thus far over the course of five years. Each CoMOOC has been run and evaluated multiple times, with an increasing number of participants, and adaptations have been made to embed the courses within the stakeholder communities, and inform the next stage of research as indicated.

The data we have collected and analysed during these projects takes the form of platform analytics, interviews, survey responses and learning designs. This has produced a large-scale dataset which allows us to substantiate our claims. As we present data in the subsequent chapters, we provide the details of the

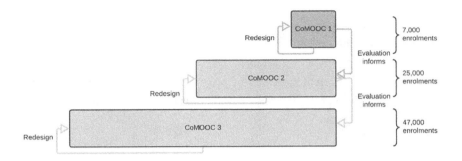

Figure 1.1 Cycles of CoMOOC Design-Based Research showing cycles of design and redesign within and between each CoMOOC.

individual projects from which they derive. All our research has ethical approval from UCL IOE Research Committee. The CoMOOCs referred to in this book are detailed in Appendix A.

We also draw on our ongoing research to develop and establish the Learning Designer as an online tool to support teachers to represent and share their best teaching ideas for online and blended learning. In addition, findings from research conducted during the COVID-19 pandemic with university staff in the UK and in Kenya also feature in Chapter 3.

The methodology of 'design-based research' points to a contrast between our methods and the educational research methodology that aims to achieve clear causal relationships for effectiveness, through the use of randomized control trials, and the methodologies that aim to identify new ways of conceptualizing how education systems and their communities work. Within our approach, we may use some of those methods, but the fundamental aim is to design, develop and test the efficacy of a specific project, or model, or initiative, and so develop design knowledge. The contrast is similar to that between science and engineering. Science aims to understand and explain the way the world works; engineering aims to build on that understanding to improve the way the world works. The initiatives we are testing are all instantiations of different kinds of teaching. By conceptualizing teaching as a design science we use the findings of education science to guide and keep improving the implementation of the chosen initiative (Laurillard, 2012). The designs use the findings, and the methods use the methods of education science, but the overall methodology begins and ends with the nature of the designed intervention itself and its efficacy in the world. The main chapters describe how this kind of evidence is generated, and what it means.

How do we do 'collaborative professional development'?

The previous section explains the methods we have used. The design knowledge that emerges is influenced by the principles guiding our methodology and is conceptualized at different stages of the research projects, according to each of the principles. Throughout the following chapters we will return repeatedly to the following concepts:

'Co-design' is the means to achieve quality because it derives from the needs of the intended participant groups.

'Deep learning for professionals' defines the high-quality and effective learning experiences perceived by the participants

'Transformative online education' and 'Social learning' take educational theory into practice to discover how to make it work effectively in local contexts and so achieve greater equity.

'Online for inclusivity' realizes the potential for online methods to achieve equity and at scale.

'CoMOOCs' adapt MOOCs to be collaborations both in their development and in their course design and operation in order to achieve quality, equity and inclusivity.

'A benefits-costs balance' for online learning and teaching ensures long-term sustainability.

'An iterative theory of change' for projects and initiatives plans the means to achieve quality, equity and sustainability.

Our focus throughout is on professional education and the collaborative development of knowledge, and not on creating courses for students at any stage of their education. The same courses may be embedded within taught courses in tertiary education and other programmes as supplementary material for students, but they cannot act as isolated educational courses for students. The model does not scale for students in the way it can for professionals, who do not need personal nurturing and can be guided to learn a lot from each other.

What is the narrative line of the book?

The book proposes some new perspectives for higher education (HE), derived from the experience we had with taking them into action, which is how we establish the evidence that they are feasible and welcomed by their respective audiences.

It begins at the heart of education, with the internal relationship between teacher, subject matter and learner. Chapter 2 argues for using the extraordinary benefits that digital technology can bring to education at all levels, and for focusing on the quality of the pedagogy that makes it special, and how it can be continually improved, at scale, in a sustainable way. The critical point here is to provide the online tools for teachers to become design scientists in their own right, developing new knowledge about digital pedagogy.

Chapter 3 uses the historic global experiment caused by the pandemic to learn the lessons of what is now possible that had not been beforehand. The evidence of how it impacted on both teachers and learners in all countries, in all sectors, is startling. It took a global pandemic for the world of education and its stakeholders to realize the opportunity for quality and equity with online learning. That's how hard it was to make the case to education leaders. That's our tragedy.

How do people experience online learning? In this book we are arguing for a very specific type of online learning, the MOOC, that has had a bad press following its over-hyped initial years, and yet is still accelerating in its attraction to both users and investors. It is still a solution for mainly professionals rather than students, and it still has the potential to improve radically what we can do for the future of online education. Chapter 4 listens to the stories of the professionals who have experienced it, and learns what it takes to ensure a quality experience.

How feasible is the universal move to online learning? It has often been characterized as second-rate because teachers and learners never meet, and as a cheap option because no estate costs are involved, and you can teach more students at the same time. Both assumptions are false. The pandemic demonstrated that when well-designed it has several quality advantages over in-person learning. It also became apparent that far from being cheap it is very time-consuming for teachers if done well. Chapter 5 takes on the issue of balancing the teaching costs against the learning benefits, to show that although not cheap, it can be financially viable. It shows the importance of understanding the significant differences from traditional 'business models' for HE, and how to assure both quality and sustainability, whether at scale or not.

The evidence presented in Chapters 1–5 shows that online learning via MOOCs can achieve quality and equity at scale, but under certain conditions, specifically, that the participants are professionals. For undergraduates, any massive solution will be inappropriate because these students are still learning, as yet uncertain of what it means to be the person they wish to become. Universities and colleges have a solemn responsibility to help their students make that journey, and that means giving them the personal attention that nurtures their developing skills and knowledge. In old technology terms, a MOOC combines a public library with a book club. This is not an education. Yet, for professionals it comes close because they have already developed their knowledge and skills, they are in a position to judge what they need, and they are valuable interlocutors for their peers. So we put our faith in the professionals in all walks of life. Chapter 6 works through the evidence we had from professionals learning in MOOCs to the development of the concept of the CoMOOC, which is designed to achieve equity by capitalizing on what they already know to bring them into an orchestrated engagement in developing their knowledge and practices collaboratively.

This is just the beginning of exploring what this model can do, so Chapter 7 tests its quality and efficacy in implementation. It situates our focus on quality, equity and scale within some of the highly ambitious mission statements from some of the world's top universities. Our mission is to enable universities to enact those vaulting ambitions. The chapter focuses on how we test the kind of value a CoMOOC creates for its participants, going beyond the immediate context of the CoMOOC to its potential impact on their own future practice and professional context. How well can the model achieve the criteria we have set?

The UNSDGs form an overarching framework for all the work we have described in the book, and clearly represent the range of different challenging contexts in which a CoMOOC must be tested for its power to achieve equity, and as a potential solution to supporting these most vulnerable professionals. In Chapter 8 we go more deeply into the particularly challenging context of refugee education in Lebanon. The scale of the compounding disasters that have hit Lebanon in recent years creates one of the most formidable contexts anywhere in the world. It is a humbling experience to even attempt to contribute to improving conditions there. To work with our colleagues there is to learn how not to lose hope. They are extraordinary. Prior to the pandemic we developed a CoMOOC on 'Transformative Education in Challenging Environments', designed to support the teachers who are coping with the extreme challenges of refugee education in empowering the children there. Such conditions are not unique in the world, and what we learned from and with these teachers has since travelled to another challenging context caused by the military coup in Myanmar during the pandemic. When the physical infrastructure crumbles, the online world can be the one stable part of a teacher's life, the only hope for sustainable support. Could this experience transfer and generalize also to other professional contexts?

That is the issue that Chapter 9 explores, bringing together the evidence from the previous chapters to speak to a theory of change for these initiatives: a methodology for ensuring that when the research creates something of value it is also sustainable.

At the end, Chapter 10 is the companion piece to this chapter: imagining a future that turns the ambitions of quality, equity, scale and sustainability into a reality capable of tackling the vast challenges of the UNSDGs. We have the evidence from the early stages of this enterprise that it could work. We have the tools to build a new and sustainable system of professional development for tertiary education that could in reality achieve its own ambitious mission statements.

Summary

In this book we are organizing the findings from our research over the past ten years, which itself was driven by the overarching framework of UN Sustainable Development Goal 4 on Education, to: *Ensure inclusive and quality education for all and promote lifelong learning.*[9]

We could see the potential for online learning to be a major force in meeting this challenge by 2030 because it had already proved its worth in contexts where it had been used well, and because it could work on the very large scale that SDG4 demands. Working with teachers in schools, colleges and universities it was clear that the support for online teaching was highly variable and mostly poor. Goal 4 required 68m new teachers to be trained over the next fifteen years. For online learning to make a significant impact on universal education and lifelong learning it was imperative to collaborate with the teaching community to build the new knowledge of how to teach in the most challenging contexts. What works for the most disadvantaged groups in education is usually equally beneficial for all. Then, transferring the model of professional collaboration from teachers to all professionals is a big step, but a smaller one than the initial challenge of trying to meet SDG4 by 2030.

Our overall argument is that one significant future pathway for online learning is global professional collaboration on a massive scale, to contribute to solving the most challenging global problems our cultures have ever faced.

2

What Is Quality Online Learning?

Introduction

This book is fundamentally about learning. That's the critical issue. If you took that word out of the title it could be about absolutely anything. The rest of the title places the learning in a very specific context – and here we mean 'formal' learning, the kind that is meant to happen in an educational context, of any type, at any age, in any area where humans learn something that another human thinks would be good for them. That is what distinguishes formal learning from 'informal' learning, the kind we do for ourselves from babyhood, as we learn how to get food, through to adulthood when anyone with an interest wants to find out what? why? how to? – whatever the content, and whether it is good or bad for us – can decide how and what to learn.

Learning in a formal learning context is different. There is a teacher, with a goal for the learner to learn, and it is the teacher's responsibility to organize the learner's environment in such a way that they succeed in that goal and benefit from the process. Here, the quality of the learning will depend both on the degree to which the goal is attained and on how it is attained in relation to what the learner can now do.

Given these basic generalities about learning, and before we tackle the quality of online learning as a specific type of formal learning, we consider what this idea of the quality of learning itself can mean in practice.

What counts as a high-quality learning experience?

When digital technology was first being introduced in education the tendency was often to work out how various technologies could be used to enhance learning. How can we use hypertext? To create multi-layered texts. How can we use microcomputers? To put a computer in every classroom. Good – although no teacher had ever asked for these capabilities. Nonetheless, as each new technology emerged the focus for educational innovation shifted towards it. That still happens. Why not start instead from what it takes to learn complex skills and concepts and then work out how technology could help to create a high-quality learning experience?

The Conversational Framework was developed to assist this process of thinking through what we know from research on pedagogy and how students learn. It distilled the different findings from studies of learning into a summary of the distinctive ways in which learners encounter new ideas and skills as they interact with the teacher, the subject matter and other students (Laurillard, 2002). The idea is that if you start from an analysis of what it takes to learn and use that to decide which technologies will enhance those different ways of learning, it will be more effective than a technology-driven approach. By starting from the learner's point of view you can challenge the technology to support what the learners and their teachers actually need.

The framework presents the interactions between teacher, learner and other learners as the three vertical cycles shown in Figure 2.1. They each operate at two levels of concept and practice, or discussion and action. The upper level represents the teachers' concepts, the learner's developing concepts and the other learners' developing concepts. The learner in the middle represents all learners. The lower level represents the use of the concepts in practice: the 'learning

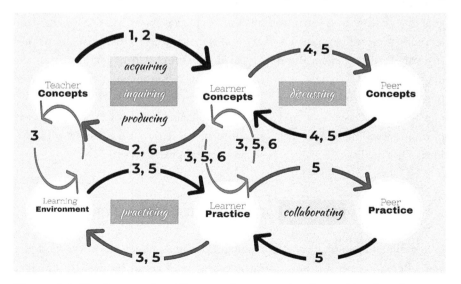

Figure 2.1 The Conversational Framework representing the teaching-learning process in action (with numbered cycles as below).

environment' embodies the teacher's idea of how all the learners engage with practice, and it also represents the learner's and their peers' developing practices.

Between these six nodes there are several cycles of interaction between teacher, learner, other learners and the subject learning environment, in both directions, characterizing six distinct types of learning:

1. Acquiring: the learner's developing concepts affect their practice, which in turn affects their concepts
2. Inquiring: the teacher presents their concepts, and the learner asks, and answers questions, makes comments and presents their ideas to the teacher, who gives them feedback
3. Practising: the teacher creates the learning environment to engage learners in the practice and use of the concept, and each learner acts to achieve the goals of the learning environment and uses feedback and reflection on their concept to improve their practice
4. Discussing: each learner discusses, negotiates ideas, asks and answers questions with other learners
5. Collaborating: learners practice, discuss and exchange or share their practice
6. Producing: each learner reflects on how their concepts and practice have developed, and represents this reflection in some way for the teacher to evaluate.

The focus for teachers, as we try to engage the learners, is to create the opportunities for interactions at both levels, to promote active learning. The role of the teacher is to orchestrate a high-quality learning experience by keeping those cycles of interaction moving, because this is how learners develop their concepts, practices and the relationships between the two. A learner may think they understand the concept of sustainability, for example, and may think they know how to recycle rubbish, but when they're not sure if this plastic bag can be recycled what principle of sustainability will guide their practice? And how will the consequences of not recycling responsibly affect their concept? The point is that when we come to apply a concept in practice, we realize the extent of our understanding or misunderstanding, and are able to 'modulate' our concepts, to strengthen or correct them. Learners should have the chance to develop the relationship between concept and practice over time. We can do that by designing each learning activity, learning session and series of learning sessions by keeping in mind how we want students to be active learners.

The 'teacher's concepts' node can be embodied in many forms: a human teacher, a book, a library, a website or an artificial intelligence (AI) tutor. The learning environment similarly will take different forms according to the nature of the subject area: pen and paper, a software app, a piece of equipment, a group, a game, a role play, a digital tool, a forest floor, and so on; wherever the learner can apply their conceptual learning and learn through feedback on their practice. A well-designed learning environment that enables learning through feedback is at the heart of the high-quality learning experience. Feedback may come from the learning environment itself, a teacher's response, a model answer, another learner or from self-review, in terms of the relationship between the learner's action and the intended goal.

So despite the name 'Conversational Framework', this is not just a conversation. The name derives from Conversation Theory (Pask, 1976), which developed a prior version of these types of teaching-learning cycles of interaction as a representation of cybernetic learning. The similarity is not surprising as the basic elements of goal, action, feedback, revised action and communication within a particular learning context are fundamental to all types of learning, although Pask was certainly ahead of his time in seeing that cybernetic learning could potentially model human learning.

How does the framework represent the quality of the learning process – and the roles that technologies can play? Given that the teacher's role is to keep the cycles of conceptual/practice development moving through the interactions they create, a simple way to represent this is to see them as a sequence of different learning types. The learner's experience is different in each case, according to (a) the type of action they are asked to take, (b) the degree of control they have, (c) the type of feedback they receive and (d) whether they act as an individual or as part of a small or larger group. The features are as follows:

Learning through acquisition

(a) reading, watching and listening, attending to input from the teacher, in print or digital texts, in-person talks, demos or videos, and digital audio formats
(b) learner-paced or teacher-paced
(c) there is no action to generate feedback
(d) as part of a group of any size of one or more.

Learning through inquiry

(a) questioning the teacher in person or online, or researching in a book or library or place or website

(b) learner controlled
(c) learner self-evaluates what they find
(d) as part of a group of any size, of one or more.

Learning through practice

(a) using the goals set within the learning environment whether physical or digital to create their actions on it
(b) either the learner or the environment is in control, or it is negotiated
(c) the learner is responding to the feedback from the learning environment itself, or from the teacher, other learners, or self-review, to improve the application of their concepts in action
(d) as part of a group of any size of one or more.

Learning through discussion

(a) negotiating ideas and plans, asking and answering questions of the teacher or other students, articulating and refining their concepts, whether in-person or online
(b) control is negotiated
(c) feedback is from the teacher or other students, or self-review
(d) as part of a group of any size more than two.

Learning through collaboration

(a) practising in the learning environment whether physical or digital, sharing and exchanging their practice with other learners, discussing what they have done, aiming to develop a joint output, in synchronous or asynchronous mode
(b) control is negotiated
(c) feedback is from the teacher or other learners, or self-review
(d) as part of a group of any size more than two.

Learning through production

(a) presenting what they have learned to the teacher or to other learners, using in-person and/or digital representations, trying to optimize their contribution
(b) the learner is in control
(c) feedback is from the teacher or other students, or self-review
(d) usually as an individual, but can be as part of a group of any size.

The point of the Conversational Framework is to clarify the ways in which the teaching-learning process goes beyond the least active form of learning, through acquisition. So the quality of the learning experience is determined to a great extent by the sequence of these actions and interactions, whether and how digital methods are embedded, and how well the guided actions and feedback are designed.

This is about pedagogy, not curriculum. One of the interesting properties of pedagogies is that they apply across a wide range of subject areas and educational sectors. All teachers share the traditional pedagogies, such as teacher presentation, question and answer (Q&A) sessions, libraries, small discussion groups, tutorial groups, student projects, educational games, practice sessions and marked assignments. Some pedagogies have been associated with a particular discipline area: problem-based learning with medicine, the Harvard case study method with business, the masterclass in arts, Socratic questioning in law (Shulman, 2005). However, while the conditions of a discipline might foster a particular method as its signature pedagogy, there is no reason why it should not transfer to other fields. We will be exploring later what can happen if you mix them up – why should a poetry class not engage with problem-based learning, or a business session not be run as a master class?

Each pedagogy can be represented as one or more learning types, which can be combined and sequenced in infinitely many ways. The process of combining learning types is the beginning of designing for learning. Learning design is the representation of the iterative processes of teaching and learning, describing the roles that both conventional and digital methods play. Since teachers first started using digital methods in education, we have developed an even greater multiplicity of ways of engaging students in active learning, because all the historic conventional methods have their digital and online equivalents, with new apps appearing all the time.

This must be the most exciting time to be a teacher since the invention of writing. It comes with many challenges and a huge task of innovation, but think of the potential.

The different levels of quality in the move to online learning

The regulatory function for tertiary education at national level provides standards for institutions that are subject to inspection and assure quality for external stakeholders – potential students, employers, regulators and government.

Standards are monitored via outcomes intelligible to all these audiences, and via the internal processes designed to ensure them (Parker, 2008).

However, these quality standards make very little reference to the nature of teaching and learning itself in terms of the relationships between teachers, their students and the subject matter, so they have little to say about the move to online learning. In the UK, for example, they contain no explicit reference to digital teaching and learning methods other than expecting, for example 'a high-quality academic experience' and 'innovative and flexible learning' (OfS, 2021, pp. 9, 26), which is not defined in any greater detail. Teachers looking to these documents for guidance on what counts as a high-quality academic experience would be disappointed. The quality of pedagogy is primarily the responsibility of the institution, while regulators take responsibility, e.g. for ensuring that the institutions commit to supporting learners, and academics are not simply dispensers or interpreters of content for passive students (Parker, 2008). This is the closest quality assurance regulations come to defining pedagogy. Here we consider the meaning of quality at the level of pedagogy.

High-quality pedagogy

The quality of pedagogy is our focus in this book, because there is so little help for teachers to ensure that quality at the level of pedagogy is able to deliver the overall quality standards being defined at the national level. The research on quality and effectiveness of the learning experience, both conventional and digital, comes from the academic community, not from the quality assurance community.

This literature formed the basis of the Conversational Framework and its expression of what it takes to learn (Laurillard, 2002, 2012). To date, the definitions of learning types we discussed above have been sufficiently generic that they continue to apply to both conventional and digital methods, so the framework can be used to challenge and test the quality of both modes of pedagogy. Each new form of digital learning tool and environment, from virtual reality to AI tutor, addresses at least one learning type and they do not yet offer any form of learning that would require a new framework.

Because the six learning types are generic, and apply to all educational sectors and subject areas, as do the established pedagogic principles, it is possible to link categories of digital tools to each type, as listed in the section 'What counts as a high-quality learning experience?' above, and more extensively in Appendix B. For acquisition, inquiry, discussion and production the generic tools for reading, watching, listening, exploring, discussing and presenting can be used in any subject area, but practice and collaboration require the kind of practical learning environment in which the student must act to achieve a goal, and use the feedback it produces to improve their action. The learning environment will vary for different topic areas – from dental students drilling a tooth to language students practising pronunciation – but this is where a digital tool can make a critical difference to students' understanding. For example:

> With a plastic mouth and tooth and a real drill, learners can make a mistake, but need the tutor to advise them on how they went wrong. With a virtual mouth and tooth and a haptic drill, everything is digital, so they can run an action replay of what they did and analyse mistakes for themselves.
>
> (Ria et al., 2018)

> If language learners use computer-assisted pronunciation they can compare visual representations of their own and a native speaker's pronunciation as a way of identifying what they need to focus on for improvement, without needing continual advice from the teacher.
>
> (Levis, 2007)

Whatever the topic, the structure of the learning environment must offer

> a task goal that the learner can recognise as being achieved,
> the means to act to achieve that goal,
> intrinsic feedback on what their action actually achieved,
> the means to keep revising their action to improve their outcome.

It is in the final two features that digital methods can excel, because they provide informational feedback that enables the learner to analyse their own mistake and work out how to improve their actions, and the means to keep practising productively, without needing help from the teacher. This is the essence of a high-quality learning experience. Appendix B provides further examples of the digital tools that best serve each learning type.

The Conversational Framework does not explicitly embrace the emotional aspects of learning, such as enthusiasm and motivation. Research on the value of different aspects of emotion in learning is still quite limited, but has shown, for example, the importance of positive emotions such as joy, happiness, interest and excitement for their impact on enhanced cognition and social functioning, increased motivation and heightened self-efficacy, coping and resilience (Rowe et al., 2015, p. 15). These are all important outcomes of a good learning experience in any context. After all, the process of learning is not always a pleasurable experience – it can make us doubt ourselves and everything we thought about the world – and It is difficult to understand how anyone can keep coming back for more learning unless there is an expectation of some pleasure at the end. In terms of the Conversational Framework embedding the emotional aspects into a learning design would mean reflecting on how best to construct an optimal sequence of learning types. A learning design that

- begins with a lecture to explain a concept (acquisition)
- then Q&A (discussion), followed by
- exercises (practice) and
- an assignment (production)

is a standard approach, for either in-person or online learning, covering four different types of learning. But a pedagogic principle, such as encouraging engagement by using an 'advance organizer' (Ausubel, 1980), would suggest beginning prior to the lecture with, say:

- an initial class discussion of how students have already experienced that concept, to attract their interest,
- a problem they cannot solve to motivate them to find out how to,
- or getting them to make a prediction they are likely to get wrong to build a sense of excitement as they listen to how the concept explains that.

These designs would insert a learning type of, respectively, discussion, practice or production prior to the acquisition of the content in the lecture primarily to turn this least active type of learning into one where the learner is attentive, engaged, questioning or analytical, in the way they listen and watch.

Taking account of emotional aspects means changing the learning design in terms of the sequence of learning types, or the guidance to students. The quality of the learning experience itself lies in the quality of the pedagogy: the learning designs developed by the teachers.

In summary, the quality of the learning experience must be judged primarily by the extent to which the teacher enables the learner to achieve their learning potential. It is the government's job to make tertiary education widely available, and the institution's task to provide the infrastructure conducive to learning, but the high-value outcomes for the learner will depend crucially on how they are taught, or rather, the way their learning experience is designed by their teachers.

Using a learning design tool to improve quality

At the institutional level tertiary education uses regulation and policy-driven guidance to set the general standards that teaching must respect. These regulations hardly impinge at all on the decisions the individual teacher has to make about how to help students learn. And yet the most profound changes to the ways we teach have been developing over the last few decades and this will continue, as the digital world gradually improves what it can do for education. So the question is, how do we advance the quality of digital learning methods?

Learning design as a quality process

During the first two decades of the twenty-first century whenever digital technologies targeted education the teacher was typically side-lined as a 'facilitator of learning', a gently restful term that disguises an immensely complex undertaking. The idea of 'learning design' took root by recognizing that the teacher has a pivotal role as the active designer of the blend of pedagogies, old and new, that is now possible (Dalziel, 2016; Laurillard, 2016; McAndrew & Weller, 2005). The phrase 'learning design' refers to a key area of emerging international research on the means by which teachers might engage in the development of technological pedagogical knowledge (Schmidt et al., 2009).

This is vital work because no-one other than teachers can realistically shoulder the responsibility of finding out how to optimize the use of digital methods for pedagogy. Unfortunately, most teachers have little discretionary time to give to innovation. In most countries teachers are expected to take their early training into their career with very little opportunity for personal development even while national policies, socio-economic developments and technologies frequently change according to social and political pressures that affect much of what the teacher can do. Given the range of possibilities for innovation the programme of action research needed to explore what is possible with digital technologies is immense. But so is the world population of teachers, across all education sectors and countries. And the members of that vast workforce are there because they have a sense of vocation to help their students learn, a passion to succeed and the continual daily practice that enables every one of them to accomplish what it takes to be an expert *'estimated [at] over 10,000 hours … for several domains'* (Ericsson, 2008, p. 992)[1] – IF they practice the right way:

Expert performance can ... be traced to deliberate practice (DP), where training ... is focused on improving particular tasks ... [and] involves the provision of immediate feedback, time for problem-solving and evaluation, and opportunities for repeated performance to refine behavior.

(Ericsson, 2008, p. 988)

Could we imagine developing the kind of teaching practice that fulfils these conditions, where teachers are able to plan, execute, evaluate and revise what they do with their students as a natural part of their everyday practice? That is part of the promise of the work on learning design.

The early projects shared the central goal of improving teaching and learning by developing a way of codifying pedagogically effective sequences of activities to make them shareable. An early initiator, James Dalziel, used the analogy of musical notation to capture the power of a representation for sharing an idea across many different contexts and interpretations (Dalziel et al., 2016). Why was sharing so important? Because it is part of any quality process.

If the teaching community is to investigate, critique and innovate with new digital methods they cannot be expected to do this as isolated individuals. It will be essential for the teaching community to somehow emulate the scientific and scholarship community familiar to academe and build that same collaborative environment for innovation that builds on the work of others. The time-honoured knowledge-building community of scholars and scientists acquaint themselves with prior work, develop their own ideas, test them and share them for others to build on. In this way collective knowledge progresses. There are many mechanisms that support the process, individual, institutional and global. The most powerful ways of making this work were the establishment of the means to communicate new ideas, through journals and books, and the means to test them, through experiment and peer review. If the teaching community is to achieve this type of quality process, we need specialized ways of representing, sharing and validating our own findings as teachers. The existing journal structures are not designed for such a community; hence the idea of a codified means of communicating innovative teaching practices through learning designs. The teacher should no longer be side-lined as simply a 'facilitator' of learning, but brought to the forefront of the digital pedagogy innovation process.

Several learning design tools have been developed to do this (Dalziel, 2016), but we focus here on the *Learning Designer* tool[2] because it was designed to support the application of the learning types defined by the Conversational Framework, and was intended to emulate at least some attributes of the scholarly journals that aim to assure the quality of the knowledge developed: the formal representation of the new idea or practice; self and peer review; and publication to the community for comment and debate (Laurillard et al., 2013).

How does the Learning Designer help to improve quality?

The tool is an interactive website designed to support teachers in developing their own learning design for some specific learning outcome(s), in terms of the teaching-learning activities they want learners to engage in to achieve them. The duration of the session could be minutes, or hours over the course of a week or several weeks. It also offers a library of existing designs contributed by other teachers which they can adopt and adapt to their own context. And from the input they provide, the tool will offer an analysis of the nature of the learning experience they have designed. The tool acts as a prompt, a way to think through their teaching ideas, and to reflect and redesign in the light of how it works out in practice. Its structure is modelled on the way the scientific and scholarly communities develop knowledge through representation (journal papers), sharing (in journals) and validation (via peer review) of their work.

The Learning Designer provides three types of screen, outlined in Table 2.1, showing the purposes of each one: the Browser screen, acting like a journal; the Designer screen as the presentation of a journal paper; and the Analysis screen as the initial feedback on the design, prior to implementation and then peer review.

This basic structure of the tool creates the conditions for building on the work of others. The Browser screen provides access to teachers' published designs. The encoding of design features on the Designer screen helps the teacher to focus on the quality of their design in different ways:

- Defining the aims and outcomes – to be able to test their design against those intentions.
- Setting the intended learning time – to think in terms of all the work the student has to do, whether in or out of class.
- Feedback on learning time created – the program calculates this important check on their intention. Teachers frequently create far more learning time than they intended.
- Representing the plan for a learning session that includes learner preparation, class time, group working and independent learning, and focuses attention on the learner's point of view.

Table 2.1 The main screens of the Learning Designer

Browser screen: the user can browse learning designs from other teachers by type of pedagogy, subject topic and education sector.	Enables a teacher to explore other designs, share their own either privately or publicly and exchange designs for peer review activities
Designer screen: displays the learning design as a timeline of teaching-learning activities with properties and learner guidance provided by the designer; it can be made public in the Browser or exported to Word or Moodle.	Represents the teacher's design in a common format representing aims and outcomes, intended learning time, context, teaching-learning activities, and for each activity: pedagogic features, text for student guidance, digital resources and Notes for other teachers
Analysis screen: the program uses the designer's input to analyse and present charts representing different aspects of the learning experience they have created.	Feedback using charts on the proportion of learning time designed for each learning type selected, and the proportion of time spent online, with the teacher, asynchronously and in an individual, group or class activity

- Drafting the guidance to the learner for each activity and assigning it specific attributes – learning type, duration, group size, teacher presence/ or not, online/or not, synchronous/asynchronous, and resources to be used. This focuses attention on what actions the learner is taking in order to learn.
- The pie chart representing the time on each learning type enables the teacher to critically self-review the quality of the learning experience they have created.

This detailed, analytical representation of a learning design then enables us to examine the nature of the difference that digital methods can make to the quality of the learning experience.

Comparing conventional and technology-enhanced learning designs

In workshops on using the Conversational Framework to guide a learning design we ask teachers to create their design for a current fifty-minute classroom session they run. A typical format is the fifty-minute lecture presentation including ten minutes Q&A. It produces a rather simple pie chart with just two colours for acquisition and discussion, the former taking the largest part of the pie. It is interesting to see the way this simple feedback on their design so often elicits the teacher's determination to make the learning experience more varied. It can be just the straightforward addition of a few online 'multiple choice questions'[3] to see the way the class is thinking about a question, or a collective 'word cloud'[4] to discover the different ways of understanding an idea, or an even simpler conventional three-minute three-person buzz group activity to generate good questions. These short active learning episodes help to focus attention for students to pause and think about their own point of view. And each of these requires every student to take part, unlike the standard question and answer session, where 90 per cent of the students essentially leave it to the rest. Appendix D shows generic versions of the before and after learning designs for the original lecture session and what it became when taken online, contrasting the greater overall learning time being guided, but with less time for the teacher being present with the students, given that the lecture has become two shorter videos, and with more active learning by the students, as shown in the contrasting pie charts.

A more complex learning session, such as a site-specific activity to develop 'an understanding of the thesis in an art exhibition', will have many more ways in which digital devices can greatly enhance how students interact with each other and the art objects they are viewing (Laurillard, 2007, pp. 164–5). The contribution from the digital activities is to offer guidance in situ and to focus learners' attention through exchanging observations and interpretations with their peers, which, being digital, can then follow through to a later class discussion. The visit becomes an actively productive learning process.

This is what we aim for, in using digital methods – a more enjoyable, effective and productive learning experience.

A quality process for improving the learning experience

The regulators of quality standards in tertiary education require the institutions to provide a high-quality academic experience, but to a great extent the institution has responsibility for what that means in practice. If teachers are to create such a learning experience, we have to take an institutional responsibility for enabling them to discover what that experience can and should be in the era of blended and online learning.

The means to engage in collaborative knowledge development

The combination of an open online learning design tool and communication technologies gives tertiary education the means to engage teachers across institutions in the collaborative development of innovative high-quality teaching and learning. The academic community has yet to negotiate what it means by high-quality pedagogy. We have proposed the Conversational Framework as one basis for establishing a critical approach to pedagogy, instantiated in the Learning Designer tool. The characteristics of the tool embody some of the established pedagogical principles to be found in the research literature (Laurillard, 2002), which apply equally to both conventional and digital methods. From these we can generate a comprehensive rubric for evaluating the quality of a learning design. Each criterion is related to one of the main references, and these serve as the structure for a standard rubric for the Learning Designer team to advise on preparing a learning design to be added to a Curated section of the Browser (that includes quality learning designs on specific themes). An example of an evaluation rubric for a learning design is given in Appendix C, as derived from the following key pedagogical principles:

1. Alignment of intended learning outcomes – activities – assessable tasks (Biggs, 2003)
2. Outcomes expressed as what the learner will be able to achieve from the activities (Bloom, 1956, Krathwohl, 2002)
3. Clear guidance to learners on how to engage with each type of learning, including acquisition (Pang and Marton, 2003; Perry, 1970)
4. Appropriate duration and group sizes for each activity, to ensure there is sufficient time and every learner can be active (Laurillard et al., 2013)
5. Use of digital tools and resources that are interactive, enhance the learning type and fit learners' capabilities (Laurillard et al., 2018)
6. Feedback to each learner for self-review, to motivate engagement (Hattie et al., 2007)
7. Follow-through from each learning activity across the sequence to motivate attention and active learning (Lo et al., 2004)
8. A balance of learning types across the session to encourage the iterative cycles of concept and practice development (Laurillard et al., 2013)
9. The designed learning time should equal the learning time available, and any discrepancy resolved.

These are the some of the pedagogic principles that would underlie a rubric for analysing a learning design (see Appendix C).

This could be a design process for an individual teacher, with external feedback coming from the way their students respond in practice. This is the norm for experienced teachers. The advent of digital methods makes novices of us all, however. To manage the continuing task of digital innovation that clearly enhances the learning experience and improves learning outcomes, we need a collective, collaborative approach to innovation across the whole teaching community. Otherwise we will miss many wonderful opportunities and leave the academic community side-lined by the technologists who will certainly step into that breach. But now we have the means to collaborate.

Sharing designs enables teachers to build on each other's work, so the Browser screen plays the role of a journal website or Google Scholar. Sharing designs in the Browser also supports a peer review process, using a defined rubric that specifies the design principles to be followed. One section of the Browser displays 'Curated designs' that have been through both peer review and a review by the editorial team running the Learning Designer website.

There are three stages of validation of the design, therefore: the immediate feedback to the teacher on the nature of the learning experience they have designed; the peer review of their design by another teacher, following an agreed rubric, and linked to the design as an additional panel on the Designer screen; and the curation by the editorial team, using a more stringent rubric prior to publication. The Browser shows all the designs made public by users. Peer-reviewed designs are listed as 'Reviewed designs', and those evaluated by the editorial team are showcased as 'Curated designs'. In this way we are developing the means for establishing the knowledge of what counts as high-quality learning designs, both conventional and digital.

The conditions for knowledge building by the community are in place, but now we consider whether it is really feasible to borrow pedagogy from a teacher in a different subject area or education sector.

Specific and generic learning designs

Teachers have shared conventional pedagogies for centuries – lectures, readings, small group work, exercises, discussions, assignments – every teacher in every subject area, at every level uses these methods. The technologies they used were similar as well – blackboards, books, pen and paper, and desks. All sectors and subject areas are now beginning to use digital technologies, and these methods still elicit the same basic types of learning, as those defined in the Conversational Framework.

Now that we can share our learning designs it becomes apparent how much similarity there can be between them, even across the divides of subject and sector. Examining a learning design for a session on a specific topic it is immediately clear that any teacher can understand it because the majority of the description is about how the student is to engage with the topic. The topic-related words are rather few, so it is quite easy to replace them with generic words, or with alternative topic words (Laurillard, 2008).

This is one example from an online course where teachers were asked to use a learning design to 'explain the concept of the water cycle' in Physics. They were given the original, and a generic version derived from it by replacing all instances of 'water cycle' with 'system'. One example of an adaptation by a teacher was for the concept 'financial statements'. To compare the two we can look at an extract from the export to Word, which records all the features of each step, together with the guidance. The second teaching-learning activity for the generic version reads as follows:

Prepare your account of the system

Practice   20 minutes   1 Student   Teacher not present   Online

Prepare your own animation describing the system, focusing in particular on what you feel are the critical factors, and the role they play. Explain just the basics, as if to someone who has no experience of the system. Use your own ppt software for this exercise, and save it for sharing later.

Investigate   10 minutes   1 Student   Teacher not present   Online

Use the ' system' video to check that you have done a good description that covers all the critical factors.

Produce   10 minutes   1 Student   Teacher not present   Online

Revise and improve your animation to make sure it is as clear as possible

The second teaching-learning activity for the teacher's adapted design follows similar instructions, replacing 'system' with 'financial statements', and the same generic digital tools, but changes the type of learning in the second step:

Prepare your account of the system

Practice   20 minutes   1 Student   Teacher not present   Online

Prepare your own animation describing the system, focusing in particular on what you feel are the critical factors, and the role they play. Explain just the basics, as if to someone who has no experience of the system. Use your own ppt software for this exercise, and save it for sharing later.

Investigate   10 minutes   1 Student   Teacher not present   Online

Use the ' system' video to check that you have done a good description that covers all the critical factors.

Produce   10 minutes   1 Student   Teacher not present   Online
Revise and improve your animation to make sure it is as clear as possible

Figure 2.2 shows how the generic and specific versions of the learning design are represented, in part, in the Learning Designer (where the greyscale learning types are more clearly represented in colours).

This teacher's adaptation shows that the existing learning design provides a kind of starter kit for the teacher thinking about a similar learning outcome in a very different field, but finding they can use a very similar pedagogy, while also adapting it to suit both their preferred task, and their shift from an online design to one that is classroom-based.

Adaptation of this kind will not always work, as some designs may be too topic-specific, and different digital tools may be needed, but at the level of describing whether the student is to plan an essay structure, or discuss the relationship between two concepts, or find out how an argument has been attacked by two

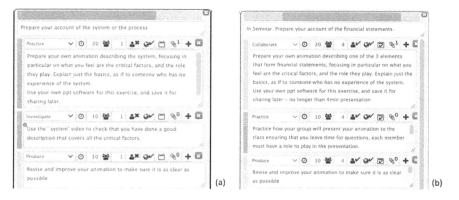

Figure 2.2 Comparing (a) an original generic design with (b) a specific adaptation to a finance topic, showing: similar guidance text; the same digital tool; changing an individual Practice step to a Collaboration among four students; changing an investigate step to a Practice of the presentation; and adding a Discussion.

different experts, the innovative sequence and style of such learning activities, and the digital tools they use, can usefully be shared. In the Blended and Online Learning Design CoMOOC freely available on FutureLearn,[5] we asked teachers from different subject areas and sectors to adapt the design shown above and to share their adapted designs on a Padlet (online pinboard) in the MOOC. The teachers' designs showed adaptations to topics as widely varied as Marx's theory of value, fractions and percentages, sink and float, avoiding plagiarism, the urinary system, volcanoes, pronunciation of regular verbs[6] – and where the pie charts were visible they were often quite different, showing that teachers will adapt a design to make it their own. We analyse this idea further in Chapter 5.

Teachers adapting a design can test their own version, revise it, share it for peer review and eventually share it back into the community. This is close to emulating the process of developing scholarly knowledge, but in the form of the professional technology practice knowledge of teaching and learning, represented as a learning design, and distributed via the Learning Designer.

The response from the teaching community

How well does this work in practice? The Learning Designer has been embedded in several of our professional development MOOCs in education, so it has been possible to test participants' reactions to the experience, through the platform data collected on what they do, the nature of the learning designs they make public, their comments in the platform discussions and their responses to post-course surveys. We come back to more detailed analyses of the teacher-participant experience in later chapters, but to address the issue briefly here, comments from the online discussion in one course[7] show that the Learning Designer tool does enable the teacher to improve their design through reflection on the analysis:

> Through reflections on my current practices, I realised that I need to add more collaboration and inquiry types of activities for the maximum student outcomes. The Learning Designer helps me to see the balance of activities in the program, so I found it really useful.
>
> (Megumin Noble)

The peer review process is valued:

> I love the Learning Designer tool, and I enjoyed reviewing teacher's designs, even if they were very different to the subjects I teach, I could find common ground
>
> (Tatiana Soler Pastor)

The improved design has an impact in practice:

> I've got lessons to plan lined up for the Learning Designer – the last I gave was observed formally towards a PGCE[8] and was very well received for the balance, variety and methodology.
>
> (Jonathan Vernon)

And teachers look forward to the community collaboration that it fosters:

> Sharing lesson designs is highly important for expertise exchange. It can bridge the gap between teaching communities and foster transnational teaching cooperation. This can create a universal experience that will benefit well-experienced and less experienced teachers as well as learners themselves. The Learning Designer can play the role of knowledge transfer tool.
>
> (Fatma Fattoumi)

That last point is exactly what we are aiming for – to emulate the time-honoured and high-quality process of collaborative knowledge development in scholarship in general.

How well the teacher's changed practice works for their students is evidence only available to the teachers themselves. A post-course survey can sometimes elicit the teacher's report on the value to their students, but our evidence of effectiveness more usually ends with the teacher's evaluation. The issue of the actual value to the end user is discussed in Chapters 7–9.

The quality criteria for improving the learning experience

To summarize, the process outlined here has several key characteristics:

- A framework for establishing a critical approach to pedagogy
- A design tool that embodies a learner-centred approach to design
- The tool is able to represent pedagogical principles and practices
- The representation of a design must distinguish conventional and digital methods
- Designs can be peer reviewed via the immediate feedback from the tool, shared designs and a rubric for evaluation
- The tool enables a teacher to adopt and adapt other teachers' designs
- It enables a teacher to share and publish their designs

We have the technology, then, to support a quality improvement process across the teaching community, as the means by which we create online learning futures of high value to learners.

Making the move to online

In this chapter we have located the responsibility for improving the learning experience with the teachers, as they are close to their students and discover on a daily basis how well their teaching is received, what seems to work and what needs improvement. In Chapter 5 we will also recognize the significant time cost to teachers of innovation.

Optimizing the move to more online learning is crucial for the way a tertiary institution operates, so it is a key strategic and policy responsibility for the leadership team. We return to this in Chapter 7.

The vision here is to bring teachers to the forefront of digital innovation, and reconceptualize teaching as a design science (Laurillard, 2012). In Chapter 7 we also return to how we do the professional collaboration that entails. In the next chapter we come back to the online learning experience from the learner's point of view, and how the teachers handled the rapid move to online during the COVID-19 pandemic.

Questions and activities

To consolidate the ideas and issues discussed in the sections above, for each one we propose some questions that might help to reinterpret them for your own teaching-learning context. How would you

1. Define the difference between formal learning in a college or university and informal learning in a personal context?
2. Interpret each of the learning types for the way students might engage with a specific topic in your field?
3. Prioritize the design quality issues for moving some teaching and learning online?
4. Use the Learning Designer to draft an alternative approach to professional development for your department or institution?
5. Adapt the rubric in Appendix C to analyse and critique a learning design for your own context?

We will do this for each chapter, and hope that the process might provide the beginnings of a framework and plan for change. And if you ignore it? Well, nothing lost.

3

What Can We Learn from the Rapid Shift Online During the COVID-19 Pandemic?

A vision for digital tertiary education

In March 2020, tertiary education achieved what had previously been considered impossible – face-to-face teaching at universities and colleges around the world was abandoned and all teaching immediately moved online. The COVID-19 pandemic was a historical watershed in the rise of online learning. The rapid shift online provided many insights into the capabilities and preparedness of staff and technological infrastructure for online teaching. This was a test case for the viability of online teaching and learning, as well as for ways to support teachers to move their teaching online.

Those insights have helped to shape this book. For example, the urgent need for professional development in online teaching and learning among the world's teachers during the pandemic required us to rapidly stress-test an approach to online professional development we had been working on. At the beginning of the first lockdown, we met online with our research collaborators in Lebanon, and made a decision to create what we call a CoMOOC – a Co-designed Massive Open Online Collaboration, in Arabic, to support teachers in the MENA region to teach online. The participants engaging in the course provided evidence that co-designed, collaborative online professional development opportunities could be used to equip professionals in crises with the skills they need, and on the large scale.

Then, as tertiary institutions around the world were able to step back and reflect on what happened, and whether they had created the kind of digital education that fitted with their mission and values and their plans for the future, researchers set out to listen to digital education leaders construct visions and strategies for transforming digital teaching, learning and research. This meant studying the work of individual tertiary education institutions. UNESCO-ICHEI

(2022) offers an especially interesting collection of case studies because they report from universities across the Global South, where even in the most difficult circumstances they were digitally transforming their approaches in the aftermath of the pandemic.

For some the transition reflected their overall strategy, for example,

- Universiti Putra Malaysia (UPM) launched a four-year strategy to plan, research and evaluate for a 'smart' digital campus, recognizing the importance of taking account of the needs of all stakeholders. The vision of UPM was to support the higher education sector in Malaysia to meet the SDGs by ensuring equitable access to quality higher education and lifelong learning.
- Ain Shams University (ASU) in Egypt created a new e-learning platform (incorporating a Virtual Microscopy Platform to support STEM subjects) to bring quality blended and distance education to their 200,000 students. ASU is committed to raising the digital competencies of both staff and students to support teaching and learning with technology.
- The Faculty of Sciences Semlalia, Cadi Ayyad University, Morocco, created an E-Labs platform because they aim to support practical study. The faculty is now focused on addressing staff and student needs in relation to both technology and training to design and implement online and blended learning effectively.

For others, the move was an opportunity to improve their approach to teaching and learning by introducing more collaborative ways of innovating:

- Universities in Zhejiang province in China formed a digital community to promote collaboration and innovation, sharing resources for general education, and exploring ways of implementing online and blended learning with MOOCs and SPOCs (small private online courses).
- The Indonesia Cyber Education Institute (ICE-I) was launched in 2021 as a marketplace for online courses to promote collective development of online learning across Indonesia. This meant that students could enrol and get credit for online learning which is recognized through certification. The ICE-I is part of a long-term strategy of 'degree modularization and decomposition' in Indonesia, making use of micro-credentials and digital badges.
- In Peru, Pontificia Universidad Católica del Perú (PUCP) focused on providing a suite of online professional development courses for teachers,

including establishing a community of practice so that teachers could support each other.

These universities have shown that despite the challenges facing them, online and blended learning can work in the Global South. Moreover, digital technology could transform universities' capacity in their 'public good' mission in an era of massive long-term increases in inequality, mobility and displacement, and health and environmental crises. Using the full range of digital technology capabilities, universities in the Global South could have a major impact on delivering the SDGs in education and health and well-being, for example, to increase access to technical, vocational and tertiary education, and to train more schoolteachers and health workers. On the other hand, without addressing some of the systemic practices within higher education that pose a persistent barrier to a deeper and more productive engagement with digitalization, universities could be hindered from realizing the potential of the digital university.

To explore these issues further, at the end of 2020, over a year since the beginning of the pandemic, the Partnership for African Social and Governance Research (PASGR) and UCL Knowledge Lab brought together leaders of digital HE in Kenya to reassess achievements and create a vision the future.[1] The priorities that emerged are insightful and can guide universities everywhere:

- Rethinking pedagogy: synchronous/asynchronous interactive teaching
- Continuous staff development: needs analysis; planning, monitoring & evaluation
- Rethinking planning: generating data for leading cost-efficient, quality digital HE
- Designing inclusive learning: embedded within a strategic plan
- Taking a learner-centred approach: underpinned by peer and tutor interaction
- Evaluating, monitoring online learning: developing quality indicators
- Collaboration and partnership: mapping stakeholders and public/private partners

Participants also reflected on how they would know that their vision for digital HE had been reached, producing inspiring images of graduates who 'will transform themselves and humanity in general'. Participants said they would know their vision was being realized when they could 'cost-effectively access quality' digital higher education without 'having challenges with devices or internet connection' and when 'learner support services are given priority'. Participants wanted to see students 'collaborate with other learners globally', feel comfortable with 'synchronous and asynchronous learning designs', able to be 'self-directed' and feel 'empowered'. Participants wanted students to be part of 'communities of practice that will last beyond their life at university'. Critically, especially for rural areas, participants wanted students to 'have affordable and reliable sources of energy' as well as 'good family support and a favourable policy environment for unhindered access to quality education online'. The vision for digital HE expressed by the representatives of Kenyan universities helps us to imagine how we can take forward the work started during the pandemic.

The pandemic also provided an opportunity to research teachers' experiences at the very moment they went online. UCL conducted a research project into university staff experiences of the pandemic: The Moving to Online Teaching and Homeworking (MOTH).[2] This research provided evidence of both the challenges that teachers face with online learning and the practices that were working well. The value of the knowledge this study provides is not limited to the traumatic period of the pandemic as it helps us better understand the future for online education. In the next section, we explain why online teaching and learning during the pandemic represented such a significant disjuncture with what went before.

The transition to online learning after the COVID-19 pandemic

In a report commissioned by the Higher Education Funding Council for England (HEFCE) in 2010 to provide an overview of online learning in the UK, a number of trends were observed. These included the insights that almost all online courses were at postgraduate level and could be described as continuing professional development (White, Warren, Faughnan, & Manton, 2010). This situation had changed little in 2018, when another UK government-commissioned report identified a gap in online course provision at Levels 4 and 5 (undergraduate years 1 and 2), with most online HE provision at Level 6 and above (final year undergraduate/postgraduate) (Zaidi & Beadle, 2018). The report also found that few tertiary education providers were planning to increase their online learning offer, and considered blended learning a more viable option for low-medium skilled learners who needed more in-person tutor support.

When online learning was adopted for all levels of education during the pandemic, this was a very sharp change of direction, therefore, unanticipated and without preparation. As a result, online learning during the pandemic represented an adaptation of the vision for online learning held by many of its earlier advocates. There was a new focus on video conferencing that was designed to replace the synchronous experience of the classroom or lecture theatre. The use of video conferencing platforms for synchronous teaching had previously been a small part of an online teacher's toolkit. Instead, online learning had more commonly consisted of carefully designed sequences of asynchronous activities. Video conferencing requires high levels of internet bandwidth, presents challenges when teaching geographically dispersed learners (e.g. on an international Master's programme located in different time zones), and the technology very frequently proved problematic for learners trying to log in via an app. This last issue was such a problem that educational video conferencing had started to move towards the use of WebRTC (Web Real Time Communication) to allow participants to meet in an internet browser window without the need to download an app to their computer. For example, Blackboard, a major player in video conferencing for education pre-pandemic, had adopted WebRTC for its Blackboard Collaborate Ultra product (Hettick, 2014). However, during the pandemic lockdowns, app-based video conferencing became the principal means by which people were able to keep in contact with each other. This increased familiarity with using video conferencing apps in everyday life made an impact on education. For example, in a review of research on HE's approach to emergency remote learning during the pandemic, Bond, Bedenlier, Marín, & Händel (2021) reported that synchronous video conferencing tools were the most frequently mentioned tool used. In particular, Zoom became the preferred app for video conferencing over rivals such as Skype, which according to Grandinetti (2022, para 13) 'suffered over time from what users described as feature creep – the excessive expansion and mutation of functionality that users don't actually want'. By contrast, the simplicity of Zoom led to its market dominance (Grandinetti, 2022; Sherman, 2020).

Another kind of simplicity also influenced the rise of video conferencing in education. Littlejohn (2020) argued that teaching through lecturing is an entrenched practice in HE teaching, and during the pandemic many teachers' initial reactions were to find ways to transport this practice from the campus to the online world. This seemingly simple move ignored the complexities of online learning highlighted in research and shifted expectations away from asynchronous learning designs firmly towards more synchronous experiences.

Bond et al. (2021, p. 19) suggest this was because teachers did not have 'extensive experience in providing other formats of online learning that make more use of the temporal flexibility inherent to online formats'. This move may have caused additional technical problems, since, in contrast to asynchronous designs, video conferencing requires fast computers and internet speeds which many teachers (and learners) were not prepared for at home. The challenges experienced by many teachers during the early months of the pandemic have been associated with the transition to using unfamiliar technology. For example, Kita, Yasuda, & Gherghel (2022) reported that Japanese faculty were more at risk of mental health deterioration if they experienced IT difficulties and inadequate support from their institutions.

Despite the initial unpreparedness of most colleges and universities for online learning, the worldwide need to improve skills, equipment and infrastructure to support it resulted in the global exposure to, and resulting acceptance of, online learning, something that would have been previously unthinkable. This experience has changed the landscape for online learning. The use of video conferencing for teaching and learning has now become established, and is now generally expected as part of the experience tertiary education will provide for online and distance learners.

Staff experiences of the rapid move to teaching online

In the early weeks of the pandemic lockdown, staff at UK universities as elsewhere around the world were required to move their teaching online and work from home before their institutions had put in place much support to help them do this. This transition was described as an emergency response to differentiate it from a planned and designed distance learning offer, and as online learning researchers we were curious to know how this was being experienced by academics and professional staff, the majority of whom had never experienced online teaching and learning before. In particular, we wanted to know what support staff needed and how best to provide this. As a result, the MOTH project to investigate UCL staff experiences was established, comprising an online survey (412 responses) and follow-up interviews (Kennedy, Oliver, & Littlejohn, 2022; Littlejohn et al., 2021; Rode, Kennedy, & Littlejohn, 2022).

Participants were asked to describe both the challenges and opportunities involved in moving their teaching online. In terms of the challenges they described, there was a lack of interaction and engagement online; problems with unfamiliar technology; increased time and resource demands; the need for professional development. Among participants perceiving there to be opportunities to moving teaching online, many experienced a relatively smooth transition, and were positive about pedagogical innovation, student engagement and the implications for the future of online learning. These findings have been explored in various publications, for example Littlejohn et al. (2021). Delving further into the findings it was possible to make links between teachers' needs for interaction and their desire to create a pedagogy of care for learners. Trying to put this in place made sense of the increased labour they reported. In addition, while all labour increased, much of it related to the emotional labour of teaching online. Finally, the smooth transitions that were reported indicated the kind of support staff needed for teaching online. These themes are discussed below.

Developing a pedagogy of care for online education

For the majority of participants who voiced concerns about moving to online teaching, the inability to achieve a similar experience to their face-to-face teaching was a key problem. Many participants emphasized that what they enjoyed from teaching was interaction with students, and it was difficult to recreate this in an online environment. Participants said that they missed the predominantly visual cues they relied on to monitor learning:

> To save bandwidth, we don't see each other. I can't see the students' reactions to what others are saying, or to what I say, I don't know who's ready to speak and who is gazing out the window. Some students say that this kind of interaction is so stressful that they do not attend class.
>
> (Elaine)

> Particularly with first year undergraduates they are often unwilling to ask for clarification, so one relies upon body language and facial expression to assess that. Not possible online.
>
> (Hugh)

> Challenges include picking up on non-verbal cues from participants in group learning environments.
>
> (Mandy)

The reduction in spontaneous interaction made the teaching much more demanding – participants used terms like 'difficult', 'harder', 'draining', 'exhausting' to describe their experience.

Participant teachers also described feeling that they were 'talking into the ether' (Ilona) or 'lecturing from a desk to silence' (Jack). As a result, participants reported missing the rapport they created in informal discussions before and after teaching: 'it's deflating at the end to just close the laptop' (Nora).

Some participants worried about the impact of online teaching on students who needed their attention since it was difficult to 'spot students who may be struggling' (Kate) or draw quieter students into a discussion. These experiences left participants feeling that the online teaching experience was 'a pale imitation of all I have strived for in my teaching to date' (Kalpen).

Kennedy et al. (2022) argued that this search for reciprocity in online teaching – teachers' need to know whether their intentions to teach have been successful by observing the impact on the students – is central to a caring approach to pedagogy. In order to create a caring relation in teaching, Noddings (2012) argues that the teacher (the carer) has to be attentive to the needs of the learner (the cared-for). The teacher needs to understand what the learner is experiencing, listening out for their 'expressed needs' rather than making assumptions about what those needs are. For example, during the pandemic institutions may have made the assumption that students' priorities were to continue their learning and therefore required academic staff to switch their lectures to an online format. However, teachers listened to students and found that their needs were for social interaction and emotional support. For example, teachers described how listening to student needs resulted in a need to change their practice:

> We supported student teachers and trainees emotionally and practically in the early days ... We have changed our curriculum so that our student teachers may feel supported and engaged with their learning and can continue to learn and make progress.
>
> (Dee)

> As some of them are in isolation on their own in, oftentimes, one bedroom spaces, they are beginning to become anxious about the lack of human contact/presence. I am currently trying to figure out different ways of offering pastoral care to them.
>
> (Tricia)

> Challenge: social connections need to be managed.
>
> (Stephen)

During the pandemic, many media reports disparaged teachers' efforts to provide online learning, and some of this attitude continues post-lockdown. For example, the former UK government universities minister, Michelle Donelan was quoted in the Mail Online in May 2022:

> She is cracking down on online-only teaching, accusing universities of 'letting students down' by placing them on a 'second track to the rest of society.'
>
> (Picton, 2022)

By contrast, the survey participants demonstrated high levels of care that they were taking to hear and respond to students' expressed needs as they moved their teaching online:

> For this reason we are and will be planning significant familiarisation activities for them. We have already begun by group meetings and one to one meetings. There is a mix of responses from students. some do not wish to be seen online which I think loses some of the value of the interaction, but is their choice. The ones who were presented with an expectation that they show themselves from the outset seem to engage better. We also found that giving every person the opportunity to speak early in a session improves engagement of the whole group. We also have to allow more time for access issues and glitches, so the plans need to include provision for later engagement if they fail to join the session.
>
> (Frank)

In the quotation above, it is clear from Frank that he does not fully approve of students not wanting to switch on cameras, but considers it their choice. In Noddings' (2012) terms, he is keeping open the door to dialogue on this issue in order to improve students' learning experience, thus maintaining a caring relation. Frank went on to describe how his experience of adopting a caring approach to online teaching has improved his teaching overall, and intends to incorporate aspects of online support into his teaching post-pandemic, demonstrating that online learning can provide a better experience for students, if carefully designed:

> I really do see this as an addition to what we already do, and will be suggesting we retain some parts for September (if back to normal) such as online discussion forums whilst the students are on placement, something that they have already mentioned.
>
> (Frank)

Noddings (1999, 2012) notes that the caring relation is not complete until it is acknowledged or received by the cared-for. Caring cannot be called caring until that happens. It is for two reasons, therefore, that the caring online teacher demands interaction with the learner. The first is the need to enact caring by listening to the learners think – which is both an intellectual and an emotional task. Through listening to the learners' needs, the teacher can think how to respond even in situations where a conflict arises such as the 'cameras on or camera off?' dilemma that has beset many online teachers during the pandemic. Like Frank above, many teachers considered that 'cameras on' was beneficial to them as teachers, enabling them to gauge learners' needs more effectively, and better for learners too because it helps them to engage. However, teachers also quickly realized that not all learners feel comfortable switching on cameras often because of their domestic location or because they are unconfident and shy (Oliveira, Grenha Teixeira, Torres, & Morais, 2021). A caring approach here could involve class experimentation with virtual background images, or discovering other ways of interacting with students that work well with 'cameras off', such as through chat, whiteboard annotations or online pinboard or quiz tools:

> For some students who feel too shy in group settings to call out answers/respond, the chat feature in most of the online platforms can facilitate better engagement.
> (Teresa)

The second reason that the caring teacher is looking for interaction is to know whether their caring has been received. It is heartening to note that many of the survey participants mentioned the appreciation of the students for their efforts:

> When we moved online, we did so with a cohort of students who knew us from multiple previous face to face interactions. And we carried those relationships, and that goodwill, online with us. Students knew these were exceptional circumstances and so gave us, I felt, a lot of leeway and gratitude.
> (Trevor)

A study of mainland Chinese learners' experiences studying online at Hong Kong universities during the pandemic shows that learners were missing the same visual cues as their teachers (Gu & Huang, 2022). Learners needed to develop their digital communication competencies in response. For example, learners reported that teachers were not able to see their confusion on their faces, and so had to find other ways to signal their needs (Gu & Huang, 2022). One learner found that questions posted in the chat during Zoom sessions had a higher chance of being answered if they phrased them in a more open way to address the whole group, since other members of the class would respond, drawing the teachers' attention to the discussion. Gu & Huang (2022) point to the multiple digital literacies that learners developed during the pandemic that helped them to learn effectively and productively despite the changed circumstances. The experiences of learners during the pandemic are discussed more fully later in the chapter, particularly their needs for compassion and communication.

The efforts to provide learners with what they needed created a great deal of work for teachers, however. Many participants were concerned about the additional work, and the next section discusses the different types of labour required in online learning and how we can better take account of these across tertiary education.

Taking account of the labour of online teaching

One of the most repeated concerns mentioned by participants moving online centred on the time it took to prepare for online teaching, which was much longer than for face-to-face:

> It is very time-consuming – written information takes a lot longer to prepare than oral information.
>
> (Keith)

> Teaching has become way more labour intensive an activity than it previously was.
>
> (Vincent)

> A lot of extra work in switching module content online.
>
> (Neil)

When teaching goes online, the time it takes changes. Labour is often brought forward, for example through recording video presentations before a session, and making sure the content is available for learners for the entire term rather than providing it piecemeal, week by week. During the pandemic, many teachers were required to move online without warning, meaning that the preparatory labour was required immediately, significantly increasing the burden of work. These experiences may be exceptional because of the urgency of the move online, but they are notable for their insight into the differences in time spent and labour intensity of creating online rather than campus-based courses

(Kennedy, Laurillard, Horan, & Charlton, 2015). These insights can and should inform an institution's strategy for creating online programmes post-pandemic, because institutions need to prepare for and cost the different types of labour involved in teaching online – the biggest expense always being the teacher's time. This is likely to require a shift from allocating funding on a regular year-by-year basis as currently happens with campus courses, and allocating extra resource for upfront development, to be recouped in the future when the resources have been developed (Laurillard, 2023). The survey participants show that this is not only an issue for the finance department, because the additional work has a big impact on the experience of teaching staff. Teaching staff benefit from an accurate appraisal of the time it takes to produce a quality course because it enables them to demand a realistic allocation of development and teaching time to do the work. It is for this reason that Chapter 5 examines this issue and provides tools to guide tertiary institutions in their approach to balancing the costs and benefits of online learning.

Emotional labour and online education

The crisis context also increased the emotional labour required for teachers to maintain a caring relation in their teaching. Emotional labour involves deliberately creating or suppressing an emotional state in oneself in order to 'sustain the outward countenance that produces the proper state of mind in others' (Hochschild, 1983, p. 7). Applying this concept to teaching in general, it is easy to see that teachers may often feel required to suppress some feelings (e.g. irritation) in order to encourage a learner who is making mistakes, or to appear lively and enthusiastic in class, despite having problems at home. Outside of work, these acts are not considered labour – for example, managing one's emotions for the benefit of friends and family is often part of the fabric of relationships. However, when done at work, this amounts to the 'transmutation of a private act into a public act' (Hochschild, 1983, p. 19). Emotional labour has often been performed by those with least power in society, and, as a result, has not been acknowledged or rewarded for the intense and personal labour that it is. For example, one of the case studies in Hochschild's (1983) book focused on emotional labour performed by flight attendants who were primarily young and female, and whose 'smiles' were considered 'assets' by the company.

In teaching, emotional labour can be considered a positive part of the role, but it can also lead to emotional burnout (Isenbarger & Zembylas, 2006). Burnout can result from the accumulated effects of emotional labour (exhaustion), but also when changes to practice are imposed on experienced teachers (Bodenheimer & Shuster, 2020). This is exactly what happened during the pandemic, and the responses from academics in the survey communicated the emotional impact of these changes in not only an increase in labour overall, but also of the emotional labour in online teaching:

> Teaching online is an entirely different pedagogy and needs a lot more preparatory work for sessions compared to classroom seminar-based work – I think the connections can be built with students but they take a lot more effort and you have to think carefully about how you present yourself and each session to ensure engagement.
>
> (Nina)

> I found the change useful in that I have learnt a lot of new techniques/tools for online teaching. This unique situation has created a great opportunity prioritising learning how to utilise platforms such as Blackboard Collaborate, which I will continue to use when you move back to face-to-face teaching. However, I have found it a real challenge to liaise with students. The pastoral side of teaching is very difficult.
>
> (Mona)

> Lack of space in my home and sometimes lack of quiet (I live in a block of flats which can be a bit noisy at times), variable quality of video link/internet and upload speeds. Difficulties in managing teaching a large cohort e.g. I run a core module which has 60+ students. I have had little training in online teaching, only online videos/tutorials which aren't ideal when we are talking about a sea change in the way teaching is being delivered and a very sudden change at that.
>
> (Linda)

These quotations illustrate that the experience of moving online required not simply technical or intellectual labour but also emotional labour, particularly as they endeavoured to adopt a caring pedagogy, for example to build relationships with learners online. Participants expressed their anxieties for themselves, for their learners and colleagues, and used highly emotive language to describe their experiences:

> I am nervous about teaching online during the summer with a completely new cohort of students, whose faces and characters I don't know.
>
> (Isla)

> Teaching online in exhausting emotionally, lack of all the 'backchannel' social cues in class, and the interactions.
>
> (Nathan)

> It was extremely exhausting and chaotic to begin with, and it is not possible to give students to the same experience and support as we can in normal circumstances.
>
> (Nadia)

As these quotations show the emotional labour (and exhaustion) experienced by participants is intricately tied to participants' desire to create a supportive environment for their learners and receive feedback from learners that this has been effective. The emotional side of online teaching and learning needs acknowledgement both by teachers and by the institutions that employ them. Not to do this allows institutions to brush over many of the most taxing aspects of teaching online, and to ignore learners' emotional needs (and teachers' attempts to meet them) in an online learning environment. Since institutional choice of technology makes an enormous difference to how comfortable both teachers and learners feel online, this must become part of the critical considerations in technology procurement decisions – technologies should be bought not simply for function but also for feel. Are they so simple to use that users will not become stressed? Do they enable learners and teachers to feel each other's presence (without invading privacy)? Do they create a joyful learning environment that teachers and learners actively want to join? If the answer is no to these questions, then technologies that may appear effective will almost certainly not be, and if they are not, then they will not be used by teachers. We know that both teachers and students want to continue with a blend of in-person and online methods (McVitty, Jackson, & Hutchens, 2021), but if teachers do not use a technology, then there is little point in an institution providing it. Instead, teachers will do the additional (unpaid) labour of improvising a solution and potentially bear the cost themselves of finding alternatives. In order to support the labour of teachers online, therefore, we need better tools to produce warm, interactive and social learning environments. Teachers should be leading these procurement decisions since managers and technicians do not experience the act of teaching online in the same way.

However, not all teachers struggled with teaching online during the pandemic. Survey participants who were already experienced online teachers reported different more positive outcomes. It is useful to identify what factors made the transition to online learning successful for these experienced teachers, and we discuss their accounts next.

Smooth transitions – what happened when things went well?

The benefits of prior experience in online teaching were evident in the responses of participants who were positive about the move online. These participants found the move online to be a lot easier than those who were not:

> I have delivered online teaching before and have worked from home a few days a week for many years, so I'm fairly comfortable with it myself.
>
> (Suzanne)

> My Masters teaching has always incorporated online elements, though I only once taught a module that was formally and wholly online. The emergency transition to working online for the last three weeks of this term's modules has not been too difficult for us, or, I believe, for the students.
>
> (Kieran)

However, even among those who did not have prior experience, many participants found teaching online a positive change, particularly those who benefitted from escaping a lengthy commute or who found working from home preferable to their previous circumstances:

> Teaching online is much easier than teaching [in the institution's] Open Offices.
>
> (Babek)

> Teaching online also means I don't have to spend several days a week sitting mostly alone in an uncomfortable, empty office.
>
> (Emma)

Some participants were surprised to find the move relatively simple, for example:

> I wouldn't have chosen it, but I think it's gone rather well under the circumstances – it turns out that the tech is up to it, we didn't really know that.
>
> (Tania)

For many participants, the move online offered opportunities to explore further online pedagogies:

> I'm really interested in pedagogy anyway, and have spent a bit of time previously exploring opportunities to teach online, so I found this shift an opportunity to put these ideas into practice. From necessity ... opportunity, and all that.
>
> (Rosie)

Where participants considered the move successful, this had often required them to develop their understanding of online learning:

> Teaching remotely is more difficult but less than I thought, and we are coming up with solutions to cope with problems. Teaching online has forced me to get to grips with Moodle.
>
> (Uri)

> Whilst it was disruptive, I have tried to see the move online as an opportunity to try out new technologies and to test their capabilities and limitations.
>
> (Larry)

> We are now using the whiteboard feature on Teams which allows us and the student to simultaneously draw and annotate images they upload. It's pretty good.
>
> (Maria)

In contrast to those participants who missed interaction with students after moving online, many of these participants described positive engagement from students, and the capacity of technology to help them feel connected to students and colleagues:

> I think for the coursework they have actually had better feedback ... some have come to more than one session and maybe find talking over the internet less intimidating.
>
> (Wendy)

> I found that students can in fact be more engaging, as those who may not ask a question in public (lecture theatre) may find asking a question online less 'intimidating'.
>
> (Terry)

> My online students seem to be happy with the personalized and swift interactions we have.
>
> (Edina)

Participants who were practised and/or enthusiastic about online teaching and learning were hopeful that the move would have a positive impact on the development of online education in the future:

> I hope that people becoming more comfortable with using technology will trigger more discussion of hybrid teaching strategies that can free up more time for interesting discussion in lectures.
>
> (Dee)

> Perhaps we have maintained some practices from the pre-technological age for too long and this is an opportunity to fast track to where we should be in terms of flexible provision.
>
> (Frances)

These participants considered it was now the time 'to take online learning seriously' since it could make 'a significant contribution to the quality and inclusivity of the education we offer' (Vera). A key question, however, is whether this ambition is shared by learners.

The next section considers the findings from research with learners during the pandemic, and how these can help shape the future of online learning.

Learners' experiences: A need for communication and compassion

Like the teachers discussed above, going online was new for the majority of learners, too. The experiences of learners during the pandemic should be considered in this context – that is, that they did not choose to learn online and were unprepared for it. There has been comparatively little research focused on learners' experiences rather than teachers', but two interesting themes arise. The first of these is the similarity of learners' concerns to teachers' – principally around the expressed need for communication and interactivity. For example, Gourlay et al. (2021) discuss learners' preference for synchronous meetings in order to feel connected to the university and each other. As reported in other studies, learners wanted to recreate the interaction available on campus (Bond et al., 2021; Coman, Țîru, Meseșan-Schmitz, Stanciu, & Bularca, 2020; Williams, 2021). These learners wanted to be able to see each other and be seen, which enabled them to feel part of a community (Gourlay et al., 2021).

The learners considered social communication an integral part of the learning process: 'rapport with the teacher and peers made students feel more comfortable to challenge and critique ideas being discussed on the course' (Gourlay et al., 2021, p. 9). This indicates that the teaching staff highlighting the importance of social communication and interactivity were being sensitive to the needs of their learners. While there is evidence, particularly at the beginning of the pandemic, that learners were critical of the lack of interaction between teachers and learners (Coman et al., 2020), it is also interesting to note that Oliveira, Grenha Teixeira, Torres, & Morais' (2021) research indicates that for many learners, communication with teachers improved during the pandemic. Teachers made an effort to make themselves available to learners:

> [D]uring this period, teachers showed greater availability to take students' questions, both by providing more time by expanding the communication channels available for this purpose. Consequently, students had quicker and better feedback for their questions.
>
> (Oliveira et al., 2021, p. 1367)

The second theme in discussions of learners' experiences is the way the pandemic focused attention on the needs of disadvantaged learners that were less visible (or unseen) before. For example, discussing the findings of the *Students Speak 2020* report, Williams (2021) argued that the pandemic was an opportunity to listen to and amplify marginalized learners' voices. The material circumstances of learners' lives could more easily be overlooked when they left their homes to be taught on campus, creating a false sense of equality among learners in the room. During the pandemic, the resource disparities between learners became immediately apparent. These included unequal access to technological infrastructure, as well as the impact of personal circumstances: 'from digital access and job stability to personal, familial, and emotional struggles' (Williams, 2021, p. 27). Such disparities affect learners all the time, not just during crisis situations, so the need to address them will not end with the pandemic. Disabled Students UK (2020) made similar points to these, whilst highlighting the additional needs and challenges facing disabled students with inaccessible online learning. Some common challenges included inaccessible content, for example the lecturer not describing what is on the slides they are showing or captions being of poor quality.

Often the problems were not discovered until disabled students themselves reported that they could not access their online teaching. However, disabled students want flexibility and compassion rather than a 'tick box' list of measures, and it is this that could offer hope for the future. The report noted that, as a result of the pandemic,

> many accommodations which have previously been denied disabled students, have suddenly been put in place for non-disabled students – from lecture recordings to coursework extensions.
>
> (Disabled Students UK, 2020, p. 15)

The COVID-19 pandemic demonstrated that universities were capable of compassion, patience, flexibility and inclusion, and it is these attitudes that must continue. Phipps (2021, para 19) argues that 'when we are inclusive by default, disabled students can use their energy for learning'.

The learners in Gourlay et al.'s (2021) study reported that as well as helping to connect participants, scheduled synchronous sessions helped with keeping to a routine. These findings relate perhaps to a lack of self-regulation on behalf of the learners new to online, which is a characteristic necessary for successful online learning. For learners who are not proficient at self-regulation, more support from teachers is necessary, and scheduled, synchronous sessions can fill this gap. Williams (2021, p. 29) reported that the most satisfied learners were those whose teachers provided regular virtual office hours, and that a mix of synchronous and asynchronous learning resources and virtual office hours 'helped them feel successful'. The pandemic has been instructive in underscoring the key role teachers play in supporting learners to learn. Far from replacing teachers, it is even more clear that teachers are required to mediate learners' encounters with technology. Williams (2021, p. 27) emphasizes the message from the *Students Speak 2020* report that students want 'faculty to be better equipped to use digital technology for delivering online courses'. By developing teachers, we can create better experiences for learners. Teachers are themselves some of the most well-equipped online learners, and the embrace of technology can also extend to teacher professional development. The next section discusses some of the insights from the pandemic that we can use to guide the education of teachers in online teaching and learning for the future.

Support for teachers to teach online

Professional development in online teaching and learning can make an enormous difference to teachers' experiences, and ultimately therefore to the experiences of those teachers' learners. Learning how to make online teaching work well – e.g. by using digital tools for interactivity, and designing these into a programme of synchronous and asynchronous learning – created an experience that was less stressful for the teacher, and more effective for the student. The real challenge that the pandemic presented for teachers in our survey was that the move online was so fast, and institutions could not match that speed with their offer of professional development. Added to this the majority of institutions had not made support for online learning a priority for their staff. As the participants above noted, teachers had not been required to 'get to grips with Moodle' and were unaware that the 'tech is up to it'. In fact, the tech has been up to it for some time, but prior to the pandemic, education's priorities were firmly campus based. Phipps (2021) reported that during the pandemic academics were aware that their institution provided support to help them use technology, but that it came in the form of lengthy documents and videos which they needed help to navigate and understand:

> We spoke with members of one edtech team who stated they had made 'loads of videos' and sent them to staff; and they had hundreds of people turn up to a webinar. They pointed to the production of videos and webinars as evidence of how busy they were, but engaging with those resources was perceived by the academics as requiring more work and time that they did not have the capacity to give.
>
> (Phipps, 2021, para 11)

Could tertiary education institutions have provided better support for teachers more quickly so that many more could have had the kind of positive experiences reported above? Yes, they could, the technologies have been available for many years, and they could have supported teachers in schools and in vocational education too. The teachers who were struggling needed immediate help from their colleagues who were more experienced, or who had found their own solutions to the challenges they faced. This is different from the traditional model of professional development that many institutions were offering. They did not need a course as conventionally conceived. Teachers needed to learn from each other, and this is where digital platforms come into their own. Perhaps one of the best uses of digital technology is to support professionals like these teachers new to teaching online. This book examines in depth the potentials of open access platforms for supporting professionals to share their practice online and collaborate on new solutions. For example, as mentioned at the beginning of this chapter, early in the pandemic we were aware that many teachers in the MENA region were moving online with no experience and no-one to help them. Within four weeks we were able to collaborate with our partners in Lebanon and Jordan to create *Teaching Online: Get Ready Now!* using the Arabic language MOOC platform, Edraak, to create an opportunity for teachers to learn how to get online, choose the right tools and understand how to design online learning. Crucially, they could share their challenges and solutions with each other. *Teaching Online* reached 47,000 teachers within a few months. If we use online platforms at scale to support teachers to teach online, then we support their learners too.

Conclusions

The pandemic offered many opportunities to learn about how teachers and learners experience online learning. Since the move online during the pandemic was in an emergency, the resulting form of online learning and the preparation of teachers and learners was rushed and not always well considered. This resulted in a major shift towards teaching through synchronous video conferencing, which was not the norm for online learning prior to the pandemic. The stress experienced by many inexperienced teaching staff is related to their growing awareness of the limitations of this medium and their attempts to use its benefits to create more interactive and social learning opportunities. These teachers needed to find out how to do this – to learn from each other and exchange their newfound knowledge. This marks a difference from traditional professional development offerings because they needed practical knowledge that was being developed in the moment. The CoMOOC model that we argue for in this book was ideal to provide this, and the CoMOOCs we launched during the pandemic reached tens of thousands of teachers around the world. They helped teachers understand the value of learning design and the combination of asynchronous and synchronous learning activities to improve the effectiveness and productivity of teachers and learners alike.

The pandemic has changed online learning for good. Prior to the pandemic many of the asynchronous online programmes in HE were aimed at experienced learners (postgraduates or professionals) for whom flexibility was the key concern. Asynchronous learning has a vital part to play in online learning in the future, particularly where these groups are concerned. To reach younger and less experienced learners with online learning requires more support however, which was provided through synchronous video conferencing. Expectations for what online learning entails have shifted as a result of the rapid transition in 2020. However, as we return to campus, asynchronous study can also be supported through face-to-face meetings where these are possible. It seems certain that in the future, we can expect more hybrid and blended course designs.

We also learnt that teaching online is not an easy option. The work changes – it is front loaded and intensive while courses are designed, and resources are created. This needs to be acknowledged by tertiary managers, and the planning for new programmes adjusted to take into account this upfront cost of teacher time. The issue is addressed in detail in Chapter 5. Doing this would enable tertiary institutions to provide staff with the time to undertake the development work, and reduce stress and likely burnout. The payoff is that once a course is created, subsequent course runs do not require the same intensity of work. Yet, there is a lot of work to do in supporting and engaging learners, and this is vital work for a caring online pedagogy. However, the emotional labour of teaching online also requires acknowledgement, particularly as it is often undertaken by the most marginalized staff.

The experience of learners will be best supported by caring educators who have access to ongoing online collaborative professional development. These teachers will learn from each other the best ways to support their learners. Relating stories from the pandemic, Macgilchrist (2020, p. 28) argues that far from needing corporate EdTech solutions, teachers' creative uses of 'a handful of carefully curated tools' in solidarity with parents without access to digital infrastructure, enabled them to keep in touch and support learners to engage in learning. The lessons learnt from the pandemic are that teachers are critically important, and when crises strike, we should look to them first for the solutions.

Questions and activities

During the pandemic, educators everywhere developed new skills, became more familiar with digital technologies for learning and changed their approach to teaching with technology. In the light of this:

1. What do you consider to be the most important new knowledge you developed during the pandemic about teaching with technology?
2. Which technologies and techniques for using them were most successful for engaging online learners?
3. Could you represent one of your most successful online activities using the Learning Designer to share that knowledge with other teachers?
4. How could your institution prioritize support for teachers using technology, taking into account the increased labour of teaching online, including emotional labour?

4

How Well Does Online Learning Work at Scale?

Introduction

This book is about how we can realize the potential of online learning on the large scale to increase access to the kinds of education needed to address the world's most pressing problems. To do this, we need to understand how online works on the large scale because this is different from how online learning works in small cohorts where a teacher is there to respond to the needs of learners. To learn in an environment alongside many others, with little personalized support, takes a degree of confidence that comes from having previous successful learning experiences. Such learners are resourceful and determined but are also usually immersed in complex professional and personal lives with many competing priorities that threaten to draw them away. To make sure that we are designing online learning experiences that work for professionals, therefore, we need to find out how participants are responding to learning on the large scale. This chapter will draw evidence from a range of adults learning through MOOCs. What can their perspectives tell us about the most valuable learning experiences they can offer?

Learning is not a simple process. Research has shown that there is a difference between active and passive learning and between an atomistic or holistic approach to learning, for example Entwistle (2018). The ways learners experience learning is accordingly varied and complex, and researchers who wanted to drill down into the practices and processes involved in learning have used the rigorous analysis of qualitative interviews to conceptualize the differences and draw conclusions. In addition, research indicates that the way students perceive a situation also affects learning (Fransson, 1977; Laurillard, 1979). Thus, qualitative research approaches developed in the 1960s, 70s and 80s to understand learning from the learner's perspective often involved not only interviews but problem-solving tasks as well. These tasks, and learners' reflections on them, helped researchers to elicit how different learners approached a specific activity like reading and understanding a written text, resulting in researchers observing 'relatively consistent variations in learners' approaches to learning and studying' (Entwistle, 2018, p. 65). Studies of learners' differing conceptions or misconceptions were conducted within the approach termed phenomenography – an open style of interviewing that encouraged learners to describe the ways 'in which phenomena [such as the concepts they are learning about] ... are experienced, conceptualized, understood, perceived and apprehended' (Marton, 1994, p. 4424).

Influenced by these approaches, we wanted to identify a method of interviewing that could stimulate and support MOOC participants to reflect on their learning experience and help us understand how they were learning on a MOOC. We considered using phenomenography although the experience in focus was not the conceptual learning in the MOOC, but the participant's different ways of experiencing this type of learning process. We were, however, concerned that MOOC participants might find it challenging to communicate their experience of learning, and were drawn to a method that would be very open, like phenomenography, and use prompts or activities to stimulate participants to reflect on and articulate the process of learning and the features of MOOC that supported it.

As a result of these deliberations, the method we decided on adapted the Repertory Grid Technique, based on the Repertory Test developed by Kelly (1955) as part of his personal construct theory of personality. The approach enables a researcher to see the world from the perspective of research participants by encouraging them to articulate the constructs they use to make sense of the people and experiences they encounter. A construct is an abstraction. A construct is also essentially bipolar: when we affirm something we also simultaneously deny something else. Fransella, Bell, & Bannister (2004) argue that this is what differentiates a construct from a concept which can be more categorical. That is, something either is or is not 'a bird' or 'a flower' but when we attribute a construct such as 'fun' to a person or an experience, then we are also saying that they are not 'boring'. We do not always articulate the contrast to ourselves, but its unstated existence makes the construct meaningful. A construct is therefore 'a way in which two or more things are alike and *thereby* different from a third or more things' (Kelly in Fransella et al., 2004, p. 6). This definition is the basis for the method Kelly proposes to elicit a person's constructs – ask someone to identify a particular group of people, for example, their neighbours or work colleagues, and then ask them to compare the ways in which two of those individuals are similar and thereby different from another type of acquaintance. In this way, the relationships between the two poles of the constructs can be explored, and the way someone sees the world can be better understood.

Using such an approach, a repertory grid can be developed, where individuals (A, B, ... F) can be compared and plotted on each of the dimensions defined by the two extreme poles of each construct, for example:

Fun-------B----E------------------F--------E---------------------------D---Boring

The repertory grid has become a research method in its own right that results in scoring the individuals in relation to construct poles. For this research, we used the repertory grid technique, but as we were interested in comparing MOOCs, not people, we did not use the scoring element. We wanted simply to elicit the personal constructs that participants brought to making sense of their experience of learning online.

The repertory grid technique typically involves five stages: deciding on the elements in terms of types of experiences to be studied, eliciting participants' constructs, completing the grid, analysing the results and interpretation. For the first three stages, we recorded the discussion as it was taking place. The approach used a form of graphic elicitation as a stimulus for the interview (Crilly, Blackwell, & Clarkson, 2006). Following this we analysed both the interview transcripts and the grids, with the interpretation focusing on the resulting construct poles in relation to the participant's ideal course.

Interviews using the repertory grid technique

In the repertory grid technique, the first stage involves selecting elements which represent a domain to be investigated, which in our case was online learning. Such elements can either be provided by the interviewer (such as family members for the domain of 'family relationships') or selected by the participant. For this project, the elements were examples of their own online learning experiences for the domain of 'online learning', and were selected by the participants themselves. Participants were given the following instructions:

> As part of the interview I will be asking you to compare aspects of up to four online learning experiences you have had and your ideal online learning experience.
>
> To help the process, before we meet could you please think about four specific instances of online learning including:

- one or two MOOCs (free online courses)
- another kind of online course (e.g. as part of a degree programme or professional development)
- any other kind of online learning experience you have had, such as Khan Academy, a self-paced e-learning unit, a webinar.

All I need is a short name or code name to identify them in our conversation e.g., 'branding mooc' or 'maths mooc'. Thanks.

To elicit the ways that participants perceived these online learning experiences – in other words, their personal constructs – a grid was created using an online interactive whiteboard (see Figure 4.1) that both the interviewer and participant could access and manipulate during an hour-long interview conducted online using a video conferencing platform of the participant's choice.

Virtual post-it notes were created for each element supplied by the participant. The participants were then asked to compare these online learning experiences using the 'triad' technique. This asks participants to name a way that two of the elements (online learning experiences) were similar and different from a third. This construct was then written on the left of the grid, and the participant was asked to supply the opposite of that construct. For example, one participant suggested that two of the online learning experiences had 'real fellow participants reading comments' and the opposite of that was 'chatbot feedback'. Thus, two poles for each construct were elicited and added to the grid. Each participant supplied around five such construct poles. Other examples of poles were:

- In-depth video ←→ Superficial video
- Real-world knowledge ←→ Theory
- Strong overall structure/plan ←→ Haphazard scattering of ideas
- Meaningful interaction ←→ Off topic discussion
- Easy assessments ←→ Difficult and too long tasks

To complete the grid, the repertory grid technique requires participants to evaluate each element they have supplied against the dimensions they have now described in terms of the two poles of each construct. As discussed above, rank ordering or rating of each element against the construct poles can be used. These approaches produce scores that could enable patterns of associations between constructs and elements to be calculated and analysed across all interviewees. However, this requires some consistency of elements between the participants, that is, the elements are supplied by the interviewer and the participant considers each in turn. By contrast, our approach was fundamentally open and explorative, and used the grid as a mechanism for eliciting participants' perspectives on the learning experiences provided by different types of online learning. As a result, number rating scales were avoided, and participants were asked to take each element (by dragging the corresponding virtual note) and position it by sight between the construct poles corresponding to how they considered the poles related to that element. The interview then invited the participants to explain why they chose that position. Finally, they indicated where their ideal course would lie on this scale. Figure 4.1 shows an example of what a completed grid looks like.

The outcomes, therefore, are both the constructs, as ways of conceptualizing the MOOC learning experience, and a sense of the different characteristics participants are looking for in their ideal course, which could influence design.

We interviewed a total of twenty-five MOOC participants using this process, who were geographically located in the UK and Europe, North America, East and South Asia, and Australasia. The participants' educational attainment level ranged from non-graduate to PhD, and included current students. However, most participants were graduate professionals. By the end of the interviews, patterns among the constructs being elicited began to emerge. Reflexive thematic analysis (Braun & Clarke, 2020) was conducted on both the elicited construct poles and the interview transcripts using Nvivo. Since the constructs were elicited from the participants themselves, using their own words, which were checked and adjusted by the participants, these were coded first. Analysis of the construct

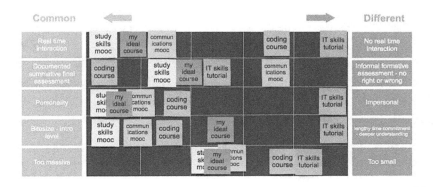

Figure 4.1 A completed repertory grid.

poles produced five themes that were discernible across all the grids. These were: deep learning, applied learning, discussion and social learning, digital engagement as inclusive learning, and learning design. The interview data was then coded within these overarching themes. The following sections focus on the ways the five themes can help to guide the design of MOOCs, particularly for those aimed at professionals. Participants have been given pseudonyms to protect their identity.

Deep learning

All the participants emphasized that the kind of learning they were looking for was 'deep learning' in contrast to superficial learning. This was perhaps a surprising finding since MOOC participants study in their own (very limited) time and it might be thought that this would incline them towards easier MOOC content. However, the preference for meaningful learning went across the board, including the desire to be challenged intellectually, for example:

> I'm not here because I want a Mickey Mouse experience either, I'm here because I want to learn something.
>
> (Anne)

> Confirmation bias I think is very powerful ... so I try very hard not to fall into that trap ... so yes, I will look out ... to try and get a different perspective, to give me a better balance.
>
> (Vincent)

> My ideal course? I would go right to the left, because I like something a bit challenging and I don't mind if I don't understand some of it.
>
> (Zack)

This theme includes construct poles participants created that reference the idea of 'serious' or 'scientific' content, with the participants' indicating that their ideal course had more challenging content:

Serious ↔ Basic (Bas)
Superficial ↔ Scientific and academic (Wen)

It was also evident that many of the participants preferred challenging content because they were confident independent learners. For example, Zack like, many of the participants, had developed capacities for self-regulation as part of his professional career:

> My job was as a design engineer and that involved a lot of thinking during the day, and one of the things I really missed was a bit of challenge.
>
> (Zack)

This led participants to favour pedagogies that, in the words of Simon, were about 'drawing it out of you' as opposed to 'drilling it into us'. This preference for active learning was seen among many participants, especially those with higher educational experience. For example, one participant (Noah) who was a semi-retired high-level consultant expressed a desire to 'be researched' which he considered the opposite of 'being fed information'. This meant that he wanted the purpose of a MOOC to be as much about finding out information about the participants as giving information to the participants:

> I get the impression that the courses are set up as an excellent way of doing a grounded theory investigation.
>
> (Noah)

The dislike of being 'fed information' was shared by a number of other participants who were also high-level professionals. For example, Una and Wen contrasted the teaching quality of various MOOCs, criticizing those who provided 'superficial' lectures:

> it seemed quite superficial, there wasn't much depth behind what they were saying ... I just kind of felt, yeah, yeah, we know that ... so it was just kind of them telling you stuff about it, I think ... it was more like the lecturer was kind of, giving like small, mini lectures that weren't particularly that good.
>
> (Una)

> The professors and the speakers, they didn't provide any sources about what they were saying, they were just giving a lecture saying this was written in this book or some scholars say – it was quite superficial I would say.
>
> (Wen)

The participants were generally seeking a deeper learning experience on the MOOCs, and for many, a challenging assessment was key to this. Noah even went so far as to say that he thought it 'absolutely essential that there's a stressful test'. Yvonne contrasted 'rigorous checking for learning' with a 'slapdash/casual approach to assessment', putting their ideal course firmly at the rigorous end of the pole. Participants wanted assessment and (possibly more importantly) opportunities for feedback, to be present within the MOOCs and had suggestions for where educators could provide opportunities. For example:

> They were talking about info graphs, and this was another missed opportunity in that course, … then we got, right, let's move on and they didn't really give the participants a chance to go and practice, to build an info graph.
>
> (Duncan)

Many of the participants stated a preference for challenging quizzes and tests, for example:

> Meaningful tests and quizzes ←→ No tests or quizzes
>
> (Anne)

> Serious test ←→ Self-check quiz
>
> (Olivia)

> Stressful test ←→ Easy quiz
>
> (Noah)

> Quizzes without grades ←→ Quizzes with grades
>
> (Raaka)

However, there is an optimal balance, as others indicated that there could be too much of a good thing, with the constant quizzes in one MOOC, for example, getting in the way of information:

> I found it quite hard to take in things because it was almost fragmented by the constant quizzes, so in the end, they kind of annoyed me, because they were like in the way of getting the information.
>
> (Fiona)

Some participants had a sophisticated understanding of the role of assessment for learning. Kath considered the role of assessment for motivating, discussing how the desire to pass quizzes was 'a very good negative inducement to read the material' (meaning that fear of failure in a quiz would prompt the reading). In contrast to quizzes, however, Jay considered peer review to be a better assessment because 'we can learn from other people's [work] even when we evaluate others'. Zack explained how the process of production helps a learner to formulate and articulate their thinking for others.

> If you are given a task, go away and read this and give us your comments, you are actually putting words down on paper or on screen, so you want it to be right.
>
> (Zack)

However, while Wen likewise understood the value of more complex learning tasks, she could not find a justification for the time involved. Wen gave an example of an exercise that involved tracking the behaviour of her social media contacts over an extended period, and suggested a scaled-down version might be a more appropriate alternative task:

> It is not difficult, because it is interesting, it is just time ... For example, just pick up – instead of ten people because I think it was a big number – I would like to pick up just 3 people.
>
> (Wen)

In summary, therefore, despite being time poor, these participants were not looking for surface learning opportunities and preferred to engage in deeper learning, deriving deeper understanding. The participants used quizzes to check their learning, but wanted the quizzes to test them seriously rather than provide easy answers. It can be challenging to create quizzes that provide serious tests, and some participants preferred the more in-depth assessment options provided by peer-reviewed assignments. These opportunities for engaging in peer review were seen to be valuable for performing the review as well as for the review that was received. However, the time that activities take was also critical – if an assignment took too long it became unfeasible for participants to complete. There needs to be a careful balance of tasks to enable participants to monitor their learning progress without making it impossible for them to complete within the time available to them.

Applied learning

In addition to a preference for deeper learning, another theme that cut across the interviews was a desire for applied learning. This is explained to an extent by the preponderance of professionals within the group of participants interviewed. Discussing knowing and learning for professionals, Fenwick & Nerland (2014) describe the importance of the embodied nature of professional knowledge, which weaves together knowing and action. Professional practice in this view is situated, contextualized knowledge. This knowledge is inseparable from learning because, for professionals, learning always involves applying that knowledge to practice. Unsurprisingly, therefore, the participants who were professionals frequently praised online learning experiences that provided them with opportunities for applied learning:

> I'd call [it] deployed knowledge and real world knowledge and that's why I really got a lot out of it.
>
> (Mike)

> Where I found the greatest benefit is, when I've been able to learn something or cover a topic and then actually go and use it.
>
> (Peter)

> These helped me dealing with my patients, so [for the] application part, I'm satisfied.
>
> (Raaka)

However, this theme was also discernible among participants who had yet to begin a professional career. Bas, for example, wanted real-world examples (with all their complexity) rather than 'artificial' cases that 'just focus on one specific thing'.

While participants found theory useful, they wanted to see how to put it into practice. Participants' ideal courses balanced the practical and theoretical, sometimes sparking their own investigation, for example:

> It gave you something more than just going away and reading an academic paper, because you had people who were, you know, engaging with it, doing it, giving you some tricks of the trade, showing you how it might work, you know, as a starting point for you to investigate further as well.
>
> (Una)

The participants who were practising professionals were able to make connections between their studies and their jobs. Sometimes this was tangential. For example, Mike was invited to take a MOOC with a view to recommending it to his colleagues. Noah found that MOOCs helped him reflect on and understand events that had occurred during his career. Hilary, a translator, gained background subject knowledge that she could apply to translation work. The application to practice was also not restricted to paid jobs. Zack, who wanted to get more involved in environmental activism, found that sustainability MOOCs helped him to put myself in the mindset of someone who is more professional in terms of thinking about the environment, so it has certainly helped me with both campaign and voluntary work.

(Zack)

For other participants, they more explicitly considered their engagement in MOOCs as a form of professional development. For example, Larry said he had no time for personal interest MOOCs, Peter found MOOCs that addressed different aspects of his research and teaching career, and Raaka updated her medical knowledge.

For the participants in the study who were seeking professional development, their capacity to apply their learning to practice was essential. In contrast, abstract knowledge was not seen as useful. Being in the company of other professionals who supported the process of application to practice or supplied more practical, contextualized examples was highly valued by this group. This relates therefore to the importance of social learning for professionals, which is discussed next.

Social learning

It was in the area of social and collaborative learning that the biggest differences emerged between participants who were professionals and those who were at the beginning of their studies in HE. The participants were recruited through FutureLearn MOOCs, which is a platform that foregrounds social learning. Discussion was important for the majority of participants, in fact for some it was the defining characteristic of learning on a MOOC:

> I think that's a key thing with MOOCs, isn't it, yeah, but that's what's different from just any kind of learning that you do on your own, the fact that you can have discussions with other learners.
>
> (Olivia)

> One thing that's different ... with the MOOCs, you have kind of a forum where you can follow people, you can post messages, you can do replies ... the nice thing about MOOCs is you get an opportunity to interact with other learners, other participants and then also with some of the presenters.
>
> (Peter)

> I joined several discussions, that was nice, many people were responding to my discussion because they were giving their comments after reading my

discussions, that felt very good – yes people are learning and people are reading my comments.

(Raaka)

However, there were some participants who did not enjoy the discussion and rarely took part:

No, I've no wish to engage in the discussion.

(Thea)

In reality, I don't want to continuously talk to people about what we learnt just because I can easily get distracted or their opinions may confuse me.

(Gini)

It is significant to note that both of these participants were educated only to high school level. Gini was planning to go to university, however, and she had taken some tentative steps into the discussion. In fact, another learner had recently responded to a comment she made, and this had a positive effect:

I got a reply to one the other day, which was great [....] because you just feel more involved in the course and like when I got the email saying, oh, you got a reply to this, it just made my comment and my contribution to it seem more valid ...

(Gini)

The discomfort that Gini felt ('a lot of these people are more intellectual than me') was echoed by another participant, Alana. As with Gini, however, although Alana tended to stay away from discussions, when she was pushed to contribute (through a MOOC activity that required it) she got more out of that course than others she had taken.

It is interesting to note the value of discussion for learning even among hesitant participants. The more confident discussion participants, however, were the professionals and postgraduate students. It seems reasonable to suggest this was the result of more effective self-regulation among these participants. Our capacity to self-regulate is 'the source of our perception of personal agency that lies at the core of our sense of self' (Zimmerman, 2000, p. 14). Self-regulation is a cyclical process that involves forethought (goal setting, planning and self-motivation), performance or volitional control (self-instruction and self-observation) and self-reflection (self-judgement and self-evaluation) processes (Zimmerman, 2000). The more experienced the learners are, the more likely they are to have developed self-regulatory skills, and this concept has been shown to be helpful in explaining 'the diversity of motivations and incentives among learners and the mutable, learner driven nature of the learning experience in MOOCs' (Littlejohn & Hood, 2018, p. 49). For those experienced learners, discussion was one of the most valuable aspects of MOOC learning:

> If you were going to make me pay for something [then] I want that level of discussion, I want that level of clarity that I can't get from a book itself.
>
> (Alicia)

> I enjoy that side of it and in posting, I think it makes me think, because I'm putting something down, so therefore I have to try and think before I do so as to what it is I want to say.
>
> (Vincent)

For these participants, however, not all discussion was worthwhile. Participants disliked discussion that was unstructured. Zack said he gave up reading reams of superficial comments where there were 'so many people saying things like "wow isn't this wonderful"'.

This point was echoed by Anne:

> If you're going to encourage discussion, you should design this so the discussion is fruitful and there is an academic point to it.
>
> (Anne)

Participants therefore valued discussion prompts that were carefully crafted to produce a meaningful, genuinely dialogic discussion:

> It's the fact that the course providers have decided, this is the issue we want them to think about here at this point.
>
> (Wen)

Some of the most productive discussions that were reported during the interviews involved the exchange of applied knowledge among MOOC participants.

> Many people who are putting up a post will put up a link to an article that they've read ... so there's also quite a lot can come from other participants, so that interaction ... [is] integral to the enjoyment factor and it can be very useful in terms of the knowledge side of it as well.
>
> (Vincent)

For Mike, this was supported by his interest in applied learning as other participants in the MOOC could share their practical experience:

> Somebody says, ok, the tool, this is how it works, ok, well, that's great, but in the real world, will it deploy in practice? How does that actually perform? because often, you know, you can go on the internet and type in collaborative tool, can't you, but ... how we're using that tool, what's the best way, what functions work for you, then you kind of get that real world [knowledge].
>
> (Mike)

> It's like a review of the concept and then how people have used it in real life and because in [the design profession] most people that do the course are either in the job itself ... I feel the conversation is useful at least for me because I'm the one who is learning from the discussion itself.
>
> (Alicia)

The discussions described by Mike and Alicia highlighted the possibilities of collaborative learning in the discussions, where professionals share their applied knowledge with each other. This kind of productive discussion addressed two aspects of learning in MOOCs that the professionals interviewed valued highly: social learning and applied learning.

A subtheme emerged strongly about the importance of having educators (or those that were representing them as moderators) participate in the discussion. All the participants who mentioned this wanted to see more participation by educators – to avoid the MOOC feeling like a 'canned course'. It is interesting to note, however, that nearly all participants were also happy with mentors engaging in discussion instead of the course educators:

> I think you just want to know that there's somebody keeping track of the discussion.
>
> (Kath)

Social and collaborative learning in open online learning environments could have enormous value for professionals, facilitating the exchange of applied knowledge and skills in a way that could be more immediate and responsive than traditional professional development in emergency situations. The theme of the value of social and collaborative learning for professionals will therefore be explored further in Chapter 6.

Digital engagement as inclusive interactive learning

The final theme to emerge relates to digital engagement as inclusive interactive learning. Many participants wanted MOOC creators to make good use of the digital environment for interaction. For example, Mike enjoyed using the colourful digital whiteboard tool during the interview which he found 'very interactive' and lamented that there was too little use of tools like that in some MOOCs:

> It was all very much black and white, very much what I'd call 2D.
>
> (Mike)

For Simon and Una a key capacity of the online environment was to enable learners to share content with each other, and online learning experiences that enabled interactive digital engagement were highly praised:

> Some MOOCs are ... much like watching a TV series on iPlayer, that is to say ... basically you have an individual experience ... and then there is the [other] experience of ... being very much aware in each interaction of what other people are doing and saying.
>
> (Simon)

> These other ones made sense to be online ... you could watch the video, you could read the text if you didn't want to watch the video, you could put up a question, you could get some interaction if you wanted it, you could look and see how other people felt.
>
> (Una)

Una contrasted a lively interactive MOOC with the kind of compliance training she was required to do at work that only taught her 'that it's a bad way to do online training':

> It's a bunch of slides that you read the information on and then you take a quiz, you could have an information sheet and get the same information ... I mean, it was online so everyone can access it, ... but they didn't use the value of being online in any kind of positive way, so they didn't even have a discussion board, they didn't have a place to ask questions, it was just you sit there, you do it, you take a test.
>
> (Una)

However, some of the participants focused more on the use of digital tools within educators' videos. For example, Ellen remembered a particular use of videos that was appealing to her:

> There's more than one lecturer ... there were lots of diagrams and some of them were animated and that sort of thing, you know, so it wasn't just [a talking head], no, but also there was a sort of performance element ... he used props, he drew on a whiteboard, they used diagrams, you know, all sorts of different things.
>
> (Ellen)

Ellen was ambivalent about the extent to which these elements supported learning. There was a sense from the majority of participants that digital capabilities should be exploited, including the capacity to link out to other resources:

> That's what the internet offers ... pointing you to something [beyond the MOOC platform] ... resources I wasn't aware of which are extremely valuable and I will go back to them.
>
> (Zack)

By contrast, however, when too many technologies or tools were used, these actively prevented other participants from learning. Participants signalled the need for inclusivity through a range of requests to create courses that were sensitive to the challenges they faced taking part in learning. For example, Thea complained about the demands that participants access external technologies:

> Things we had to access from the internet, ... and they were all difficult to get to work.
>
> (Thea)

Similarly Anne highlighted a course that required a Pinterest account to take part:

> It was clear they were losing students over the need to use Pinterest in order to get the homework done.
>
> (Anne)

Participants were also critical of the gratuitous use of multimedia, when simpler media forms would have been more fit for purpose. For example, the use of videos where text alone would have done, or where there were unjustified effects such as background music:

> The Compliance Training was … just words on PowerPoint slides … you could have read it off a paper more easily.
>
> (Una)

> If you want me to read, I would prefer to read a paper, not this … screen.
>
> (Camila)

For Thea, this was not inclusive. It made it difficult for her to learn because it interfered with the way she processed the information:

> Why do they have to put the background noise, music, etc, in the video, to make it difficult to hear? It doesn't contribute anything to it and it just makes it infuriating.
>
> (Thea)

The length of videos was also considered potentially problematic if they were too long.

The contexts in which participants were learning needed to be taken into account. For example, some participants viewed content on a mobile phone, while travelling or during lunchtimes at work:

> I like the videos but the downside with them was, I can't always access videos at work, which is where I did a lot of my MOOC work.
>
> (Kath)

> I would like to have the … option to just kind of quickly get something out of it while I'm on the go, or while I'm, I don't know, like, doing the laundry or things like that, the tiny slip of time.
>
> (Hilary)

For them, and for working professionals who fit in MOOC learning between other commitments, alternative forms of access, like the transcript, are crucial. Raaka, a medic from South Asia, explained the appeal of a MOOC for a busy professional:

> I am a working professional. I am working in the field of mental health so after working I don't get time to go anywhere to do a course, so in my convenient time if I can do a course that can enrich me, in a convenient place and time, so that's the best solution – my option is these MOOCs.
>
> (Raaka)

Raaka used her mobile phone with the sound off so as not to disturb her family. As a result, features such as transcripts, or subtitles on videos, or audio versions, are important forms of inclusive access that enable participants to make the most of the little time available to them to study.

MOOC platforms also provide digital certificates of participation. Despite the wide use of MOOCs for professional development, there were mixed views about the value to participants' careers of gaining digital certificates and the purchase price was a considerable barrier to professionals located in the Global South. Jay and Raaka, both located in South Asia, noted the escalating costs of MOOCs:

> When I did the MOOCs at the beginning they were absolutely free, but now I can see some they have fees.
>
> (Jay)

> It is not possible for me to pay for all the courses 4,500 is a lot of money here, maybe not in UK or other countries.
>
> (Raaka)

Jay continued to study by taking advantage of promotions or financial aid offered by platforms such as Coursera or FutureLearn.

The language and terminology used in MOOCs was also mentioned as having an impact on inclusivity by a number of participants – albeit in slightly different ways. Alana created the pole:

> Fun – easy to follow ←→ complicated language
>
> (Alana)

explaining that since English was a second language, academic or specialist language made it difficult to follow. The challenge to understand terminology of different disciplines was also highlighted by native speakers such as Zack, Duncan and Anne who felt that avoiding jargon and specialist vocabulary was key to keeping MOOCs truly open. The design implications of this are that educators should take care to define specialist vocabulary where it is essential, and as a consequence of this participants using auto-translation are more likely to see the appropriate meaning.

Despite major advances in auto-translation, MOOC platforms have done little to incorporate this capacity into their platforms. While there is nothing to prevent participants from installing Google Translate into browsers to leverage the capacity of these tools for increasing inclusivity, there is arguably more that

MOOC platforms could do to support the many participants who are learning in a second or other language.

If taken seriously, digital engagement brings participants into membership of a global community of learners despite their physical separation and despite the competing pressures on their time. The capacity of the platforms to make the most of multimedia to provide stimulating and engaging activities is central to the experience of all participants. Participants actively wanted the platforms to exploit the full potential of the digital to create vibrant and social learning experiences. While using too much multimedia when it was not necessary detracted from the learning experience, offering alternative forms of digital engagement, with the learning needs of participants in mind, improves inclusivity. There is more work to do to find ways that MOOC platforms could use digital technologies to provide more engaging and inclusive learning experiences for their participants.

Learning design

Some participants mentioned the learning design of the MOOC explicitly or by implication – generally appreciating a sense of logical structure or narrative. For example, Bas, who was a current undergraduate, appreciated both a logical structure 'where you would have to build your knowledge from the beginning to the end' and a 'thematic' approach that focused on exploring a specific theme via case study:

> You still need the thematic aspect where you say, okay, let's say the example of Syria, where either we have conflicting data or we have something else.
>
> (Bas)

Other participants like Noah emphasized the need for narrative:

> They could have, what I call, storyised it more, so build a story around [the content]
>
> (Noah)

These reflections show a kernel of understanding of learning design, and most of the participants were aware that there was a structure. Some participants did not appreciate an approach that was too 'standardised, formulaic' (Mike):

> So a video to start off with, we'll give you some text, you'll do a reflection and … then the next section we'll do no video, but some text and exercise and reflection

and then just repeat those two things back to front over a period of about seven sessions per week.

(Mike)

Participants who were education professionals were most likely to notice, appreciate or criticize the design of this structure, but not exclusively. These more experienced learners were able to offer re-design suggestions for improving the courses. For example, Wen suggested most courses had a similar structure made up of videos, texts and links to other material, but she liked those with tasks for learners, such as 'compare these two articles or just write a small text about this topic'. These are the kind of active learning opportunities constructed through cycles of interaction discussed in Chapter 2. These courses she preferred, but for her to complete the tasks she had to recognize their usefulness. Vincent preferred more collaborative designs where educators engaged with contributions from the MOOC participants:

> MOOCs that work best for me, that I've found, have been where there have been a number of contributors ... a mixture of videos, articles to read and discussions with contributors, where they have batted back and forward contributions that have come from the learners, from the participants and these have been more enlightening to me.

(Vincent)

Duncan observed that the learning design of a communication MOOC missed an opportunity to involve an element of practice that would have improved it:

> They were talking about infographs and then we got, right, let's move on and they didn't really give the participants a chance to go and practice, to build an infograph.

(Duncan)

The participants who were able to offer learning design suggestions are those who had a good deal of insight into their own learning. This revealed that MOOC participants were aware of the different ways that asynchronous learning in MOOCs could be designed, and they favoured approaches that invited them to be more active and involved in dialogic exchange, able to contribute their own knowledge to that of the educators. The observations of MOOC participants are in line with the views of educators and learners reported in Chapter 3, who were searching for opportunities for interaction online. Moreover, these suggestions could be supported by embedding the Conversational Framework into the learning design of MOOCs, and the design implications of the findings are presented next.

Design implications

This chapter presented an examination of the way MOOC participants construed their learning experience. The results enable us to go some way towards answering the question that the chapter poses, 'how well does online learning work at scale?' The experiences of MOOC participants indicate that online learning can work very effectively for many, particularly those with an advanced level of education and experience as a working professional. However, there are design implications that emerge from the interviews that would support these learners to learn better.

To create a learning design that engages professionals, the following characteristics are required:

- A sense of real-time interaction
- Productive structured discussions (with educator or mentor presence)
- Deeper leaning with meaningful opportunities for feedback
- Development of practical applied knowledge
- A clear narrative structure
- Digital engagement and inclusive design (including accessible content, timings and scheduling)
- Effective use of video communication
- Opportunities for interactivity (both digital and communicative)

The sense of real-time interaction creates an exciting environment where professionals feel that they are joining others around the world to share knowledge and learn what their counterparts are thinking and doing. Embedding opportunities for structured discussion, ideally with an educator or mentor to monitor, makes the most of the opportunity that real-time interaction provides.

We have shown that professionals take their learning seriously, and want to be provoked and their learning extended through deep learning experiences, so they also want some kind of feedback to check they have really learned something. Professionals are not content with abstract knowledge and want the application to practice to be made explicit.

The key difference in learning on a MOOC rather than from an isolated YouTube video or reading a book is that a learning journey has been designed for participants to follow. When a clear narrative is discernible, it is easier for participants to see the journey laid out for them. In addition, the design needs to take advantage of the digital environment, be digitally engaging and inclusive, for example by adapting to the little time participants have to devote to learning. If it does not do this, the participants will fall away if they are confused or encounter problems with access.

Videos need to be engaging and succinct, because of the multiple pressures on the time of participants. The design of activities that make participants feel that they are not alone, but are studying alongside many others with similar pressures is also critical to help them engage (Liyanagunawardena, Kennedy, & Cuffe, 2015). This is why activities that ask them individually to contribute in relatively straightforward, low-risk ways, for example to add a word to a word cloud, or post a link to a Padlet, provide such good value for MOOC participants. When participants see all the others' responses and realize they have access to a wealth of knowledge provided by a global community of learners, they know they are in the right place and are encouraged to exchange more.

Everything needs to be designed from multiple perspectives – those with prior knowledge, those without, those working in a second or other language, those who have specific needs or competing demands on their time. This may seem impossible, but it is the biggest design challenge of a MOOC. Designing for difference is a major driver for MOOCs, and it needs to be acknowledged, at least in the ways we communicate our expectations of learners, that we are taking into account their variable situations in the way we design the course.

In Chapter 2 we explained that active learning is required for a high-quality learning experience. In Chapter 3 we saw that online learning experiences during the pandemic underscored the need for interactive and engaging pedagogy. This chapter has explored the pedagogical features that are most important to a professional participant in a MOOC.

We used the design principles presented in this chapter to guide the co-design of RELIEF Centre MOOCs with professionals in Lebanon and the companion MOOCs on FutureLearn. On the basis of this evidence, these design features are likely to produce MOOCs that will be of most benefit to professionals. The next chapters share some of the insights we gained throughout the CGHE and

RELIEF Centre research about how to implement these principles within the design of open, online professional development, and their value for participants and their communities.

Questions and activities

The research presented in this chapter derived five themes that were critical for professionals' positive learning experiences in a MOOC: deep learning, applied learning, discussion and social learning, digital engagement as inclusive learning, and learning design. How would you

1. Use these themes as a way of analysing MOOCs being offered by your own or another institution? Does this approach indicate whether the learning experience provided in the MOOC will support professionals effectively?
2. Undertake your own research on the experience of groups of online learners (you could focus on professionals, or another type of learner, e.g. undergraduates or postgraduates) by using the repertory grid approach? To what extent are your findings in line with those presented here?

5

Balancing Learning Benefits and Teacher Workload for Quality Online Learning

Introduction

As discussed in Chapter 3, the rapid and radical shift to online teaching during the COVID-19 pandemic inevitably impacted teachers' workload in the short-term rush to provide online teaching – and find out how to do it at the same time. The shock to the tertiary education system was immense as institutions scrambled to develop central support for teachers and students, trying to equip them with both infrastructure and the skills to use it, while most had to fall back on their own resources and the teachers' commitment to serve their students well. The system owes the teaching community an acknowledgement of their extraordinary effort, as the reports in Chapter 3 have shown (Littlejohn et al., 2021; McVitty, Jackson, & Hutchens, 2021; Rode, Kennedy, & Littlejohn, 2022).

There was a second, milder shock in that period, the surprising realization that online teaching and learning has a lot to offer. No-one wanted to downplay the disadvantages of enforced separation, but equally tertiary teachers found an unexpected excitement in what was now possible. Using the institutional Learning Management System (LMS) they could reach into their students' personal study time and guide their learning in ways they had not previously discovered. Online and digital methods were no longer seen as a second rate or merely cheaper alternative to current conventions, but rather as a cornucopia of valuable tools and resources, creating unexpected opportunities for their students to have a higher quality learning experience than conventional methods alone could ever achieve (Laurillard, 2022).

Teachers and students alike want to continue with online methods, to find the optimal mix of campus and online. For both groups there is also now a dawning awareness of what this means for their workloads. Teachers need more time to develop digital methods that guide a larger proportion of their students' study time towards more active learning (Smith & Traxler, 2022). Students notice there is more for them to do. They enjoy the greater flexibility, interactivity and creativity afforded by digital methods, but expectations of them are changing towards more active, collaborative and social learning, demanding more of their time than was the case with the widespread reliance on their 'self-regulated' learning, as we saw in Chapter 3.

The pressure of this demanding workload also had the effect of increasing anxiety for many students who were already trying to cope with the mental and physical stress of lockdown (Idoiaga et al., 2022), although the caring and responsiveness of their teachers played a strong role in relieving them (Barros-Lane, Smith, McCarty, Perez, & Sirrianni, 2021). The return to campus teaching that now integrates more online learning will need careful planning with both teachers and students to manage this new balance of workload.

In comparison with the dominant learning experiences pre-pandemic the variety of blended learning combinations will be hard to track in terms of how teachers and students distribute their time, how much time they spend and how valuable it is to them. A high-quality learning experience depends on that balance. The same applies to professional development courses, even though they do not typically promise the personal feedback and mentoring that students can expect. An important question follows: do the increased benefits for learners warrant the additional workload for teachers using digital methods? This is where we think through the answers.

Tracking the learning benefits

The national regulatory bodies' concern with the quality of the learning experience requires tertiary institutions to provide data on how much time students spend on different types of learning. 'Seat time' or 'contact time' bedevilled the early years of online methods because all that institutions were accountable for was the time students spent with the teacher, and this had to be recalibrated for wholly online and asynchronous courses (Powell, Helm, Layne, & Ice, 2012). Course modules were created and approved to show that there was an intended spread of student activity across the main categories of lectures, seminars/tutorials, lab/studio, field work, independent project work, independent study and assessment. The latter three constituted the great majority of learning time for subjects that had no labs, studio or field work, and this study time was informed by but not supported by the teacher, so that teacher time in most cases was more or less commensurate with the hours spent on lectures, seminars and tutorials, plus the time spent on grading assignments. It was feasible to assume that a standard tariff for teacher workload for an average class size was a reasonable and efficient approach to costing a course, with suitable adjustments for the subjects where labs, studios and fieldwork were standard. Of course, the approach took little account of digital methods, but although they have been used in tertiary education for several decades, they are even now scarcely represented in costing models, or are confined to online tutor/student contact, again focusing only on the time the teacher is 'with' the students.

In reality, digital methods bring with them the opportunity for teachers to spend time on guiding the work students do as 'independent' or 'self-regulated' learning: that is 'supporting' rather than merely informing what they do. Prior to this, students were often left to work out for themselves how best to supplement the teacher-led learning sessions with their own partially formed ideas of what it takes to learn at the tertiary level.

With an LMS and a variety of digital tools available, the academic can go well beyond providing reading lists and assignment rubrics to designing in some detail how students can be invited to engage with the subject matter using a variety of digital tools and online methods, as we have seen in Chapter 2 'The different levels of quality in the move to online learning' and 'Using a learning design tool to improve quality'. This is how we increase learning benefits to create a more productive learning experience with students doing more active learning, but at the cost of the additional teacher workload entailed.

The current course costing tools do not help with understanding and optimizing this balance.

Problems with the current costing models for teaching

Business modelling for accredited programmes must take account of the academic and professional services costs of both development and delivery of the teaching, and of how that staff resource is deployed for different course models, over several runs of the constituent courses. The teaching staff resource in any education institution is very high and bears a clear relationship to the number of students who can be recruited to a course and the fee they must be charged to break even. Unless we understand the true cost of staff time in terms of the activities involved in supporting all the students on a given course, the business model is at risk of overloading teachers and driving the quality down.

First, we must establish the basic parameters of teaching cost, which are common to all types of course, campus or online, student, postgraduate or professional.

Any analysis of teacher workload must account for the *fixed costs* of development of all aspects of the course – curriculum, outcomes, materials, activities, assignments – and the *variable costs* of teaching support – the hours per student, or per student group needed for running and updating the course. The development is an initial workload that is 'fixed', i.e. the same no matter how many students are recruited. The support workload is 'variable' according to the number of students in the cohort, the size of the different kinds of group, how frequently they meet and the number of hours the teacher is active in updating the content and materials, interacting with students and grading assignments. Once these parameters are assigned, the rest is just arithmetic.

There is also an important numerical concept to bear in mind: economies of scale depend on the size of the cohort. An example will help to make the point. Imagine a short course of just twenty lectures. There is a great difference in the financial viability of these three different ways of running it, shown in Table 5.1.

- For Course A the lecturer needs four hours to prepare each one-hour lecture, so with only ten students, needs a break-even fee of £250, for a teacher cost of £25 per hour.
- Course B has a lower development time, and with more students achieves a greater economy of scale that allows for a much lower fee.
- Course C has the same high ratio as A of 4:1 development hours for the lectures but can achieve an even lower break-even fee than B because of the large cohort.

Table 5.1 Comparing the main parameters of teaching cost against student fee

Course	Dev't hours	Support hours	Students	Teaching hours cost per student	Break-even fee @ £25 per hour per student
Course A	80	20	10	100/10 = 10	10 * £25 = £250
Course B	30	20	25	50/25 = 2	2 * £25 = £50
Course C	80	20	100	100/100 = 1	1 * £25 = £25

- In Course C the economy of scale achieved does not compromise the quality of teaching because the teaching development cost is the same as A. It also allows the fee to be even lower, and therefore more inclusive.

This kind of simple spreadsheet tool does not make design decisions but does support decision-making because the arithmetic is not easily imagined. It allows the teacher to decide what trade-offs to make. For the Course A students, paying a high fee to be in a small cohort might be worthwhile. The Course C lecturer who needs four hours of prep may prefer to offer the lectures to a larger group and recruit more students to keep the fee even lower. All three are reasonable designs, but the choice of parameter values greatly affects the financial viability.

This is not an issue that teachers attend to very much, beyond estimating the number of students they hope to attract when they apply for course approval. They are not invited to. It has typically been left to the professional service staff to check financial viability, using their standard course costing models to define the course fee.

The historic tariffs still being used to estimate the teacher time needed for planned teaching and learning activities are no longer fit for purpose with digital teaching. The approach of traditional costing models of teaching is top-down and based on organizational units of cost: estimate the number of academics at each grade and the proportion of their time that is allocated to the programme against the expected annual intake. There is no breakdown of the nature of the teaching activities involved, except a small allocation in the year prior to the initiation of the programme.

How useful will standardized costings be in the new world of blended and online learning design? As we have seen in Table 5.1, even a lecture cannot be standardized when there are so many different analyses of the workload they require. The argument has always been that it will 'all come out in the wash': i.e. although some lectures require a lot of work, they balance out those that can be repeated without preparation for years. So, we don't wash our dirty linen in public, and conveniently ignore all those discrepancies. In a context where digital innovation is driving workload, that is a high-risk strategy.

The early approaches to a costing model that would be neutral with respect to conventional and digital methods went beyond the traditional approach of using organizational units as cost parameters, in which teaching cost became a single unit covering the costs of lectures, tutorials and marking, without further differentiation. The more realistic way to cost teaching used 'activity-based costing' (ABC) models, which instead break down the costs of a single process, such as providing a lecture, and estimated development time, delivery time, the provision of the lecture theatre for the student numbers, for what period of time (Ehrmann & Milam, 2003). If the estate costs are low in comparison with staff costs, then the 'time-driven activity-based costing' model is sufficient, estimating only the unit cost of developing the teaching, and the time required to deliver it (Kaplan & Anderson, 2004). As we saw in the example above, this simple analysis is enough to show how changing the values of these cost drivers can have a significant effect on viability in relation to income.

Around the same time, to go beyond the traditional approach, a 'technology costing model' was developed that was based on ABC but taking into account the size of the student cohort, allowing it to test the effects of scaling up (D. Jones, 2004). However, it made the assumption that online courses can offset the high cost of development with high student numbers. This is possible for a fixed cost resource such as a lecture, where the development cost is the same no matter how many students are there. It is not realistic when so many teaching-learning activities (TLA) in tertiary education are based on one to one or small group engagement with the teacher.

There is a further major problem with all these approaches to a cost-benefit analysis of teaching: there is no representation of the *benefit for students* in terms of the quality of their learning experience. A more recent application of the ABC model in HE describes it as a cost-benefit analysis, but still models only the financial benefits of being able to plan for a break-even or profitable course (Sorros, Karagiorgos, & Mpelesis, 2017). We have no examples of cost-benefit models from the students' point of view, except in terms of the fee they pay.

If HEIs wish to use technology to scale up student numbers, or increase the quality of learning, or both, then it will be essential to understand the relationship between teaching costs and learning benefits (Laurillard, 2007a; Robinson, Winthrop, & McGivney, 2016). There are considerable differences in the learning experience of a lecture, a lab, a field trip, a one to one tutorial, a video, an asynchronous discussion group, a peer review task and a multiple-choice question test. All have their special advantages, and these need to be well-balanced for the students to have an enriching learning experience. Equally, there are considerable differences in the teaching cost of developing and supporting each one. So, we need four basic requirements for a twenty-first-century course costing tool. To cope with the new demands and opportunities it should

- provide an equal and consistent analysis of both conventional and digital methods
- represent the benefits to students of the different methods
- estimate both development and support costs of teaching the different methods
- estimate the differential effects of student numbers and group sizes.

The cost of developing conventional methods tends to be much lower than for online methods because the latter are new, there is little support for teachers to learn how to use them, and they afford more ways of supporting students' independent learning, which takes time. This means that the distribution of staff time for an online course must be tracked over several runs, whereas currently we cost conventional teaching on an annual basis. Current costing models do not take account of these complexities.

It will not be possible to plan and manage academic workload for teaching in a time of change unless we use a methodology that properly represents what teachers actually do. The changes to teaching methods will create unpredictable disruptions, and we will need to know how to optimize the value of digital methods, and how to improve the relationship between teaching costs and learning benefits, especially with respect to online learning.

Features of a useful costing model for teaching

The alternative we propose is to take a more bottom-up, teacher-led approach to costing and planning teaching and learning as a form of ABC. The teacher would be able to cost each type of teaching activity in terms of their own development and support time, based on their own expectations of student numbers, intended learning outcomes, forms of assessment, types of pedagogy and mode of study. Giving teachers the autonomy to plan and manage their own workload would enable them to tailor their ambitions and plans for a course according to the time they have. It would be their responsibility to define the nature of the learning experience and test the kinds of learning benefits they are providing against the time it takes to provide that teaching. This is a 'benefits-oriented cost model', where the focus is on the benefit that accrues to the quality of the learning experience (Laurillard, 2007a). It is a balance that makes most sense in the hands of the teacher. The next section details the approach.

The Course Resource Appraisal Modeller

The idea for a benefits-oriented cost modelling tool for teachers arose because of the growing recognition that digital methods were not properly costed within current tools, primarily because this very different way of engaging with students was disrupting teacher workloads (Laurillard, 2007a). Thinking in terms of 'seat time', or 'contact time' as a suitable lens for understanding online learning ran counter to the whole point of digital pedagogies (Laurillard 2007b), which are particularly valuable for supporting independent learning beyond the classroom.

When the disruptive technology radically alters the pedagogy a new type of business model for teaching is inevitable. Equally radical was the idea that a cost-benefit analysis should go beyond financial considerations to address other forms of benefit to students, even though the quality of the student learning experience was becoming a primary focus for HE (NCIHE, 1997).

Teachers do not typically engage with course costings, but this had to be a tool for teachers because the knowledge of how any teaching-learning activity might work resides with them. Academic administrators and policymakers wisely decline to interfere with pedagogy.

The idea of the Course Resource Appraisal Modeller (CRAM) was to unpack the costs of teaching methods and link them to the related learning benefits for both conventional and digital methods.[1] It models the relationship between the fee income available for teaching, the costs of teaching over three or more runs, and the planned learning benefits in terms of types of learning activity. It enables better planning and design decisions to be made, which then feed into the overall costing that includes administrative, non-staff and indirect costs (Kennedy, Laurillard, Horan, & Charlton, 2015).

The decision architecture that underlies the CRAM modelling tool provides four analytical features that enable the user to enter their own data:

- For a course or module, decide: student numbers, fees (the proportion that relates to teaching) and duration in credit hours.
- Estimate the distribution of course credit hours across the range of TLAs: types of campus sessions, online sessions and assignments.
- For each TLA, decide on the learning experience in terms of time on different learning types, group sizes, teacher presence or not, and whether online or not.
- For each TLA, estimate the teaching time for preparation and support, and assign the different staff teaching roles, over several successive runs of the course.

The first two bullets are the standard decisions made for the course approval process, but with the explicit inclusion of a choice of digital methods. The latter two are the decisions teachers necessarily make in planning the course teaching, but they do not typically articulate or record them. Even teachers themselves have little idea of how much time they put into the many different activities that are part of teaching. At least being invited to estimate them brings their workload into explicit consideration.

How does the CRAM tool help with balancing teaching costs against learning benefits?

The relationship between teaching costs and learning benefits

This section describes how the Modeller works for the teacher or team using it for planning any type of course, and why its various features are important for understanding both costs and benefits. It looks at five ways in which it invites the teacher to use design features that either improve the learning experience, or the teacher workload, or both.

How does deciding on different learning types help to assure quality benefits for students?

For each TLA the teacher can either select a given one with pre-set values that can be edited, or define their own from scratch, such as '*Creating and sharing text, images, or video to document their practice*', and can then define the proportion of each learning type. For this TLA it might be 50 per cent collaboration and 50 per cent production, with the interaction defined as social, and the duration as, say one hour per week for three weeks. This is sufficient information for the tool to sum the proportion of each learning type being used by students across the whole module, expressed as a pie chart. Figure 5.1 shows an example for converting a generic design for 'understanding the topic' from a campus lecture session to an online session, which has had the effect of increasing the amount of guided learning time and increasing the proportion of active learning for that topic.

The data input by the teacher shows similar visual representations of the proportion of time spent doing individual, small group, or whole class work, and with or without the teacher present.

The tool tracks the quality of the learning experience being designed in terms of these three parameters:

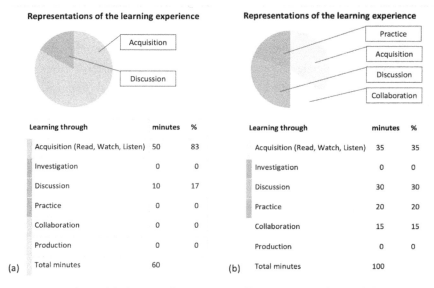

Figure 5.1 Shows (a) the overall proportion of learning types for the f2f session and (b) the overall proportion when converted to online, increasing the proportion of active learning through Practice, Discussion, and Collaboration and reducing Acquisition.

- proportion of time spent in passive (Acquisition) vs active (other) learning,
- proportion of social learning (with peers), and
- amount of access to the teacher.

The teacher may take exactly the opposite approach to this conversion design, and respond to students' requests for more social learning on campus by converting the campus lecture session into more active learning with students together in the classroom, and guiding the learning through acquisition, via reading, videos and individual practice, online at home.

The point of articulating all these decisions is that the teacher can receive immediate visual feedback on the nature of the learning experience they are designing and continually adjust the values to fit their overall intention.

It is good practice in thinking about any learning design, or challenging teaching context, to ask 'how could technology help?'.

The CRAM tool offers a selection of existing TLAs that include both conventional, online and blended methods which already have their parameters defined for

- the proportion of learning types they encourage
- group size: individual, group or class work
- online or not
- feedback from the teacher, peer or program

It therefore encourages the teacher to consider including a blend of both types of method.

The move to online teaching affords a wide variety of digital pedagogies, so this makes it important to model the effects of moving some of the variable costs of individual feedback and formative assessment[2] by the teacher to alternative digital methods. One example would be 'peer review prior to assignment', a TLA organized by the teacher as an online student-only activity for students to

- produce the initial draft of their assignment, according to the rubric,
- review and discuss each other's drafts according to the rubric,
- reflect on the feedback, and on reviewing their peers' work, and
- revise their assignment draft.

In this sequence of learning through Practice and Discussion, the students learn how to improve their work, and the teacher receives better quality assignments to mark. The teacher uses the online environment to support the students' learning, the only additional time being to set it up on the LMS. Individual feedback from the teacher is very costly, so this is a valuable way of optimizing the teacher's time on feedback once the peer feedback has helped with the more obvious problems. It both reduces their own workload and increases the learning benefit. The cost-benefit analysis will look good. For professional development courses that offer no individual feedback, a peer review exercise is a good way of giving feedback to the participants. They often experience it as a valuable way of engaging with their knowledgeable peers in the community within a MOOC or other type of online course.

Digital methods also offer automated feedback, the most common of which is the ubiquitous multiple choice question (MCQ) quiz. They are good because students like them – they offer active learning with immediate feedback, and in formative mode they can be repeated until they achieve 100 per cent, which is rewarding, and will help them discover that they do not know as much as they thought, which is helpful. On the contrary, MCQs are not good because they invite a reliance on guessing. A simple way to avoid this is the 'concealed multiple choice question' (CMCQ), which conceals the options and invites an open answer first, and then reveals the options for the student to select the one they now think is correct. It is difficult to score the first answer, because they are open answers, so it is only partially automated. However, these can be useful for the teacher to browse through, as a way of tracking misconceptions, and generating new plausible options. And the students receive feedback in the usual way for the MCQs.

The 'plausible distractors' among the multiple choices create another problem: if students are invited to give credence to an incorrect answer, how do they then erase that reasoning? Even with immediate feedback there is a risk that the plausible reasoning for why that could be right might stay with them.

The balance is finely judged: the learning benefit is individualized and mostly good, especially when using the CMCQ, and the teaching cost of creating a quiz is fixed for an activity that can then be reused many times in the formative mode. In many contexts it will increase quality without much teaching cost. So when the teacher designs automated feedback into the teaching plan on balance the cost-benefit analysis will tend to improve.

How do learning designs benefit from incorporating digital methods?

It is difficult to imagine one that could not. Learning a physical skill that requires equipment? Learning how to think fast in an argument? Learning how to perform in front of a difficult audience? In all these cases the real practical experience of interpreting, deciding, acting, evaluating and adapting are vital for developing those skills. But teachers always blended real practice with preparation and reflection. Now those activities can be enhanced if they are done online by, for example, analysing videos of skilled and unskilled practice; using a digital simulation to experiment; taking more time asynchronously to discuss alternative perspectives; analysing the playback of their own practice. These and many others are all ways of extending the place-based learning beyond the place.

For each of the conventional pedagogies below it is possible to imagine significant enhancement (+) of the learning experience by using digital methods to extend the learning beyond the classroom without a significant increase in teacher workload:

Guided inquiry: Essay title with rubric and reading list

+ A protocol for doing an effective web search to identify their own additional resources.

Tutorial: Tutor-led discussion with small group

+ Prior asynchronous discussion among the group to construct their own discussion topic.

Practical tuition: One-to-one advice and guidance to each student

+ A video of this for the vicarious tuition of the other students who probably need the same kind of guidance.

Student-led content production: Group work to develop an article summary

+ Posting their summary to the class website for each group to view all summaries prior to a teacher-led class discussion.

Teacher-led field trip: Supervised group observation and interpretation

+ Use of app to provide access to guidance, group contact to compare observations and interpretations, uploading of answers to questions and quizzes, links for a class discussion post-trip[3].

Supported lecture: Individual exercise, lecture and marked assignment

+ Collaborative exercise, online access to lecture definitions, automated formative quiz prior to submission of the assignment.

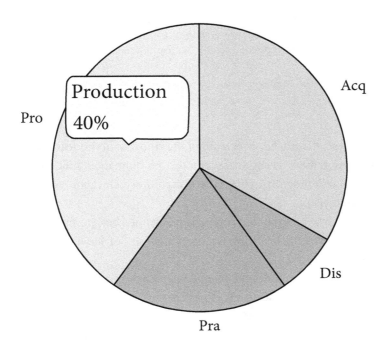

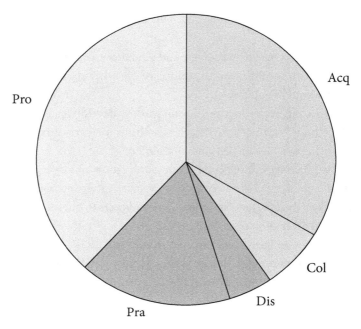

Figure 5.2 Both learning designs show the same proportion of acquisition learning but there is one hour more of supported learning for the blended design; (a) and (b) show the distributions of types of learning, with additional collaboration possible in the blended design.

Supported lecture (f2f): 2hrs 30 mins Supported lecture (blended): 3 hrs 30 mins

In each case, the teacher is extending the students' active learning time and its value beyond the conventional method, for a quite modest addition to their workload in designing the online tasks – each of which can be reused in many different contexts.

Figure 5.2 compares the conventional and blended designs for the 'Supported lecture' in terms of the Learning Designer analyses[4] of the learning types they support (see Chapter 2).

In all the above examples the blended approach is designed to increase the pedagogic value of the learning experience by providing additional online guidance for the work students do away from the teacher, supporting their independent study, and thereby scaffolding the kind of work they need to do for self-regulated learning. Designing the additional online tasks into the LMS is not especially onerous. These designs, once perfected, become an efficient design process for the teacher because they define their own generic digital pedagogies. By sharing such designs, for example, through the Learning Designer, they become even more efficient, sharing the costs of innovation. So the cost-benefit analysis will improve over time in the form of lower costs and increased learning benefits for all the participating teachers.

Why should the teacher estimate the costs of both preparation and support time?

We cannot rely on these blithe assurances that the design time for new digital pedagogies is not onerous. Part of our argument here is that we need to understand properly the full teaching costs of moving to online if they are to be optimized. For this reason the fourth analytical feature of the CRAM Modeller focuses on the fixed costs of preparation and variable costs of support, which can both change radically for digital methods.

Another part of the argument is that the true costs of teacher time are too individual to be standardized. Providing the Modeller as the means for the teacher to estimate their own preparation and support time is the most reliable way to do this. It will be inaccurate, but it provides the means for the teacher to learn over time how to make it more accurate, and it will never be as inaccurate as standard tariffs would be.

There are several ways in which the fixed costs of preparation can be high. For those most frequently encountered there are also ways in which they can be ameliorated.

Innovation of any kind presupposes a learning curve. So institutions must provide efficient, asynchronous, online guidance to support teachers' learning[5]. Academics are very time poor, and will not want to read much, but do welcome intensive and highly practice-oriented advice and exercises. In Chapter 2, a quality process for improving the learning experience section we saw an example of how the Learning Designer assists teachers in sharing and building on each other's new pedagogies by offering both specific and editable generic versions of a particular type of learning design. This could be done for any one of the 'enhanced' digital pedagogies shown above.

Digital methods often require expert digital content creators, such as a video crew, or digital designer, so institutions must ensure there is sufficient central institutional resource to support all teachers in learning to develop their own digital methods, where feasible, and encourage the sharing of exemplars to build widespread excellence. A fast-changing field will demand continual updating of some resources, making it difficult to achieve economies of scale over time. However, if student cohorts can increase in size there are potential economies of scale for all the fixed costs of preparation time.

The variable per-student costs of support are for large classes, small group work on tutorials, seminars, labs, studio work, fieldwork and marking assignments. They are all related to the size of the cohort, the size of the small groups, the time needed for teacher presence in classes, groups and places, and for giving individual feedback on assignments. The teaching-related part of any fee will include the cost of teacher hours spent on those support activities, so the more students the more fee income there is to pay for that time, assuming it has been costed accurately. These costs could be reduced by making classes and groups larger, but this impacts on the value of the learning experience, giving less access to the teacher, and a reduction in benefit.

Despite the supposed quid pro quo of student fees paying for per-student support, the cost of individual feedback is often reduced by giving this kind of work to lower cost staff or graduate students, again reducing the value of access to the teacher. This is why there is such interest in Artificial Intelligence (AI) methods that can personalize feedback to students. Alternatively, digital methods could automate individual feedback, where the improvement in quality would be most likely to come from providing additional formative feedback to students via automated methods (Ke & Ng, 2019), while maintaining the majority of the feedback input from human teachers. This strategy might use the AI-based feedback as a useful exercise prior to submitting an assignment for marking, just as we have seen above in the prior 'peer review' activity designed to improve the quality of an assignment. These prior review activities both create an additional learning activity for the student and tend to reduce the time needed to comment on it. Thus a blended approach can maintain or reduce teacher support time while also increasing learning benefit.

The complexity of these different kinds of trade-off between teacher time and student learning benefit makes it essential that the decisions are in the hands of the teacher, if there is to be any hope of optimizing the cost-benefit analysis.

How do cost-benefits change over time?

It's useful to turn these potential trade-offs into illustrative numbers. In this worked example the numbers used are based on real cases, but they are essentially illustrative, not necessarily typical. The range of contexts for teaching is too

Balancing Learning Benefits and Teacher Workload 99

great to be worth averaging. Instead these illustrative examples are designed to stimulate the rethinking we all need to do in our respective local contexts.

One key issue needs attention: the initial fixed cost of creating digital methods is usually greater than for conventional methods, although the value to students in terms of active learning supported should be greater. Figure 5.3 and Table 5.2 illustrate the point for one way of converting a campus-based lecture session to a wholly online session.

They compare teaching costs and learning benefits for a campus-based f2f session:

Fifty-min lecture and ten-min Q&A session
with a wholly online session where the campus session has been adapted as:
4 x five-minute videos with
4 x five-minute quizzes that students have to repeat until they score 100 per cent,
a twenty-minute reading, and
a live thirty-minute online discussion with the teacher.

As Figure 5.3 shows, the teacher preparation time in the bar charts on the left is much higher for the online session for Run 1, but updating is lower for the later runs, so the overall increase is proportionally lower, and amortized over the three runs. The support time where teachers are present with students is halved for the online session, but is used entirely for teacher-student discussion.

As Table 5.2 shows, the teacher time is increased because they have designed the online work by the students to provide 50 per cent more supported learning time than the campus session would, being time-limited. The student learning

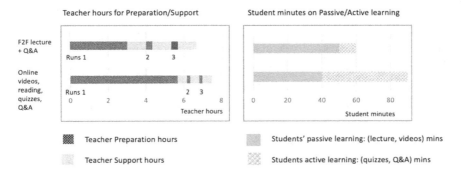

Figure 5.3 Comparing teaching time and learning benefits for a lecture given on campus and online, where the total supported learning time and the proportion of active learning is much higher for the latter (see also Table 5.2).

Table 5.2 Comparing campus and online estimates of teacher time and learning time, for 3 runs. Teacher time increases 7% for online with a 50% increase in supported learning time

	Campus lecture session teaching times	Student learning experience, Active (A) and Passive (P)
Run 1	To prepare 50-min lecture + 10-min Q&A: 3 hrs Support lecture, Q&A: 1 hr	(P) Listening: 50 mins (A) Q&A: 10 mins
Run 2	To update 20 mins Support lecture, Q&A: 1 hr	(P) Listening: 50 mins (A) Q&A: 10 mins
Run 3	To update: 20 mins Support lecture, Q&A: 1 hr	(P) Listening: 50 mins (A) Q&A: 10 mins
Totals	**Teacher time: 6 hrs 40 mins**	**Learning time: 60 mins** **Active: Passive = 10: 50**
	Online lecture session teaching times	**Student learning experience**
Run 1	To prepare 4 x 5-min videos, 20-min reading, 4 x 5-min quizzes: 5 hrs Support 30-min Q&A online: 30 mins	(P) Videos, Reading: 40 mins (A) Quizzes, Q&A: 50 mins
Run 2	Update guidance on digital resources, reading, quizzes: 20 mins Support 30-min Q&A online: 30 mins	(P) Videos, Reading: 40 mins (A) Quizzes, Q&A: 50 mins
Run 3	Update videos, reading, quizzes: 20 mins Support 30-min Q&A online: 30 mins	(P) Videos, Reading: 40 mins (A) Quizzes, Q&A: 50 mins
Totals	**Teacher time: 7 hrs 10 mins** (+7%)	**Learning time: 90 mins** **(+ 50%)** **Active: Passive = 50: 40**

time in Figure 5.3 is categorized in the bar charts on the right as passive (blue) for lecture, videos, and readings and active (orange) for the quizzes and discussions. The bar charts show both the increase in supported learning time and the improved proportion of active learning. In this example, do these learning benefits warrant the 7 per cent increase in teacher time?

The benefit to students comes from both the increase in supported learning time and the considerably improved ratio of active to passive learning. We must also take due note of the comparisons of just the first Run of each session. In that case the teacher time would increase from 4 hours to 5.5 hours, an increase of more than a third in teacher time. That is why it is so important to plan for the longer term, if these learning benefits are to be sustainable. For topics where the content changes rapidly it will be important to reduce workload by making more use of existing sources of content illustration, if possible, even if the basic pedagogy remains similar.

This approach is the simplest that a quantitative cost-benefit analysis could be for an activity as complex as teaching and learning. These tables provide an intelligible way of thinking through the trade-offs that all teachers must make – and do make implicitly every day – as they juggle the demands of teaching, research and the increasing administration needed.

Future costing tools?

Our argument is that we need costing tools for course business models that derive from a fundamental rethink that is now long overdue in tertiary education and has become urgent, given the potential and complexity offered by digital methods. The CRAM tool illustrates this but is still embryonic and needs full development to be integrated with institutional finance systems. A tool of this kind, together with a Learning Designer design tool, enables teachers to plan and develop innovative blended and online learning while also sharing the burden of innovation across the sector. We discuss this further in Chapter 9.

For professional development, especially online and via MOOCs, this approach to course costing is essential, because it is importantly different from teaching students. Without the need for personal nurturing and support, which most such courses do not provide, the cost structure is very different, being focused almost entirely on fixed development costs, with the variable costs and recurrent costs of re-runs being proportionally very low. A MOOC for professionals with 1,000 participants will have similar educator involvement in discussions as one for 10,000, because the focus is on peer interaction as much as with educators. The business model for MOOCs should therefore be very good, in terms of educator costs vs scale of reach. The critical variable is the proportion of participants who pay a fee for certification and permanent access, an issue we come to again in Chapters 7, 9 and 10.

The institution that embraces this issue and plans for it thoroughly and openly, building on the foundation of the academics' experience and expertise, will thrive and take the lead on creating the high-quality and sustainable learning experience in the coming years.

Future modelling

How will institutions manage the complex implications of all the different assumptions involved in designing and running a course? Using the CRAM tool for each new programme under consideration they could test, for example, the effects of having no overseas students for campus-based courses against normal numbers of overseas students for wholly online courses. This would be useful if circumstances such as a pandemic, or a conflict, meant that a high proportion of overseas students would be unable to travel to a campus-based course. Alternatively, it could test whether it would be feasible to broaden access to well-qualified but poorer students. By providing a mixed-mode version of a course they could enable both home and overseas students to study one or more years of their programme wholly online, thereby saving on the students' costs of travel and accommodation, and improving equality of access to tertiary education.

Using a benefits-oriented cost modelling tool institutions would be able to develop alternative business models to assess the teaching costs against the learning benefits of moving to blended and wholly online courses, and to campus and mixed-mode programmes for the immediate and longer term. Prior estimates are inevitably untried and uncertain, but once the course is running, whether on campus or online, the course team can return to the initial course model and update its assumptions in the light of experience. In this way the community would build its own knowledge base for improving the cost effectiveness and value to learners of the new kinds of programmes and courses being developed.

The further critical task is to develop professional services costings, properly adapted to the constraints and opportunities of the digital world. Professional services, like teaching, would be subject to both fixed and variable costs. Education has already been making considerable investments in digital infrastructure and automated processes, often achieving greater efficiency by pushing a lot of the work of data collection and input to academics and students, without necessarily accounting for the consequent reduction in *their* efficiency. An adapted benefits-oriented cost model for professional services would begin with an analysis of the fixed and variable time costs of management and administrative work but would also estimate the resulting timesaving and service benefits to academic staff and students.

The move towards digital methods has two main effects on study at the tertiary level. It makes both wholly online and mixed-mode models of accredited programmes possible, both of which will be key solutions to the problem of making admission to HE more equal. What would a modelling exercise tell us?

Modelling a wholly online mode of study

It would be possible to market wholly online courses to attract a larger and more inclusive group of home and overseas students, because without the high costs of travel and accommodation they would be more affordable. For professional development courses, such as MOOCs, the absence of venue provision and catering also allows more affordable and inclusive pricing. Once wholly online courses are developed, they can be run with the same numbers, or scaled up to much higher numbers than campus-based courses, because there are no campus restrictions on numbers. The critical limiting factor becomes the number of qualified staff available to act as tutors or mentors.

The Modeller can test the impact of wholly online programmes in terms of the likely increase in the two types of staff time, for course development and for student or participant support, and on the expected increase in fee income, while also modelling the impact on the learning experience.

It is important to understand that in the current standard tertiary teaching mode the variable costs (e.g. tuition and marking, which vary with the size of cohort) dominate the fixed costs (e.g. lectures and reading lists, which require the same time to prepare and present, irrespective of the size). If per-student variable costs are high the increase in income for scaling up student numbers is relatively low, as there is only a low economy of scale on the fixed costs. For this reason, in many universities the variable costs of tuition and marking are given to lower paid staff, such as graduate students, early career researchers and contract tutors. Unless they receive good professional development for these skills there is a risk of reducing the quality of the learning experience. Alternatively, by modelling an increase in digital pedagogies it is possible to reduce the variable support costs while maintaining high-quality student support, as discussed under teacher support time above.

For professional development MOOCs, there are very low per-participant variable costs. Being 'massive', they do not offer personalized or one to one tutorial support, the dominant cost is the fixed cost of initial development, while the per-run cost of hosting the course, and the time offered by mentors to engage in discussions, can be limited, rather than necessarily being commensurate with the scale of participation.

Administrative and management costs for running wholly online courses, like teaching costs, are radically different for online courses, and also need careful planning and modelling, especially where administration costs run so high (L. Jones & Cunliffe, 2020). This is true also for the mixed mode, which is discussed in the next section.

Modelling a mixed mode of study

The other alternative design for an accredited programme is 'mixed' or 'hybrid' mode, where students can study a mix of some modules or years wholly online and some campus based. If the student can spend only part of their study on the campus, this reduces their overall costs while enabling them to have the full campus experience at some stage in their study. The mixed mode could also be used to explore the relation between limited campus attendance and larger-scale online attendance patterns.

Other staffing for administration, registration, well-being, library and IT services, career advice and course guidance services, etc., and non-staff and indirect costs, should be examined in detail for any major move to online courses for three reasons:

1. some services will be done in very different ways for wholly online students
2. some will incur variable costs in a similar way to the campus teaching model, and
3. more teaching staff may need to be recruited and managed if numbers are high.

If administrative systems incur high variable costs that are not all scalable these additional costs must also be carefully modelled against the course income. Estate costs are very low for online courses, when library and IT costs have been accounted for, but of course are an essential element of any comparative modelling with campus courses. If an institution intends to emulate social and cultural elements of the campus experience for online students, this may be included in Estates costs, or perhaps in 'well-being' costs, to acknowledge these as important components of the student experience.

The institution will need to plan where they can achieve economies of scale, and the extent to which they can emulate the campus experience. Non-academic costs can easily dominate, so it is essential to interrogate them if there is any prospect of running wholly online and mixed-mode courses as cost-effective programmes. As any major move to online programmes would have a significant impact on the roles and responsibilities among both academic and professional staff, the role of senior management and institutional governance will be crucial. They would need to work closely with the academic and professional communities, organizing the professional development of teaching colleagues, and engaging their experience and expertise in collaborative and realistic planning and costing for the new programmes (Laurillard, 2023).

Concluding points

As an institution prepares to move to a broader offering of wholly online and mixed mode courses, the associated costs in terms of staff time will change their structure. This chapter reflects on what this means for teaching time, and its potential importance for administrative and management staff time.

The main messages for moving to online and digital methods are that

- Existing course costing tools are not fit for purpose as they do not provide a consistent metric for planning staff time across both conventional and digital methods.
- Preparation time is concentrated prior to the course start, putting a heavy investment load onto the first year, which must be amortized over later runs, higher student numbers, and the sharing of generic innovative learning designs.
- It becomes essential to differentiate between the staff time for fixed cost preparation and presentation, and variable cost student support, because these costs change dramatically when moving online if student numbers rise.
- Every institution will need a project to develop a costing tool adapted for the digital world, to account for teaching, administrative, management and non-staff costs, using a consistent metric across all conventional and digital methods of preparing and supporting both teaching and the professional services to courses.
- Course teams must have a keen awareness of the potential for digital methods to improve the learning benefits for students while also innovating to exploit digital methods for reducing teacher time.
- Digital methods can improve inclusivity, as we discussed in Chapter 2 as a key aspect of the quality of education. That is a significant increase in the benefit for students.

- Use an appropriate benefits-oriented costing tool to model the scenarios for wholly online and mixed-mode programmes, along with investment in marketing these new products.

Tertiary institutions that fully understand how teaching and professional staff spend their time, to what benefit for students, will be well equipped to drive the changes that the digital world will bring to tertiary education. Those that fail to update their costing of staff time will either fail or will exhaust their staff.

Questions and activities

There are several ways you could follow up on the ideas presented in this chapter. For your own context, how would you

1. Assign responsibility for remodelling the costs of (a) teaching and/or (b) professional services to help your institution move to more blended and online learning?
2. Use this kind of modelling to plan courses for (a) students and (b) professionals?
3. Use or adapt sections of this chapter to bring the issues to the attention of colleagues?
4. Use the CRAM tool to think through the planning for a new module or course?

6

Co-designing Collaborative Open Online Learning for Professional Communities

Introduction

The COVID-19 pandemic has necessitated the urgent need for professional development at scale, especially in the areas of healthcare and education. While the pandemic has been a unique event, global crises involving health, conflict, displacement and the natural environment are not – and occur with increasing regularity, all requiring professional development across a wide range of areas immediately and at scale. In this chapter we introduce the idea of the CoMOOC, a special type of 'collaborative' MOOC, designed with and for professionals as a form of social and collaborative learning that could offer a solution to this global need. This chapter builds on the research findings in Chapter 4 about how professionals learn and outline the co-design approach that is critical for incorporating a professional community's needs and commitment during the design process. Learning designs for CoMOOCs are discussed, examining the ways social learning and collaborative knowledge exchange for professionals can be supported. Drawing on evaluation data from a CoMOOC designed with teachers in Lebanon, the chapter argues that several factors would better equip professionals at scale for the global challenges ahead: more effective design of MOOCs (e.g. as CoMOOCs), the importance of co-design, foregrounding and encouraging meaningful discussion, collaboration and digital engagement. Attention to these design features would support 'deep professional learning' to meet the expressed needs of professionals, reported in Chapter 4, for deep learning experiences.

The non-negotiable features of scaling up open, online professional development

The origin of MOOCs lies in the free online courses for programmers, given by some of the most famous names in the field, which generated active cohorts of >100,000 learners (Shah, 2020). This phenomenon gave rise to massive investment and the rapid development of the first education platforms able to support so many learners at any one time: Coursera, Udacity and EdX (DeSantis, 2012; Kolowich, 2012). The basic idea was that the unique features of being massive, open to all and online – as well as free at the point of use – heralded a new progressive dawn for open higher education. Their viability depended on requiring only initial fixed costs for a course design that would be appropriate no matter how many learners enrolled. Once the videos, quizzes, readings and exercises were developed, there was no further input from the educators, and learners could talk among themselves in the discussion forum. In this way, high quality education from the top universities could be accessed by learners, for free, anywhere in the world.

For those of us interested in professional development for people trying to work in the most challenging contexts, this was an important model. However, when MOOCs were later heralded as a disruptive force in education, many educators were highly sceptical, arguing that the pedagogy employed by most MOOCs was not at all progressive, but behaviourist in orientation (Conole, 2016). Moreover, research indicated that MOOCs were unable to fulfil expectations of widening access to education, since demographic analysis demonstrated that participants were already highly educated:

> MOOC students have very high levels of educational attainment: 83.0% of students have a post-secondary degree (2 or 4 years), 79.4% of students have a Bachelor's degree or higher and 44.2% report education beyond a Bachelor's degree.
>
> (Christensen et al., 2013, p. 4)

MOOCs as originally conceived have experienced what List (2022, p. 13) terms a 'voltage drop' in attempts to scale an idea. Voltage drops occur for a variety of reasons, which include testing the idea on participants who are not representative of the population, and being mistaken about what is non-negotiable within the key 'ingredients' of the idea to be scaled.

In relation to the first of these reasons, MOOC participants were not representative of the general population in any way. They were confident and accomplished learners, who enjoyed learning for fun, or for career progression. However, their career progression motivation – professional development – is an indicator of an unanticipated 'spillover effect' (List, 2022, p. 91) from the initial plan of sharing undergraduate-level education with the masses online, to a phenomenon that the process of scaling has made more visible. These kinds of spillovers or externalities often derail the process of scaling, as professionals' needs have now done to the traditional MOOC. Spillovers are not necessarily negative, and can help to show the audience for MOOCs more clearly, in this case, that: MOOCs will not be appropriate for everyone, but they can be what educated professionals need, as we saw from the interviews in Chapter 4.

What is also critical is that the 'ingredients' of a successful MOOC for professionals are identified clearly. MOOCs have many shared characteristics: they use online platforms, they feature videos and other resources, they enable commenting or discussions, they have quizzes and they are free at the point of use. But what are the critical characteristics? What are the non-negotiable ingredients of a MOOC learning design for professionals that will make it work effectively for everyone? This is particularly important, because although MOOCs for professionals already recruit tens of thousands of participants, they could be scaled up even further, as the modelling in Chapter 5 shows, to reach the millions of professionals who are not currently engaging in MOOCs. In emergency situations, such as the COVID-19 pandemic, for example, governments need a way of equipping professionals quickly and at scale. In these cases, governments need to know what is non-negotiable about a learning design that is able to engage millions of professionals in learning, because as the evidence from professionals learning showed in Chapter 4, MOOCs vary a great deal in their efficacy.

In the early stages of the RELIEF research, introduced in Chapter 1, we held many meetings and ran workshops with many participants in Lebanon, discussing the concept of MOOCs for professionals. We had lengthy debates and found that stakeholders in Lebanon were very open to the idea. However, during discussions we discovered that 'MOOC' meant different things to different people. The term has been used to refer to scaled up, open, online courses on dedicated platforms, but can conjure the idea of a course dominated by videos, with little opportunity for interaction. In addition, the first experience of online learning for many people has been a MOOC. This meant that for some people we talked to, any online learning experience was included within the term 'MOOC'. While we were talking very specifically about MOOCs featuring social and collaborative learning designs, our interlocutors could be imagining a very different design. As a result it took a long time for all of us to exchange our preconceptions and visions for the kind of MOOCs we had in mind. We realized it is necessary to be precise in specifying what is being meant by a MOOC for professionals. As a result, we decided that a new term, connected to the idea of a MOOC, but making its key ingredients clear, was necessary to communicate the essential learning design. In this chapter, we present the non-negotiable ingredients of what we call the 'CoMOOC', a co-designed, massive open online *collaboration*. Only when these essential features are present can the idea of a MOOC truly scale for the newly identified audience of well-educated adults who need professional development offered in a flexible online mode.

Before we can define the necessary features of a scalable design for open, online professional development, we must first understand the needs of the professionals they will engage. The next section explores the learning needs of professionals – especially those who are working in challenging contexts, and for whom urgent professional learning is crucial – to understand what kind of MOOC will work for them.

The learning needs of professionals in emergency situations

What kind of knowledge do professionals need?

We are now facing unprecedented social and environmental challenges, to which education can offer part of the solution. The forms of education that prioritize plurality, diverse knowledge, networking and problem solving for diverse constituencies can develop the world's capacity towards new paths to a vision of prosperity not based simply on economic growth, but on an inclusive prosperity founded on the flourishing of both the people and the planet (Moore, 2015). Such an approach must begin by allowing professionals who influence working practices on a daily basis to come together to revalue communities and environments and develop diverse but locally appropriate holistic solutions, rather than replicate standard developments.

To achieve this step change, 'businesses, governments and civil society actors are equally called upon to pursue a more sustainable path forward' (Scheyvens, Banks, & Hughes, 2016). The UN has acknowledged the transformative solutions being presented by businesses 'helping to lift people out of poverty through social enterprise or developing green products and processes' (United Nations, 2013a, p. 3). Social entrepreneurship (SE), for example, needs not be viewed as top-down solutions 'sold' to communities, but can be stakeholder oriented, working with communities from the bottom up, since their success is seen to be dependent on collective solutions (Chandra, 2018; Nicholls, 2010). Education needs to engage exactly these actors to support them in innovating solutions in practice in a way that can sustain both social and business goals, and to do this at scale.

Learning as action in the world

We need education to engage professionals in lifelong learning capable of developing their capacity for creating and sustaining stakeholder-oriented solutions to social and environmental challenges. The kind of knowledge they need is the applied and transdisciplinary knowledge to be able to make decisions and take action in complex situations. Such knowledge requires collaborative learning opportunities relevant to the practical needs of the professionals for action in the world (Hager, 2004). Professional learning needs to be holistic, integrated and contextual, for making judgements that alter the context in which they work. Professionals and practitioners must work across discipline areas, and face a greater degree of urgency and immediacy in their decision making (Nicolini & Roe, 2014), often requiring rapid and responsive education to inform their daily working activities.

A situated learning approach to professional development emphasizes the importance of participating in communities of practice (Hager, 2004). This kind of learning fosters active participation within a larger community of practice. This helps professionals to build collaborative knowledge of generic principles through creating and exchanging stories (Brown & Duguid, 1991) as real-world case studies of the effects of changing actions in the world. Professional knowledge has to be dynamic and responsive as 'professionals constantly need to learn fresh knowledge to solve the new problems' (Milligan & Littlejohn, 2014, p. 199). Professionals' capability in self-regulated learning (Zimmerman, 2000) is critical to their ability to update their knowledge whenever it becomes necessary.

Professional education must therefore support learners with practical knowledge and skills to tackle challenges they will face in the course of their work. To summarize: to reach the large scale, the support for this kind of learning has to be open and online, and the non-negotiable educational experiences must be

- co-designed with professionals to ground them in case studies from practice.
- designed for social and collaborative learning.

These characteristics correspond with the demands of the interviewees presented in Chapter 4 for deep, applied and social learning opportunities in MOOCs. In response, we can conceive of a model for professional education that combines these elements into a form of 'deep professional learning'.

What does this mean in practice?

Co-designed with professionals: to create learning experiences embedded in current practice, co-design is vital. Co-designing with professionals and those responsible for professional education in a local context can not only create high quality courses that are based on current practice, but can show something of the range of local conditions, enabling it to be more easily embedded in that current practice. The curriculum, activities and content can be co-designed with groups of the target professionals themselves.

Through the process of co-design, case studies grounded in practice can be developed to allow professionals to share their stories and solutions – in writing or on video. Co-design provides access to networks where contacts with relevant professionals can be established, practices filmed and interviews conducted.

Designed for social and collaborative learning: interviews with professionals in Chapter 4 indicated that many MOOC participants learnt as much from other participants as from the educators. In the case of co-designed learning for professionals, it is possible and necessary to design in this kind of collaborative learning from the start, so that the co-design of applied knowledge solutions is extended to all those who join a course.

Learning needs to be open and online so that scaling up means that it reaches as many people as possible, wherever they are; that is, not the tens and at most hundreds of participants that are typical of professional education courses. Professionals are increasingly busy, and can rarely dedicate time away to study. The interviews reported in Chapter 4 showed professionals snatching time away from work – in quiet moments or while travelling – to engage in learning, often using a mobile phone. Online learning allows for both scale and flexibility, but both the learning and interface designs are critical to supporting this effectively. For example, learning needs to be designed to enable the professional to engage in brief chunks of time and the digital experience needs to be designed as suitable for low bandwidth and the small screen of a mobile phone.

In other words, to achieve a deep professional learning experience that works at scale, a *co-designed, collaborative MOOC* is required – something we refer to as a CoMOOC. The development of a CoMOOC, therefore, involves two intertwined processes – co-design with community stakeholders and the design and implementation of a social and collaborative learning experience. The next two sections will explore these features in more depth.

The importance of co-design

Our approach to co-design combines learning design with community-based participatory research. Community-based participatory research involves conducting collaborative research with communities who are affected by the issue under investigation. The particular orientation to community-based research adopted within the RELIEF Centre is to go further than involving community researchers as data collectors, and instead involve community researchers from the beginning of a project in the design of the research itself – an approach they term 'citizen social science' (Mintchev, Baumann, Moore, Rigon, & Dabaj, 2019). The first steps of designing a CoMOOC work to this principle and therefore engage a range of stakeholders to explore the feasibility of a CoMOOC in their particular context, assessing needs and constraints (e.g. access to digital infrastructure, appetite for online learning, characteristics of potential participants and urgent challenges to be met).

Within our research conducted with the RELIEF Centre, for example, we held workshops with communities of teacher educators in Beirut and Beq'aa in Lebanon, drawing together stakeholders from universities, government and NGOs involved in refugee education (Kennedy & Laurillard, 2019). Within these initial workshops, the concept of a CoMOOC can be explained and an outline curriculum can be co-designed by collecting together the topics considered most important by the community stakeholders. For example, stakeholders contributed a list of topics for community-based research MOOC that emphasized the development of communication skills for both asking questions and effective listening, to build trust in the community and to enable researchers to adopt a 'spirit of inquiry' so they could dig below the surface. Key challenges or specific needs can be also addressed. For example, the requirement for dual language CoMOOCs (i.e. in Arabic and English) was identified in the RELIEF workshops, and became a key design criterion for all our work. While the need for adequate digital infrastructure was important and not necessarily always available, the appetite for online learning among the stakeholders meant that workarounds were possible; for example, by providing access to content through blended learning sessions run in campus-based workshops.

The next phase of co-design involves learning design workshops to stimulate 'design thinking' (Cross, 2011) for developing an educational experience that is able to reflect and scale up successful practices. These workshops enabled stakeholders to come together physically or virtually to design the content for the CoMOOC which included identifying professionals to interview for the videos, as well as discussions, activities and exercises which would support participants to engage with the CoMOOC content and share their own expertise and experience. For this stage, we have drawn on paper-based workshops such as the ABC workshop (Young & Perović, 2016) and online adaptations of them (e.g. a Miro-based workshop that we made available for re-use https://miro.com/miroverse/co-design-storyboard/). The later stages of the co-design approach are described in Chapters 8 and 9.

While these workshops have been useful for ideation around the narrative and structure of the CoMOOC, when we needed to go deeper into the learning design for the individual weeks, we used the Learning Designer tool (see Chapter 2) to develop and represent the learning activities for each week, and gathered feedback from stakeholders as we went. The learning designs created this way have enabled us to implement a learning design-led experience on different platforms despite the platforms' different affordances. For example, rather than starting with features the platforms offered, we design social learning and collaboration into the core of the CoMOOC experience, supplementing the platform capabilities by embedding external tools (e.g. using word clouds, polling tools and online pinboards; see El Moussaoui, 2022 for illustrations). The next section examines the digital solutions we design to create the collaborative learning experience that is central to a CoMOOC.

Social and collaborative learning design

In Chapter 4, the value for professionals for taking part in social and collaborative learning in open online courses was explored. Professional participants, such as Vincent and Zack, highlighted the importance of social learning, and the ways that this led to shared knowledge building:

> [T]he interaction with people from different cultures, different countries, the ability to bat ideas backwards and forwards perhaps with others, that has been, has added a considerable interest and at times, specific knowledge has come from that.
>
> (Vincent)

[I]f a student does actually point you in a new direction or says 'have you seen this YouTube video' and you click on it and you find that's enlightening, [...] you store that away on your knowledge base.

(Zack)

In emergency situations, such as conflicts, environmental and health crises, like the COVID-19 pandemic, the knowledge that professionals need is only partly supplied by the educators. Experts can supply principles and evidence from research, as well as expertise in the pedagogical design of learning; but in crisis situations, professionals need immediate access to what Mike (in Chapter 4) referred to as 'deployed knowledge and real world knowledge'. This is the knowledge that can only come from professionals on the ground, in the thick of it. The value of the co-design approach is that it supports the curation of this knowledge by going to community networks and identifying professionals who can share their practice, and so build community knowledge. CoMOOC learning designs created with the community are then able to support other professionals to engage with this knowledge, and add their own. This can happen in two ways: creating videos of professionals and creating collaborative activities in ways that enable other professionals to respond.

Leveraging the possibilities of digital engagement to create social and collaborative learning in asynchronous environments requires learning design. Learning design aims to represent an educator's pedagogy (including the way the educator uses technology) in a format which is shareable and adaptable by others. Digital tools for learning design (such as the Learning Designer in Chapter 2) support this process and provide design analytics which the designer can use to improve the design. Learning designs for current CoMOOCs are available in the Learning Designer. The following sections highlight the main features of these designs.

Professionals as experts

The widely accepted model of the MOOC is heavily video-led, and the content of MOOC videos tends towards 'talking head' academics giving short lectures. Despite the popularity of video lectures, evidence shows that learners rarely watch more than a few minutes (Guo, Kim, & Rubin, 2014). It is critical, therefore, that video minutes count, particularly since video creation always represents the greatest investment of time and money.

For teachers wanting to learn about teaching they find other teachers' practice both authentic and applicable. During the COVID-19 pandemic, when all teachers found themselves in the challenging context of discovering how to teach online, a CoMOOC for the Centre for Global Higher Education (CGHE) was developed in collaboration with teachers experienced in digital methods.[1] Their video case studies demonstrated the contextualized solutions, which were represented as learning designs that could be adapted by participants for their own contexts, and then shared with others (as detailed in Chapter 7). The videos were from peers who spoke from experience, and this resonated with participants. Alumni then volunteered for later runs to act as 'Mentors' to help with participants' discussion points, the peer review for community sharing process and the revisions for improving the course, engaging in the full range of collaboration.

For CoMOOCs aimed at a professional learner, often in the midst of an emergency situation, it is vital that video resource is used as effectively as possible to impact on their immediate practice. For RELIEF CoMOOCs, the co-production of videos of professionals working with challenging communities resulted from a process of participatory research, whereby our co-design partners were able to identify professionals engaged in *Community-Based Research, Transforming Education in Challenging Environments* and *Sustainable Energy Access for Communities* who could contribute to the videos. Prior to the pandemic, we were able to take a professional video crew out to film professionals where they were working, such as Syrian refugee teachers in NGO-run schools in the Beqa'a region of Lebanon. This opportunity enabled us to understand exactly the context and challenges involved in providing quality education for refugee children in a caring environment. The teachers we interviewed expertly and creatively made the most of the few resources at their disposal to teach children who had been traumatized by conflict and migration. The NGOs MAPs and Jusoor introduced us to their teacher contacts, and we discussed the kind of practice they wanted to highlight prior to conducting the interview on camera. By videoing interviews with these teachers, who were also able to share their own community-based research experience, we could create CoMOOCs where professionals taught other professionals, and the authentic voices of teachers with few resources could inspire others in similar settings to do the same.

This approach is risky and time consuming because the video content cannot be specified in advance, but it is vital to a co-design approach. We transcribed and translated the video interviews and compiled a storyboard for the final video which combined video clips from interviews with an introduction to the clips from one of the Lead Educators. Supplementary video material (B roll) was added to give context to the topics discussed by the teachers. The videos were edited in the style of short educational documentaries, with CoMOOC educators appearing in the videos only to introduce the professional experts and provide a narrative structure. Even after the pandemic hit and professional location-based video became impossible, we were able to continue our approach by asking professionals to create their own videos and editing them afterwards. This approach, which is even more cost-effective, means that co-design can be conducted remotely, and quality co-production remains feasible.

Social learning through case studies

The second key feature of CoMOOC learning design is the interweaving of discussion and collaboration activities around video and written content focused on case studies from practice. Online platforms have varying affordances for discussion and collaboration. For example, the design of the FutureLearn platform is based on social-constructivist pedagogy, influenced by the Conversational Framework (Ferguson & Clow, 2015). This has resulted in user comments being available underneath each individual 'step' (unit) of learning, which may also include a video, a text, an activity or a combination of all three. This creates an immediate link between content and discussion, and the functionality cannot be switched off. Other platforms, such as the Arabic language platform, Edraak, provide discussion forums separate from the content.

An aim of our design-based research methodology within the RELIEF Centre was to achieve an equivalent learning experience within a multilingual cross-platform environment. Since commenting is integral to the FutureLearn platform, the design challenge is to manage it in a way that promotes learning. In the early years of the MOOC phenomenon, many learners were taken aback by the volume of comments. As MOOCs have mushroomed, only rarely do individual courses attract 10,000s of participants at any one time, and so the discussion has become less overwhelming. However, the quality of that discussion is often in question. Several of the interviews in Chapter 4 rated discussion highly but pointed to the need for structure and direction to be provided by the educators. For example:

> If you're going to encourage discussion, you should design this so the discussion is fruitful and there is an academic point to it [...] in the sense of the individual students being able to learn from each other's thinking.
>
> (Anne)

Anne went on to explain that one course she had taken had discussion prompts which were 'terrible ... very self-evident, simplistic trigger questions that don't lend themselves to further elaboration'. Olivia was also critical of 'rambling' discussion where 'you can make any comment you like', and was appreciative of educators who would

> ask a specific question to point the discussion in a certain direction, so 'we want you to comment on this' or 'we want you to answer that question', or 'consider this issue' or 'give examples from your own experience' – and that's much better, because it focussed the discussion.
>
> (Olivia)

In order to scaffold discussion in both platforms, therefore, we needed to focus always-on comments on the FutureLearn platform through well-designed, stimulating and enticing discussion prompts (see Figure 6.1); and to achieve the same effect in Edraak, we first modified the platform design so that the discussion forum was pinned beneath the content step. This made a substantial difference to the learning experience in Edraak, since most courses consisted of videos and quizzes only. We evaluated the effect of the design on the level of participation in discussion in the two platforms, and found that, despite the lack of experience of discussion in the Arabic MOOCs, an equivalent proportion of participants took part in discussion in each platform. For example, during the first run of *Community-Based Research: Getting Started*, 14.9 per cent of participants on the Edraak platform made at least one comment, similar to the 15.8 per cent of participants on the FutureLearn platform (Ismail, 2019). This indicates that it may be possible to overcome platform limitations if educators have a clear learning design and the motivation to implement it.

We also modified the functionality of both platforms to create more opportunities for peer collaboration and exchange. For example, embedding Padlets (online pinboards) and polls, including word cloud question types, enabled participants to share ideas and practices in a simple, immediate and very visual way. To get this right requires finding tools that do not provide additional entry barriers (such as an additional login) or the effect can be to confuse participants moving from one platform to another. In this case, the capacity to embed such tools (rather than link out to them) in Edraak created a smoother experience than FutureLearn. Often these collaboration tools were combined with opportunities to practice concepts – for example, we created an exercise to rate influence and interest of stakeholders in community-based research using a 2 × 2 grid, where the final outcomes showed the difference between individual

Exercise

On this Learning Types and Learning Technologies Padlet, you will find 6 columns for each of the 6 learning types. Add a post underneath each learning type with your suggestion for a digital tool that could support that type of learning - you might need to scroll across to find all 6 types.

If you are mentioning specific tools, why not add a link to them too, so other people can investigate? On Padlet, you can create a thumbnail image of a website by clicking on the link icon at the bottom of your post and pasting the url into the box that appears. Then explain why the tool is good for that type of learning.
If you are already using a tool someone else has suggested, rate your experience of the tool by clicking on the stars (1 star = poor, 5 stars = very good) and reply to the post and tell us a bit about your experience with it.
If you can't think of a digital support, add a conventional technology – this helps us see some of the parallels between old and new technologies for education.

Over to you

Look at others' suggestions on Padlet.
Did you see any suggestions you think you could use? You might want to expand on your own use of these tools, and share any tips for using them.
Are there other digital tools you know of that you cannot fit to a learning type? You can also make these suggestions here.

Figure 6.1 An activity in Transforming Education for Challenging Environments CoMOOC

and accumulated ratings. Padlets enabled various activities, from knowledge building around digital technologies in practice, to sharing the outputs of participants' research. Collaborations also stimulated interaction in discussion, particularly word clouds and polls, where participants could participate anonymously in a polling activity and subsequently become emboldened to join in a debate. An example is shown in Figure 6.1 where an exercise featuring a Padlet is arranged in the 'shelf' format (featuring columns titled with each of the six learning types), and a discussion activity follows on from a video on the Conversational Framework. Participants are invited to add a post beneath each column with an example of a learning technology that could support that learning type. Then participants are asked to rate the technologies and describe their own experience with the technology. The 'over to you' invitation to the discussion asks them to reflect on the Padlet and discuss more tricky issues.

This teaching and learning activity illustrates two aspects of designed activities that are critical to the CoMOOC.

Collaborative learning activities

Both the Padlet activity and the discussion activity carefully and specifically prompt participants to engage with each other in structured ways. This makes it easier for participants to know how to respond and creates a more meaningful and interactive discussion. Inviting participants to share their experience is particularly fruitful, since this is an area that they feel comfortable to share (it is not a test) and it results in collective knowledge building (see below).

As each participant adds an individual post, the activity creates a collective knowledge base that is more useful to all the individuals than if they were working alone. In addition, participants gain some feedback by upvotes or by comparing their own suggestions with others and seeing if they were on the right lines.

Structured discussion

This involves two aspects: an invitation to take part and a discussion prompt. Participants are coaxed into making a post: the language invites, rather than instructs, participation. In an open learning environment, no one has to participate if they do not want to; but more than that, the gentle suggestions are designed to acknowledge that it can be daunting to add one's voice to a public board, as we saw in Chapter 3. For example, discussions are signalled by phrases such as 'Over to you' and are structured so that participants are guided to respond in specific ways. In addition, this is beneficial for participants who are hesitant to post. In Chapter 4, interviewees reported that they got more out of MOOCs where they had been prompted to take part in discussions, even though they were not previously inclined to do so.

For example, in Figure 6.1 the participants are invited to review the suggestions on the Padlet (from the collaborative exercise) and discuss what could be used in their own practice. Participants are given a few different ways into the discussion to take account of the range of experience and expertise, but the discussion is directed rather than left open. Chapter 4 showed that unstructured or 'off topic' discussions were seen as superficial and not valued, whereas structured discussions were considered fruitful and capable of producing the deep professional learning experience that the participants wanted.

Laying out the details of our learning design of this activity demonstrates how online teaching can be considered a design science (see Chapter 2). In summary, the critical design features for a CoMOOC are

Design phase

- **Co-designed with professionals** – so grounded in case studies from practice, for co-designed videos
- **Designed for collaborative learning** – at scale, so therefore open and online

Designed activities

- **Collaborative learning activities** – using mechanisms for community knowledge building such as Padlets, polls, word clouds or peer review activities
- **Structured discussions** – where participants are gently invited to take part with explicit prompts to guide the discussion.

By using these features to design an experience that combined pedagogy and technology, we were able to enhance participants' digital engagement with the platform, and create a sense of social presence within the CoMOOCs. But how successful was the result? Design science also requires us to take a researcher perspective and consider the evidence about the effects of our design. In the next section we present participant perspectives on the features of the CoMOOC.

Evaluating social and collaborative learning features

Feedback from post-course surveys gives an indication of the success of the learning design, but can fail to provide an examination of the precise formulation of design elements that characterize the CoMOOC. In order to address this, we included a short survey in week 2 of *Transforming Education in Challenging Environments* that asked for participants' feedback on elements of the collaborative learning design that we particularly wanted to test. We received 880 responses from participants in the Edraak version of the CoMOOC and 134 from participants on the FutureLearn version, totalling 1014. We invited participants to rate the three core elements of our learning design – co-designed videos, discussion and collaborative activities – in terms of their usefulness in supporting learning. Then we asked participants to explain their answers. The participants' ratings and their explanations are discussed below (pseudonyms have been provided).

Co-designed video

The first element we asked participants to rate was the type of videos, which deliberately focussed on teachers themselves discussing their work in challenging environments. We wove together short clips from interviews conducted with teachers in Lebanon, which were introduced by one of the lead educators on the CoMOOC. As explained above, the video interviews were the result of participatory research with the educational community in Lebanon, particularly with the Syrian refugee community, but also with teacher trainees at Lebanese American University and Palestinian educators from UNWRA schools in Lebanon.

The feedback from the collaborative learning evaluation survey was overwhelmingly positive with 88 per cent participants across platforms rating the videos very or extremely useful, 12 per cent rated them somewhat useful and 1 per cent rating them not very or not at all useful. Participants explained that they found the teachers' authentic narratives from practice useful:

> You've spoken to real life teachers in the field and so often evidence-based theories/ideas are never ever portrayed in the real world. So, it's inspiring to see such practice in the real world with real people who will honestly tell you how it's going, what they're trying and how they're adapting.
>
> (Jessie, FutureLearn)

> It is very useful for people with experience to share with us, and you can benefit from their experiences and the situations in which they are going through.
>
> (Nour, Edraak)

Participants commented that they were able to learn from the practical experiences of teachers, and were inspired by teachers working in difficult conditions without resources.

> Useful videos, especially since it shows that the teacher can teach in the worst conditions and with limited resources, since the teacher is creative and is not

hindered by anything, as long as they believe in the importance of science and education.

(Farah, Edraak)

The videos are very clear to follow and combine narrative and teacher experiences very effectively. It is hugely beneficial to learn from teachers working in challenging contexts. This makes the course relevant and practical.

(Marion, FutureLearn)

This did not, however, mean that they were not applicable to teachers in different circumstances, and some participants noted that although there are many different challenging contexts, they are able to apply the insights to their own situation:

[T]he videos provided multiple perspectives of educators from different contexts and this is very good as it mirrors the different challenges educators face and since moocs have versatile participants each one will find a learning experience that mirrors [their own].

(Jackie, FutureLearn)

The experience of every teacher cannot be generalized to everyone, but it could be a key to urge the teacher to address their own problems.

(Majd, Edraak)

Suggestions were to include more voices of learners and more practical teaching situations, which would be the ideal.

The process of co-designing video and including the voices of professionals themselves is an effective way of creating the conditions for the kind of deep professional learning that the participants in Chapter 4 were seeking. The evaluation shows that this approach was considered authentic, useful and inspiring by participants.

Discussions

While the teachers in the videos discussed their own practice, we invited the participants to join in the conversation and share their experience and insights with others. The majority of the participants (74 per cent) rated the discussion very or extremely useful for their learning across both platforms, 24 per cent rated them as somewhat useful and 2 per cent not very or not at all useful – the proportions were very similar between Edraak participants and FutureLearn participants. This was an important finding, since the FutureLearn platform is better designed for supporting discussion as an integral part of the course. As we noted above, comments appear beneath each content step in FutureLearn, and have an easy-to-engage, social media feel, whereas threaded discussion forums are separated from the main learning area in Edraak. However, the modifications we made to the Edraak platform, including pinning the discussion thread beneath the content, enabled us to mirror, as best we could, the smoother and more inviting discussion affordance of the FutureLearn platform. This change in combination with the inviting and explicit discussion prompts created an environment where teachers were encouraged to interact with each other.

The evaluation indicated that this was successful. Participants said that they valued learning through discussion in relation to having their viewpoints challenged, learning from others' experiences and found ideas they could apply in their own practice:

> My experience in discussion was more beneficial than learning on my own.
>
> (Rayyan, Edraak)

> The discussion is very good in order to exchange experiences and benefit from the experiences of others from different countries. It was a wonderful experience for me.
>
> (Zein, Edraak)

> The discussion enriches my experiences and information and makes me benefit from what others say or to evaluate my experiences and reuse other teaching methods.
>
> (Jamal, Edraak)

> It makes me review some strict convictions I have.
>
> (Siham, Edraak)

Participants also noted that they were able to grow in confidence themselves, and that the design of the discussion had had an impact on their approach to learning online:

> The discussion has a great benefit in exchanging information and it also gives the student great confidence in themselves.
>
> (Ehsan, Edraak)

In fact, although I have registered in many of the courses on this platform, I participated actively and enjoyably in this course, the mechanism that the course follows to offer and then indirectly pushes the learner to participate in the discussions and answer the questions was wonderful, which gave me the audacity to participate in the discussion forums. For other courses …

(Almas, Edraak)

Similar comments to these came from participants in the FutureLearn platform. For example:

It is very helpful to read about the ideas, concerns and challenges of other teachers around the world.

(Alva, FutureLearn)

I've learned from others' experience and the strategies they use at their schools, I've also known that I'm working on the right track and the problems I face usually are common problems with students throughout the world wide.

(Ollie, FutureLearn)

Not all participants were confident to take part, however. Participants were sometimes intimidated by the number of comments, and others preferred to read comments from mentors. Nevertheless, some participants who did not comment affirmed that they learnt from discussion even without their own active participation.

Several participants were able to articulate the value of this kind of learning for isolated professionals in challenging environments, however:

I think everyone has something to contribute at some point, even if not every time. Some people are definitely less able to offer examples and suggestions, when they lack actual experience so far. Others contribute 'extra' – and thoroughly deserve the 'likes' they receive! Having educators and mentors endorse and add to comments themselves gives the rest of us a definite boost and feeling of 'real time' learning, with real people helping us and taking an interest in us!

(Jodie, FutureLearn)

I think that this is very important for teachers as teachers work in isolation they close their doors in their classrooms so unfortunately rich experiences are not shared; however MOOCs offer them this window.

(Cleo, FutureLearn)

Even for participants who felt they were not sufficiently experienced to contribute to the discussion, they found that reading the comments from others was useful:

> [W]hen I myself cannot bring anything to the discussion it is eye opening to read what other teachers have said.
>
> (Danni, FutureLearn)

Discussion is vital for professionals to exchange stories from their practice, try out ways that suggestions from other participants might be applied in their context and build community knowledge together. Participants are generally confident in taking part in social learning, even when, as with the Edraak participants, this was not the norm. A social learning design reduces the feeling that participants are studying in isolation, and it helps to achieve a deep professional learning experience by introducing new ideas and challenging existing ones.

Collaborative activities

Related to the social learning design, we also asked participants specifically about the collaborative learning elements – the use of word clouds to give a quick representation of what other participants were feeling, polls to compare a participant's individual view to that of the crowd and the Padlets for building resources together. Across both platforms, 77 per cent found them very or extremely useful, 21 per cent somewhat useful and 1 per cent not very useful.

The collaborative activities were enjoyed by participants who valued them differently and in combination with discussion:

> It gives more benefit than just writing in a discussion, in addition to knowing the opinions of learners in general through voting, so it gives a quick look at the learners' orientation.
>
> (Duha, Edraak)

> The Padlets, Polls and word clouds act as an effective tool to visually understand the differing perspectives of those on the course. These tools are a very effective way of taking in a small amount of information in a short space of time.
>
> (Kerry, FutureLearn)

> The Padlet exercise enables me to learn about the activities that other teachers perform in their classroom.
>
> (Ali, Edraak)

Many of the teachers were inspired to use the same tools in their own teaching. There were a few who experienced technical challenges, but more who benefited, and some who appreciated the opportunity to engage with tools and platforms without having to contribute an account, which they did not feel ready to do. Overall, the feedback not only indicated that these design elements were effective for the learning of participants, but they endorsed the different kinds of value that the elements can bring to construct a social and collaborative online learning experience.

Scaling online community knowledge building with the CoMOOC model

This chapter has delineated the non-negotiables in the design of a CoMOOC. We do not argue that any or all MOOCs are going to be successful for scaling up professional development in a way that supports a professional community to build the knowledge it needs. We know that MOOCs cannot reach everyone, but they can reach educated professionals. CoMOOCs offer access to the kinds of knowledge and skills needed by professionals at the time they need it. Examples of these situations are to be found in the many conflicts and crises that the world is witnessing on an increasingly regular basis. Since these learning opportunities are online, they can reach professionals where they are. While the technological infrastructure may be too poor to rely on for access to online learning for everyone, professionals tend to have access to the internet and their own devices. This has opened up the online space for professional development. The case studies collected in UNESCO-ICHEI (2022) show that universities across the Global South were able to provide online professional development to their staff to prepare them for online and blended teaching during the COVID-19 pandemic.

Often, however, the kinds of knowledge and skills needed by professionals in crisis contexts are those that are emerging from the professional community itself. This knowledge is still being developed in practice, has not been published and has not yet reached teachers. This is why co-design for collaboration is so important. CoMOOCs are not simply vehicles to share degree-level training with professionals outside the walls of the institution, although they are effective in doing this. CoMOOCs are able to foreground the expertise of the professional community itself. This can be done by developing written and video case studies showcasing how professionals themselves are addressing problems on the ground. Importantly, it can also be done through inviting other professionals to share their own knowledge and skills through stories and examples in discussions and collaborative activities. This process can build community knowledge quickly to address the pressing challenges, speeding up the exchange of applied knowledge and supporting its adaptation to new contexts.

In the teaching context, this process can use the representation of teaching knowledge in the form of learning designs. Learning designs enable teachers to articulate and share the activities they have designed for learners, along with their contexts, and the technological tools that support them. Other teachers are then able to adapt those learning designs, for example, by replacing the concepts being taught in the original design with concepts that they wish to teach, while much of the pedagogy remains the same (see Chapter 2). The learning designs facilitate sharing at the level of teaching ideas rather than teaching resources which are difficult to reuse without understanding their context, and often are not designed for adaptation. For other professions, knowledge could be made shareable in a similar way. For example, the concept of a design pattern which has influenced the development of learning designs, derives from the field of architecture. Alexander, Ishikawa & Silverstein (1977) presented solutions to common design problems which they abstracted into a set of design patterns. The accumulated community-authored resources within a CoMOOC could be made available outside the MOOC platform, for example, through tools such as the Learning Designer.

The CoMOOC model will be fundamental for equipping professional learning at scale for the global challenges ahead. This chapter has provided evidence that in order to scale online professional development, the non-negotiable features of the CoMOOC include the foregrounding and encouragement of meaningful discussion, collaboration and digital engagement. The CoMOOC must also be co-designed with professionals and stakeholders from the target participant group, which not only enables the designer to develop an in-depth understanding of the needs of the intended audience, but encourages community stakeholders to feel ownership of the joint venture. This is essential to embed the CoMOOC into the community, and sustain itself long term. Mentors drawn from this community will also keep the CoMOOC alive and support it to adapt itself as situations change. The focus on collaboration in the design of learning activities, and the active engagement of peer knowledge sharing by content contributors and participants make the CoMOOC an ongoing collaboration, reaching more and more professionals who can benefit and contribute. These features will create the deep professional learning experience that participants need.

This chapter has presented the essence of the CoMOOC model. This is a new departure for online professional development, and we have presented evidence that it not only works, but is highly valued by the communities it can reach. Not all MOOCs are the same or can achieve the same results. However, by opening up to the large scale, co-designing social and collaborative learning experiences with and for professionals, and using case studies of professional practice, the CoMOOC model can provide a powerful mechanism to support communities worldwide to address the challenges that beset them. We strongly urge governments and agencies to consider this model for professional development at scale.

Questions and activities

To consolidate the ideas and issues discussed in this chapter, here are some questions or activities that might help to reinterpret them for your own teaching-learning context. How would you

1. Extend our description of professional learning needs to fit those you are familiar with?
2. Reflect on the value of discussions and collaborations you have had with peers in terms of your own skills development for your own professional development?
3. Redesign MOOCs you have used or created for professional development using the core features of CoMOOCs?
   - Co-designed with professionals with case studies grounded in practice
   - Designed for social and collaborative learning
4. Consider using these two design tools for planning your next MOOC? The Miro Co-design Workshop template (https://miro.com/miroverse/co-design-storyboard/) and the Learning Designer (learningdesigner.org).

7

The Evidence of Impact for Co-designed Massive Open Online Collaborations on the Sustainable Development Goals

Introduction

Many universities and colleges provide ambitious statements of their mission for the global impact they intend to make. Here are some examples from some of the top twenty universities in the world:

> to advance knowledge and educate students in science, technology, and other areas of scholarship that will best serve the nation and the world in the 21st century.
>
> (MIT)[1]

> establish a high level of global consciousness and an international vision ... work together to solve common problems facing humankind.
>
> (Peking)[2]

> world-class research and education ... which benefit society on a local, regional, national and global scale ... committed to equality of opportunity, to engendering inclusivity ...
>
> (Oxford)[3]

> engaged with the wider world and committed to changing it for the better ... for the long-term benefit of humanity
>
> (UCL)[4]

With such ambitions, it would be appropriate for universities to use the UN Sustainable Development Goals (SDGs) as a framework for their intended contributions to a collaborative global response to these challenges. Even when their ambitions are more local, or national, they must surely include the mission to educate the world, to assist in the professional development of the millions of skilled employees who each have a part to play in meeting the UN goals. Tertiary education is responsible for the great majority of employees in these roles in both the public and private sectors. SDG4 on Education is to 'promote lifelong learning opportunities for all'. SDG13 on Climate Action alone will need to educate everyone on the planet, which excludes very few professionals. But as we saw in Chapter 1, very few of the top universities are highly ranked for their contribution to the SDGs.

This is an enormous challenge for the tertiary sector. They are not alone, because most large organizations offer professional development to their employees at all levels to some extent. The burden of professional education can be shared, but its renewal and further development will be a key responsibility for the tertiary sector.

SDG4 also aims to 'Ensure inclusive and equitable quality education'. In 2016 it identified 263 m children out of school[5] leading to the aim of 69 m new teachers by 2030 to achieve universal basic education. How is the sector to manage that?

In fact, since 2016 progress has been negligible, due to a range of location-specific reasons such as disabilities, conflict, climate change, gender, the journey to school, etc.[6] And progress has worsened further since the pandemic left some 1.6 bn children and young people out of school. Meanwhile the progress of access to digital devices has been improving at a much faster rate, even for the developing world, which from 2010 to 2014 accounted for 82 per cent of new internet users across the world.[7] The conclusion of the 2014 UN Broadband Commission was that connected devices could be the solution for out-of-school children.

As we discuss in Chapter 8, learners who are displaced from their education institutions, for all these reasons, at whatever age, will find that an online education space will be their most stable learning environment. Wherever there is connectivity and a suitable digital device, there is the possibility of access to education. It is a shocking fact that digital access is progressing more rapidly for the most disadvantaged groups than is classroom access. It is time to recognize this terrible fact and respond to its implications.

We have established that globally, tertiary teachers need access to quality professional development to exploit fully the educational potential of digital technology, and that collaborative MOOCs reimagined as Co-designed Massive Open Online Collaborations (CoMOOCs) have the potential to achieve this. Note that this is not an argument that MOOCs can revolutionize tertiary education. They are not suitable for students at any level, who need one-on-one nurturing and feedback. But the optimal way to help students at any level is via their teachers, so the priority for tackling any educational challenge at scale must be teacher professional development (TPD).

This approach also offers the potential for scaling up professional development in many areas other than education, such as engineering, climate action and health care – indeed all the professions that play a part in meeting the UN SDGs.

We demonstrate the effectiveness of the CoMOOC as a model for other forms of professional development, and show how this combination of collaborative MOOC design and a 'value creation framework' provides the evidence that managers and policymakers need if they are to apply the approach to all forms of professional development that can be offered online.

How realistic is this as a programme of work? In their critique of the role of universities in the digital divide and their responsibility for helping to reduce global inequality, Hill and Lawton offer a sobering conclusion:

> In spite of far-reaching international teaching partnerships and international cooperation in research, higher education is hard-wired to the pursuit of economic nationalism. For those who believe that growing inequality is a problem worth tackling, this is the opposite of what the world needs from higher education.
>
> (Hill & Lawton, 2018, p607)

Our argument is that in mission statements, vision statements and identified research and teaching challenges, universities do make strong commitments to contributing to fairer societies and to orienting their research towards making the world a better place. Government pressures certainly tend to prioritize contributions to the national economy, but reducing inequality itself makes a positive contribution to national prosperity. We should therefore be able to plan a way forward that enables universities to fulfil their ambitious commitments through real impact. We propose online professional development as a general model for one significant way to do that. That is why the final part of this chapter is about leadership and governance.

The UN SDGs as a framework for professional development: A critique

The UN SDGs were agreed in 2016, following the final year of the Millennium Development Goals (MDGs) that were due to be achieved by 2015. The new goals became more onerous after the increase in inequalities across the world following the financial disaster of 2008, and the difficulties encountered in the MDGs making real impact, despite many local successes (Nanda, 2016). Then the two years of the pandemic took a terrible toll on the most vulnerable populations around the world. Prior to 2020, as António Guterres reported, there had been 'progress in poverty reduction, maternal and child health, access to electricity, and gender equality, but not enough to achieve the Goals by 2030' (United_Nations, 2021, p. 2). Post-pandemic, however, even these gains had been lost completely, for example:

> For Goal 1: 'An additional 119–124 million people were pushed back into extreme poverty in 2020'.
>
> (United_Nations, 2021, p. 8)

> For Goal 4: 'An additional 101 million or 9% of children in grades 1 through 8 fell below minimum reading proficiency levels in 2020'.
>
> (United_Nations, 2021, p. 11)

Similar figures were reported for all seventeen goals. What is worse, as Guterres points out in his powerful Foreword:

> Had the paradigm shift envisioned by the 2030 Agenda for Sustainable Development been fully embraced for the past six years, the world would have been better prepared to face this crisis.
>
> (United_Nations, 2021, p. 8)

Could our societies be capable of making the massive paradigm shift *now* needed across the world to meet the SDGs? Governments ultimately bear the brunt of this responsibility, but their work comes from all their constituent global actors: local governments, civil society, business, science and academia. The tertiary education system in every country is essentially an organ of the nation state, even though universities and colleges typically assert their independence. Government institutions and industry alike depend on them for research-based knowledge and on the tertiary sector as a whole for the education of the nation's workforce. And many HE institutions have a global awareness and reach that makes the sector a powerful actor. So what can they contribute?

There are no plans of action or guidance on the interventions needed in the UN reports. Their role is to negotiate and promote the goals, which can then 'trigger practical solutions that governments, businesses, and civil society can pursue with high priority' (United_Nations, 2013, p. x). We have to devise our own interventions. In this book we are looking explicitly at practical solutions for TPD at scale, triggered most recently by the sector's discovery of the value and further potential of online learning, and at extending that model to all other areas of professional development. The greatest challenges the world faces in the coming years in building a decent living for its population are well-defined in the UN SDGs. They are a valuable tool for thinking through what our sector can do. The tertiary sector has the primary responsibility within government policy for delivering basic and lifelong learning for SDG4, and (through university research) is a major contributor to the practical solutions needed across all the other sixteen SDGs. We have a responsibility to contribute to the paradigm shift.

That means developing minds – new concepts, skills and methods – for creating sustainable change, and making this happen on the large scale, "and for professionals in all areas". We have the technology, as the previous chapters have shown, albeit still in their infancy. We do not yet have the knowledge and skills. Considering just TPD, the teaching profession as a whole, across the world, discovered a lot about the value of digital methods during the COVID-19 pandemic, and now has a sense of their potential, but although its members are generally reasonably digitally literate now, there has been very little opportunity or support for developing the skills and knowledge needed to optimize online learning. Who is to teach the teachers? Even the UCL Institute of Education, the world's number one faculty of education, offers digital methods as only a small fraction of its initial teacher education courses, and runs very few professional development hours for its staff.

Knowledge development in the sciences and humanities uses academic books, journals and conferences as the means to conduct validated expert knowledge and understanding, but the practice of teaching has developed no such mechanisms. General methods are offered briefly in the teaching-oriented staff development courses in universities and colleges, but university teachers in the research-oriented universities are almost completely neglected. Central support teams and enthusiastic teachers have managed their own knowledge development. They enabled the sector to just about function in offering online learning during the COVID-19 pandemic (Smith & Traxler, 2022), but none of these practices have had well-funded projects for the ongoing development and discovery of the most effective online learning methods. This is despite the radical changes in what technology has to offer over the past two decades, so it is likely they never will. The education of university and college teachers in digital teaching methods is not a priority in a world that has been so heavily impacted by recurrent disasters.

The question 'who teaches the teachers?' has no answer yet because we have done so little to develop this area of knowledge that the classic form of research-based knowledge passed on through courses is not feasible. The teaching profession now has to devise its own community knowledge development programme as a priority role in our professional work, just to manage the need for digital methods in our own teaching. For HE researchers to provide online professional development that contributes to the learning needed for the SDGs is a further burden for the sector, but they would also benefit from a streamlined CPD-at-scale model if we could achieve that.

So far even the research-oriented universities are not doing well on contributing to the SDGs. Since 2019, the university rankings have added an 'Impact' ranking, which assesses universities in terms of their contributions to the SDGs in research, stewardship, outreach and teaching. Of the universities ranked in the top ten for the standard categories of teaching, research, knowledge transfer and international outlook,[8] only MIT appears in *the first 200* for impact on the SDGs,[9] and yet these are the very universities that commit to ambitious global challenges for their mission statements. The SDGs provide a demanding framework because it is unflinching. Our sector should be using it if we are to make any real impact on improving the world.

Unfortunately we have no clear guide on how to do it. The Brookings Institution report on the US progress towards the SDGs advocates many technical imperatives but offers no advice on actions to make change happen on a global scale (Pipa, Rasmussen, & Pendrak, 2022). Among its recommendations is the aim to 'Expand awareness and knowledge through education and professional development', which is good, but translates to the action:

> Design training, tools, and curriculums for civil and foreign service officers that leverage the SDGs to spur innovation and new approaches in program design and policy development.

That is, to 'equip government officials to develop policies and practices that result in greater return on investment of U.S. financial and political capital', which was not intended as the point of the exercise, and to 'prepare the next generation of public sector leaders for multi-disciplinary problem-solving', which is good, but a long time to wait (Pipa et al., 2022, p. 21). There is no sense of the scale of the problem to be solved now. The mechanisms and drivers of change suggested as solutions are conferences, local fellowships, revised staff performance reviews, SDGs integrated into internships for initiatives such as the Presidential Management Fellows (Pipa et al., 2022). These are the recommendations from the world-renowned thinktank, whose mission is to 'provide innovative, practical recommendations for policymakers and the public' so that the United States can establish 'explicit benchmarks for progress' in its contributions to the SDGs. The richest country in the world has to be more ambitious.

For practical action we can look to the World Bank, which has created a $54 bn fund for sustainable development projects across twenty-seven 'currencies' (World Bank, 2020). This kind of funding is several orders of magnitude away from what universities and colleges, even if they act together, could ever muster. The driver of change here is investment, through bonds, in projects that create and demonstrate the value of, for example, innovative mechanisms, such as new practices, digital tools and interventions to create jobs and services in selected localities. The impact is sometimes sustainable and incorporates a 'knowledge product' that can be shared with others. Scaling up is always intended; for example, for a web-based tool for rooftop solar PV potential mapping that will 'support the scale-up of affordable and clean solar energy in a potentially high growth market segment' (World_Bank, 2020, p. 21); for a GIS[10] data collection tool that will 'benefit private sector companies wishing to scale up' (World_Bank, 2020, p.23); for a platform to stimulate economic growth and employment opportunities for refugees and their hosts, which has 'potential to scale up, and is global in its vision' (World_Bank, 2020, p. 39). The World Bank has the 'twin goals of ending extreme poverty and increasing shared prosperity' and uses the fund to work with client countries 'to deliver on the Sustainable Development Goals (SDGs) through knowledge-sharing, capacity-building, data, financing, and partnerships' (World_Bank, 2020, p. 3). It must necessarily use that vast fund well, to create a long-term return, so the focus must be on financing and partnerships that will continue to benefit both public and private sectors. But the scaling up has yet to happen, and these initial stages have been achieving on the scale of 10s of trainers trained, or 100s of businesswomen supported. A newsletter as a knowledge product reaches 8000 subscribers. The scale of the SDG challenges runs in the many millions for every one of them, and yet the concluding statement of the report maintains that the World Bank fund

> continues to develop unique tools, knowledge products, and partnerships that are critical in keeping us on track to achieve the global goals by 2030.
> (World_Bank, 2020, p. 42)

There is no discussion of how the transformation from tens and hundreds will scale up so rapidly to be on track for reaching the millions. Those mechanisms are yet to be discovered or funded.

The digital world does work on the scale of millions. The technologies we discuss in this book are designed to enable knowledge to be negotiated, evaluated, shared and contested on a massive scale, if we choose to harness their potential. The World Bank's vast funds could be directed in some small part towards discovering not just the knowledge of what works within a locality but also to orchestrating the development of knowledge as a trans-global collaborative effort, on a scale that is fitting for the scale of the challenge. Collaborative professional development as a means of knowledge building is potentially feasible now. The next sections marshal the evidence so far.

Collaborative knowledge building for the teaching community

There has been some progress towards collaborative knowledge building for the teaching community, but we have a long way to go. The nature of scientific collaboration could offer a guide to what is needed for improving practice because it is a well understood model of what we are now trying to foster for teachers. It has four interdependent elements: knowledge, people, networked communications systems and resources for the research (Marginson, 2021a). But the collaborative development of knowledge we envisage for teachers at present does not have the sophistication of three centuries of scientific practice. Of those four elements the teaching community has only two: people and resources. We have neither the well-articulated knowledge nor its curation by the networked communication systems of journals and conferences in operation since the original transactions of the Royal Society. Representing knowledge in science is unproblematic: it is represented in journal papers and reports, available for others to build on. Teachers have no such means to articulate and share their knowledge of how to teach. They have themselves and their colleagues as the 'people', and their teaching and learning environment in an institution with students as their 'resources for the research'. How close are we to the model that scientific knowledge represents? How might we develop the articulated knowledge and the networked communications?

Over the last ten years, the progress in the literature on teacher professional learning and development has been to recognize that, given the richness of teachers' own knowledge and experience, developing teacher knowledge is something better done *with* rather than *to* teachers (Kennedy, 2014). Teacher co-learning is now an established model, from informal exchanges within teachers' schools, to more formalized networks, courses and workshops featuring peer coaching and collaboration (Avalos, 2011). The need for such a 'subject-centered socio-cultural approach' to teacher professional learning has been identified by Eteläpelto, Vähäsantanen, Hökkä, and Paloniemi (2013, p. 58), and will be necessary to 'promote teacher educators' professional agency if we are to realize new ways of implementing teacher education' (Hökkä & Eteläpelto, 2014, p. 49).

Research on professional learning communities for teachers shows that if they are well-supported, with sufficient time allocation, it is indeed feasible for teachers to collaborate on improving outcomes (Darling-Hammond, Hyler, & Gardner, 2017), and use online social learning environments to support their professional networks and knowledge exchange (Khalid & Strange, 2016; Lantz-Andersson, Lundin, & Selwyn, 2018; USDoE, 2014). A review of the main characteristics found in ninety-nine studies of online teacher communities of practice networks found there was rather little research on this as a form professional development (Macia & García, 2016). Digital methods are increasingly being used to support teacher professional learning; but while the networks are beginning to develop, it is only on the local – not the global – scale, where the need really lies.

We also have to ask what kind of knowledge we need to build. A recent review on evidence-based knowledge for teachers argues for going beyond the chimera of discovering and demonstrating 'what works' to implementing policies that include the practice of collaborative and research-based designs as TPD (La Velle & Flores, 2018). The authors propose a research-based knowledge enhancement model that develops teacher knowledge through knowledge of research and through their own reflections on its transfer to practice, followed by evaluation or local action research. Their urgent challenge for teacher education is 'how knowledge is acquired and utilised by teachers' (La Velle & Flores, 2018, p. 526). The journey from *acquired* via *mobilized* to *utilized* knowledge is complex. 'Knowledge mobilisation' involves the 'interactive, social and gradual nature of the connection between research and practice which goes beyond a one-way process' (Levin, 2013, p. 1). This is because the instantiation of research findings in local contexts does not work straightforwardly. Teachers should be part of a two-way process: to engage in feeding back their own findings on implementation to researchers and to their peers as part of the knowledge mobilization process. Good. But the La Velle and Flores model keeps the 'reflection on action' stage of knowledge generation within the teacher – with no extension to sharing this new knowledge.

For so many of these approaches, the focus is only on teachers' own local knowledge, with no expectation they should see their work as 'part of the civilization-wide effort to advance knowledge frontiers' (Scardamalia & Bereiter, 2006, p. 98). Why not? If researchers do not listen to that return process of reporting back on the utilization of research findings, the teacher's voice is essentially lost because their focus is confined to informal reflection, or solutions to inform practice within their own classroom context. Instead, teachers could be supported to make broader contributions to educational knowledge (Peel, 2020; Richardson, Macewen, & Naylor, 2018) or become part of a community in the sense of developing 'a shared identity around a topic or set of challenges' (Wenger, Trayner, & de Laat, 2011, p. 11).

In all these studies of the need for teacher engagement with research and community-based learning, there is no proposal that teachers could go beyond their own practice and location to build a sense of community for exchanging new ideas and developing new forms of practice. We need to combine support for teacher innovation to develop the 'adaptive expertise' needed to manage rapid change (Schwartz, Bransford, & Sears, 2005) with a pedagogic approach that would encourage teachers to experiment and develop pedagogic knowledge themselves as a community effort. We also need to exploit the capabilities of the digital world to enable us to do this at scale.

How CoMOOCs can improve professional practices

Is it feasible to construct appropriate representations of teaching knowledge, along with the networked communications for sharing it and building on the work of others? At least we have the technology.

In Chapter 2 we use the Learning Designer to represent teachers' technological pedagogical knowledge of how they design digital methods to achieve their intended learning outcomes. In Chapter 6 we introduced the CoMOOC model as a way of orchestrating the process of teachers building on the learning designs of other teachers, adapting ideas to their own context and sharing their own tested practice with their peers. In this section we evaluate how well a course designed with these features would add value to what teachers are already doing.

Critical design features for a CoMOOC

The previous studies of teacher professional learning show that a teacher-centred approach is important. Here we propose a larger ambition, that it could go beyond the current trend of engaging teachers with existing research and move towards teachers doing the 'peer knowledge building' described in Chapter 6. We need the Learning Designer to act as a boundary object for teachers. As Star (1989) recognized in scientific collaboration, scientists do not necessarily share the same model but they can nonetheless cooperate by creating 'boundary objects' – such as data records, lists of species for collecting, policy documents (Akkerman & Bakker, 2011) – representations of knowledge that are 'plastic enough to adapt to local needs and constraints … yet robust enough to maintain a common identity across sites' (Star, 1989, p. 46). The Learning Designer tool in Chapter 2 affords the dialogical learning mechanisms of a boundary object that teachers need if they are to share ideas about learning design across the very diverse contexts of institutions, subject areas and education sectors (Akkerman & Bakker, 2011).

The design tool as the means of representing knowledge then has to be embedded within a formal process capable of organizing the successive community activities involved in knowledge building: browsing, adopting, adapting, testing, revising, peer reviewing and publishing. For this we use the form of a CoMOOC, not just as a course, but rather as science and scholarship use the academic journal system: to enable teachers to build on each other's work, through 'collaborative activities', and create transformative learning experiences even in the most challenging of environments (Pherali, Abu Moghli, & Chase, 2020).

The reason for experimenting with these large-scale platforms derives from our report on the need for large-scale TPD (Laurillard, Kennedy, & Wang, 2018). From a review of over 100 articles and reports on 'learning at scale' studied between 2008 and 2017, we identified three actions needed in terms of progressing equity, quality and efficiency on

- technology – to bridge the extensive digital divide,
- pedagogy – teachers being able to own and develop the digital pedagogy innovations that will continue to be needed as digital innovations progress and
- community – shared and localized versions of generic principles of practice.

Teachers can do little to affect the first, except through demanding better technology. The latter two findings have inspired our further work on investigating the CoMOOC form.

In the case study illustration here, the course sets out to scaffold the work of teachers as they progress from conventional to digital methods on the basis of using the Conversational Framework as a guide for both methods (Sharples & Ferguson, 2019), enabling teachers to convert from the familiar to the new digital opportunities via a common theoretical basis.

A case study illustrates how the critical design features of a CoMOOC, in bold, work in practice.

Case Study: Teaching Online (in Arabic on Edraak for teachers in the MENA region)

The context
There was an urgent need to support teachers navigating the shift to online teaching caused by the pandemic-related closure of schools in Lebanon and the Middle East and North Africa region (MENA), a situation similar to the rest of the world, though typically within more challenging contexts. Most teachers had moderately reliable internet access. Most children had at best smart phone devices.

What we did – key features of a CoMOOC
Co-designed with professionals, with the same team from an earlier LU-LAU-UCL collaboration on a MOOC for TPD, working entirely online to create during March 2020 a free online course, launched in April 2020, to support teachers across the MENA region converting to online teaching during the COVID-19 pandemic.

Established an eight-hour **free and open online course** on the Edraak platform, in Arabic, for teachers in all schools, teaching all subject areas, in the MENA region.

Co-designed videos to make it **grounded in case studies from practice,** contributed by LU teachers during the pandemic, to show examples of how they used digital tools for different types of learning.

Collaborative activities – using the Learning Designer enabled participants to articulate and exchange their ideas and practices in the form of their own learning designs, prompted by what they saw in the videos.

Teachers were **invited to share and comment on their designs** on Padlets.

Peer interactions were prompted through polling activities, for example, where participants were asked to rate the most important features of online learning (and then wrangle over the final order in a discussion). Most steps posed questions and topics to encourage **structured discussions** for teachers to share their own experiences of digital learning, challenge the points made in the materials and ask for help or ideas relating to their own practices.

The Learning Designer site collected all the designs that teachers chose to make public as an example of dynamic **community knowledge building**.

What happened
The course attracted 12,300 active learners in the first three months, 51 per cent female. An in-course survey showed that 92 per cent were able to apply what they had learned, for example, in terms of their changes in practice:

> I became more aware of some aspects of planning and more aware of supporting the class with some educational programs.
> Developing solutions that were previously complex and have no solutions.
> Moving from traditional methods to distinctive innovative methods of introducing the student and the parent in the educational process.

For the interactive exercises Padlets were used to collect 150 comments on issues such as 'the challenges you face in teaching online', and 700 recommendations for 'a tool you would recommend to others',[11] while the Learning Designer tool was used to enable participants to exchange learning designs.

A post-hoc analysis of the time spent by the different contributors to develop the first run was costed at only £5400, due to the relatively lower cost of staff in Lebanon. Running the two-week course with a total of twelve-hour support per run cost £200, which was the same for each run. After ten runs, with a total of 23,000 active participants (~50 per cent enrolments), this gives a per capita cost of £0.33.

By this means, therefore, the combination of the CoMOOC and the Learning Designer can support community knowledge building for the new digital pedagogies that teachers are now creating and exploring, modelled on the combination of journals and research papers that serves science and scholarship: 'Scientists are organised in global epistemic communities that codify their knowledge in peer-reviewed articles published in specialist international journals' (Wuestman, Hoekman, & Frenken, 2019, p. 1772). For TPD it is a process very much in its infancy, but it does address Marginson's four elements of scientific collaboration (Marginson, 2021b):

Knowledge – from the collaborating educators and contributing teachers
People – the participants
Networked communications systems – the CoMOOC
Resources – the learning designs, videos, articles and tools in the course

This is fundamentally different from the 'cascade' model of TPD, which easily fails to deliver because the ideas and practices lose the characteristics of the original learning encounter as their transmission moves further down the hierarchy (Kennedy, 2005, p. 240). If we remove the hierarchy and create instead a single-step dialogic process similar to that for journal publications – from contributors to readers and back – then we allow a more collaborative approach as discussed in Chapter 4 (Hunzicker, 2011), and are 'empowering teachers to focus more on action research' (Bett, 2016, p. 9). This is why the CoMOOC model is capable of improving TPD. Its impact in practice is considered in the next section.

Evaluating impact on knowledge and practice

To judge the impact of a CoMOOC we need the evaluation framework to be appropriate for testing the two actions defined in the previous section:

- Teachers to own and develop their digital pedagogy innovations
- The teaching community to share and localize their digital pedagogy designs

We chose the Value Creation Framework or VCF (Wenger et al., 2011) as an appropriate test of the type of community of practice we want to build (Dingyloudi, Strijbos, & de Laat, 2019). Our aim was to test the extent to which the CoMOOC model achieves the full range of value creation.

The VCF (see also Chapters 8 and 9) defines five cycles of value to its participants: from the *immediate* value generated by participation at any level in the course, through the *potential* value of what they learn, to the *applied* value that comes from their own practice of digital pedagogy, to the *realized* value of an improvement in teachers' own performance and the *reframing* value of developing a new way of thinking about teaching and learning. This second case study uses participants' reviews and comments in the CoMOOC to illustrate these forms of value, achieved for the highlighted design features.

Case Study: Blended and Online Learning Design (in English on FutureLearn)

The context
By the end of 2020, teachers still needed a lot of support for the shift to online teaching caused by the pandemic-related closure of schools, colleges and universities across the world. This course ran from the beginning of 2021.

What we did – key features of a CoMOOC
Established during the pandemic a twelve-hour **free and open online course** on the FutureLearn platform, for teachers in all sectors, teaching all subject areas.

Co-designed videos to make it **grounded in case studies from practice**, contributed by teachers in all sectors to show how they used digital tools for different types of learning.

Collaborative activities in the Learning Designer enabled participants to articulate and exchange their ideas and practices in the form of their own learning designs, prompted by what they saw in the videos.

Teachers were **invited to** share and comment on their designs in the form of **structured discussions** on Padlets.

Each step posed questions and topics to encourage **structured discussions** for teachers to share their own experiences of digital learning, challenge the points made in the materials and ask for help or ideas relating to their own practices.

The peer review process **prompted peer interactions** by guiding participants through creating two learning designs for different purposes, according to a given rubric, reviewing at least two other designs (sent automatically by the platform), and revising their own in the light of that experience as well as the feedback they received.

Participants were **invited to** submit their design for the Curated Designs section of the website, reviewed to a stricter rubric by the Educator team, contributing to **peer knowledge building**. We know from Chapter 4 that professionals favoured the MOOCs that invited them to be more active and involved in dialogic exchange, and to contribute their own knowledge to that of the educators.

We also encouraged **peer knowledge building** by asking participants to recommend useful digital tools they had used, with a brief description. These contributions were organized into a table of community-recommended tools with their links – gradually growing with each run of the course into a shared community database of useful digital tools.

The Learning Designer site collected all the designs that teachers chose to make public as an example of dynamic **community knowledge building**.

In the final step, participants completing the course were **invited to** apply to be a mentor for later runs of the course, to join and enhance the **structured discussions**. As we discovered in Chapter 4, participants were pleased to have the input from mentors, not just educators, in the discussions.

What happened

The course attracted 11,000 active learners over twelve runs and received 96 per cent 4- and 5-star ratings.

Review comments often referred to the *Potential value* of the tools and skills being learned:

> well designed, educational and thought provoking in all aspects of teaching and has changed my approach to lesson preparation and the way students are assessed.
>
> (Stephen N.)

> It was amazing! I learn a lot about the lesson design [sic] and the contents were relevant to face online and blended classroom. Thank you so much.
>
> (Louis J.)

Several of the 164 reviews illustrated the *Applied value* of teachers' new competence in digital pedagogies, and their appreciation of the practical understanding they derived:

> Where once we only wobbled intuitively, without a secure compass, now we navigate with certainty: online and blended learning and teaching have their rules and recommendations to maximize the learning experience of all educational levels.
>
> (Esther G.)

> develops practical skills on how to organize learning effectively.
>
> (Natalia S.)

Evidence of the *Realized value* of improving teachers' practices came from comments within the step discussions where teachers were asked to work on revising their current practices:

> I've got lessons to plan lined up for the Learning Designer – the last I gave was observed formally towards a PGCE and was very well received for the balance, variety and methodology.
>
> (Jonathan Vernon)

> Through reflections on my current practices, I realised that I need to add more collaboration and inquiry types of activities for the maximum student

outcomes. The Learning Designer helps me to see the balance of activities in the program, so I found it really useful.

(Megumin Noble)

The *Reframing value* that develops a new way of thinking about teaching and learning came through in many of the reflective comments at the end of the course:

such an interesting and relevant course. It has really challenged me to reassess how I teach and has certainly sparked my interest in learning more about blended and online learning.

(James Lea)

Thank you! Now I think I can re-analyse my courses with a new and more informed perspective.

(Elena Forasacco)

The course encouraged its teaching community to share and localize their digital pedagogy designs with activities to create and share their own learning designs, either developed from scratch or adapted from existing designs on the Learning Designer website. Initially they posted a link to their design on a Padlet wall, and >150 designs were shared. The peer review process required them to submit the link to a design, then review at least two others according to the given rubric and then invited them to make their revised design public, and also submit it for the Curated Designs section of the website. At the time of writing, seventy designs had been made public and twenty submitted designs had been accepted for publication in the Curated section, with several more waiting for Educator review.

In practice the course was developed and run entirely with teachers and academics volunteering their time and contributions. A post-hoc estimate of the time spent by the different contributors to develop the first run was costed at £18,000 for UCL academics and the teachers from other universities, colleges and schools involved. Running the three-week course with a total of twelve-hour support would have cost £2000 per run, which was the same for each run. For FutureLearn, teachers can opt to pay £54 to upgrade for a certificate of completion and permanent access. After twelve runs, with >9000 active participants, and a real income to the university of ~£8000 (from 310 upgrades, and after 50 per cent goes to FutureLearn), this gives a net cost of £3.90 per active learner.

A second example of community knowledge building is the accumulation of recommended digital tools and resources. After twelve runs of the course the table has over sixty contributions.

The case study illustrates how the course has enabled teachers to develop their own digital pedagogy innovations. The second objective is also being achieved in the customizing and sharing of teachers' digital pedagogy designs in an enduring collection of community knowledge on the Learning Designer website. The costing analysis also demonstrates the financial viability of the quality at scale that the CoMOOC model achieves. The up-front development cost of £18,000 is high for a three-week course, but very worthwhile in terms of the value to participants and the per capita costs. The costings include the annual costs for updating the course with new videos and digital tools, to maintain its longevity. The business model would require 650 participants to upgrade, in addition to the 310 already persuaded, so we have achieved less than one-third of the number needed to break even. The optimal business modelling for MOOCs is still under debate, with the main platforms tending to opt for higher-income/lower-volume solutions, such as micro-credentials. There is little interest, for example, in experimenting with the elasticity of fees by varying the fee according to country, to increase numbers. The current fee of £54 is difficult even for teachers in the UK, especially when the benefit of a certificate is undervalued by most of our education institutions. In some countries it means a lot but would be completely unaffordable.

Tertiary institutions face this dilemma, therefore, in deciding whether our grand challenges and ambitious missions should be achieved via the CoMOOC model. At least our case studies demonstrate that it offers a solution that is relatively low cost and high value.

Future leadership

In this chapter, we are proposing an online professional development model, the CoMOOC, as one significant way in which tertiary education institutions can contribute to nations' prosperity by reducing inequality. Universities are comfortable that they do this through contributions to research in the full range of disciplines contained within the UN SDGs. But most universities outside wealthy countries focus primarily on teaching, not research (Malee Bassett & Anderson, 2021). All these staff constitute a great community who now need to innovate in all their methods of teaching and must support the development of that new knowledge throughout the teaching profession in all sectors. The only viable means for the global teaching community to achieve this is something like the CoMOOC model, which orchestrates and maintains the development of high-quality community knowledge on the large scale.

The tertiary sector overall is not developing strategies beyond those that support their own staff in managing this transformation. Senior leadership teams are strategizing but tending not to take the opportunity to learn from their academic staff who used the pandemic years to experiment and learn something of how to teach online, and who have since been focused on desperately supporting their own students' recovery of lost learning. Perhaps we must rely on the most senior form of leadership within the institutions, the governing body. Governance certainly has the task of holding the executive to account in terms of the highest level of descriptions of what the institution is: its aims, methods and outcomes, and financial viability. The governing body can therefore take on the responsibility for what we might call 'digital governance'. They would have to persuade its executive to learn from their staff how best to deploy both conventional and online methods and use this to promote large-scale professional development as a priority for the institution's contribution to the UNSDGs (Laurillard, 2023).

The problem is urgent, and its scale is immense. In her powerful summary of the lessons from the pandemic, Roberta Malee Bassett, the global lead for tertiary education at the World Bank, details the students who are most vulnerable, due to access, disability, location and socio-economic group, for whom the move to online education has left them even further behind their privileged peers. She concludes that tertiary education leaders must direct their promise of technological innovation in learning and skills development towards these most vulnerable students if they are to sustain their fundamental values of equity, assured quality and social responsibility (Malee Bassett, 2020). Professional development operating on the large scale would help to mobilize the vast community of tertiary teachers into developing the best methods they can, collectively and collaboratively, in response to this challenge.

MOOCs have had a bad press since they suffered from the initial hype that they could bring university access to students everywhere. Of course they cannot. University education requires labour-intensive teaching, nurturing and assessment that does not scale. Professional education does not have the same requirements, because professionals are experienced, knowledgeable and able to help each other through the process of knowledge building.

The maxim that *knowledge is power* is continually reinforced by a university system that maintains an elitist control over the development and dissemination of the knowledge it creates. That power must be shared more widely if universities are to have any hope of contributing to the scale of the challenges set by the UN SDGs. Collaboration is essential, not just across the tertiary education sector, but also beyond – to the professionals who are the stakeholders in the validated knowledge being produced in its journals and the human capability of its graduates. The CoMOOC model has exactly the same potential for general professional development as we have shown it has for teachers. The instantiation of knowledge in a shareable digital form will be customized tools such as the Learning Designer – types of case study, action plans, protocols, etc., as appropriate to the discipline. The remainder of the features of the general form of a CoMOOC illustrated in the two case studies above is transferable to any other professional context. The process of creating and sustaining such a model is the subject of our Theory of Change, proposed in Chapter 9.

Questions and activities

Here are two suggestions for following up on the ideas presented in this chapter. For your own context, how would you

1. Plan for contributing to one of the SDGs relevant to your field through online collaborative professional learning?
2. Use or adapt the critical design features for a CoMOOC that would work well for professionals in your own field?

8

Transformative Online Education in Challenging Contexts

Introduction

A key application of online learning is the role it can play in addressing some of the most challenging educational problems. SDG4 represents one such problem that HE must lead on and is the focus of this chapter. The evidence of what online learning can contribute is focused in this chapter on the studies we have carried out in some of the most challenging contexts for education. While the detail may not be relevant to other educational contexts, we use these studies to draw out the generic transferable principles for methodology and action that successful online learning initiatives need to address if we are to make significant and lasting contributions.

The continuing problem of education disrupted by mass displacement is the context for this chapter. Over half the world's refugees are children, with the majority likely to spend their entire childhoods away from home with limited access to education. In the Syrian crisis alone, over 3 million Syrian children have dropped out or are at risk of dropping out of school within Syria or in neighbouring host countries (UNICEF, 2016). In conflict-affected communities, the numbers of teachers are reduced through displacement, intimidation, or physical and psychological harm. This loss of professional knowledge capital needs to be rebuilt.

The problem is not confined to countries in conflict. Even in peaceful developed countries the climate crisis is leading to increasing numbers of displaced people and communities. There are many other contexts in which learners are denied an education due to their physical situation, such as lack of proximity to educational institutions, physical mobility problems, people in prisons, long-term illness, caring responsibilities and women unable to leave their home, where digital methods are the only reliable and stable means of providing education. Teachers can have an enormous impact on the lives of such children, providing continuity and support for physical, cognitive and social needs, along with education. However, teachers of vulnerable children and young people, including refugees, but also those with disabilities, caring responsibilities or who live in other types of challenging environments, are very often not well prepared for this responsibility. This may be because they are new to teaching or lack experience with vulnerable children or both. We show that this situation risks reproducing hegemonic approaches to education which do not enable children and young people to flourish. The need for transformative teacher professional development (TPD) for both qualified and unqualified teachers in such contexts is paramount, but it is teachers themselves who have to develop the knowledge of what works in practice. A recent initiative, building on our work, is the TPD@Scale Coalition,[1] a grouping of Ministries of Education which has compiled a report on how teachers might be supported for *Learning at Scale for the Global South* (Laurillard et al., 2018).

In crisis settings, technology is often proposed as a means of supporting education. This can involve the development of digital programmes or apps that have been developed elsewhere and brought in from outside, often bypassing the teacher. Yet, it is here that the expertise of teachers is required, because they know the children and young people, and the contexts of their lives. They know what is likely to work and what will not. This chapter demonstrates how a knowledge of learning design can support teachers' professional development in transformative online and blended learning in the context of mass displacement, thereby improving the educational chances of the most marginalized children. We will show the impact of involving teachers in designing education with technology in emergencies and prolonged crises, and how CoMOOCs can support this process.

Transforming the role of the university to deliver on the SDGs

The provision of outward-facing services to the economy, community, society, social justice and the world all feature in the top ten goals within university mission statements, along with services to students, research and education (Seeber, Barberio, Huisman, & Mampaey, 2017). As we face unprecedented social and environmental challenges, the public service mission for HE has become ever more pressing, and events such as the COVID-19 pandemic have underscored the key role universities can play by mitigating the impact of crises and preparing and planning for alternative global futures. The UN SDGs provide a valuable framework for the ways universities can deliver on their public service mission, and provide a reference point for how digital education technologies might play a role. One explicit aim, of course, is SDG4 to ensure inclusive and equitable quality of education and promote lifelong learning for all. Access to education is vital to enable people to navigate through the growing uncertainties characterized by global challenges (OCDE, 2018). Recognizing the specific value of tertiary education for sustainable development, the UN has included within SDG4 the need to 'ensure equal access for all women and men to affordable and quality technical, vocational and tertiary education, including university') (United Nations, 2013, p. 19). This means we have to address all forms of inclusivity, as defined in Chapter 2 – demographic background, gender, culture and language, and disabilities (cognitive, emotional and physical) – to provide equitable access. Achieving this aim requires significant scaling up of technical, vocational and university education.

Education for professionals as a driver of sustainable development

Harnessing the power of digital technology to enable universities to work at scale with local and global communities would enable universities to transform higher education's capacity to drive the sustainable development agenda, in line with their collective mission statements.

The forms of education that prioritize plurality, in the sense of diverse knowledges, networking and problem-solving for diverse constituencies, can develop the world's capacity towards new paths to a vision of prosperity not based simply on economic growth, but on an inclusive prosperity founded on the flourishing of both people and the planet (Moore, 2015). Such an approach must begin by allowing professionals who influence working practices on a daily basis to come together to revalue communities and environments and develop diverse but locally appropriate holistic solutions, rather than replicate standard developments. To achieve this step change, 'businesses, governments and civil society actors are equally called upon to pursue a more sustainable path forward' (Scheyvens, Banks, & Hughes, 2016). That includes universities and colleges, and all their disciplines.

Currently many of the initiatives within education for sustainable development have sought to raise awareness and understanding of the issues at stake across all sectors. However, the role for universities is to develop professionals' capabilities for responsible action as envisaged in the Education for Sustainable Development (ESD) roadmap by increasing access to technical, vocational and tertiary education, and training professionals and paraprofessionals in key fields (UNESCO, 2020). We need a holistic and cross-disciplinary approach to meeting the SDGs, since the SDGs are inevitably interlinked.

Digital education is the only way tertiary education can deliver on the SDGs at a scale commensurate with the global demand (Laurillard, Kennedy, & Wang, 2018). While many universities are explicitly strategizing their engagement with the SDGs (Owens, 2017), without an aligned digital strategy it is not feasible to scale up to providing everyone with access to conventional quality education in the skills needed. Universities and colleges must forge more flexible and reciprocal relationships with their alumni and other professionals, to share the results of academic research and learn from professionals' application of ideas to practice.

Despite this clear need for ongoing professional development, universities too regularly end their relationships with professionals on graduation. Instead, universities could benefit from a highly productive two-way exchange of knowledge with professionals. Practitioners in business, industry, government, investment, NGOs and like are ideally situated to make use of academic evidence, and their situated knowledge could inform tertiary teaching to make it more relevant to the practical challenges they face in their work. We do not envision tertiary education as appropriating the domain of traditional workplace training but rather propose that they establish a genuine knowledge exchange and collaboration with practitioners, as is argued in Chapter 7. Digital education can facilitate this new role for universities in driving professional education, speeding up and scaling up collaborative learning applied to meeting the SDGs.

Digital support for teaching in challenging environments

In this chapter, we present one area of professional development (teaching) that can be effectively speeded up and scaled up using digital technology. We show the detail of how this can be done with teaching, and then illustrate how it can be applied to other professional contexts. The professional development of teachers who are working in (often protracted) emergency situations caused by conflicts or natural disasters is an area that demands the attention of universities and colleges, and where digital education is an obvious fit. For just education alone the sector shoulders the responsibility for educating another 69 million teachers by 2030 to achieve the goal of education for all.[2] Whenever mass displacement occurs as a result of crises, climate disasters and conflicts, the need for teachers is exacerbated. Trained teachers in such contexts are always in short supply. The flow of displaced people puts pressure on existing education systems who struggle to cope with the numbers and needs of refugee children, who may be traumatized or have missed sometimes extended periods of education. Teachers within communities on the move may no longer be available, because their skills mean they have migrated separately and settled into new occupations, or because they may have been intimidated or traumatized themselves (Burns & Lawrie, 2015). In addition, teachers working in the context of mass displacement may lack professional status, suffer from poor pay and conditions, and may lack contextualized professional development (Pherali, Moghli, & Chase, 2020).

Such teachers need access to contextualized professional development, and to learning from peers in similar circumstances. Pherali et al. (2020) argue that teachers should be supported to become transformative intellectuals, who can in turn support their learners 'to question hegemonic narratives that restrict their ability to transform their social, cultural, and political conditions' (Pherali et al., 2020, p. 152). This is a marked difference from uncritical or accommodating teachers who are averse to taking political action, and may reinforce the hegemonic power relationships by requiring learners to accept rather than critique their social position or the content of the curriculum. Instead, teachers can be encouraged to consider their agency not only within the classroom but within the wider environment surrounding the child.

How might this be supported? Pherali et al. (2020) argue that ecological systems theory (Bronfenbrenner, 1979) can provide a tool for teachers to both recognize the different systems of influence on the child, and identify forms of action in response. Bronfenbrenner (1979) argued that interacting systems surround each person, that influence them and that they can influence in turn. These systems, surrounding every individual, child, or adult, include the microsystem, mesosystem, exosystem, macrosystem and chronosystem. For the child these are defined as follows:

- The microsystem is the immediate context: family, friends, school, workplace.
- The mesosystem is where two or more microsystems interact, such as parents coming to school.
- The exosystem is the wider society, including political systems affecting education and media communications for parents, teachers and learners.

- The macrosystem includes the ideologies or values of a particular culture.
- The chronosystem refers to life events, such as conflicts or disasters, and life transitions.

Each of these systems constructs the context within which the child learns and the teacher teaches. Teachers can exert influence in all systems not only in the microsystem (e.g. the classroom), and this model can be used to identify the action that can help a teacher understand better how to support their learners and each other. Moreover, learning about how other teachers have operated within the ecological systems to make changes could benefit not only teachers' classroom practice, but their relationships with parents, families and community leaders, and their ability to organize themselves to address poor conditions, or the separation of refugee children and teachers from the state systems (Pherali et al., 2020).

The kind of professional development that could support teachers to become transformative intellectuals needs to reach into communities where professional development is hard to access, and provide opportunities for teachers to share their practice with each other. Digital education could reach these professionals in the form of a CoMOOC because teachers are experienced self-regulating learners and are often eager to learn from their peers. Through co-design the knowledge that has been accumulated by teachers on the ground can be shared with others through a CoMOOC. The CoMOOC social learning design is ideal for this, since teachers, even those in the most adverse contexts of mass displacement, should be empowered to support each other and take action, as Pherali et al. (2020, p. 167) explain:

> The notion of teachers as transformative intellectuals rests on the assumption that teachers in refugee contexts do not simply rely on external support to enable positive change in their practice; rather, they operate as proactive individuals who draw from their wealth of previous experiences, insights into the host community they live in, and available resources, networks, and circumstances.

Collaborative activities and discussions within the CoMOOC can provide an inclusive space for all teachers to leverage the wealth of knowledge that exists in the community but is not otherwise easily accessed. While poor digital infrastructure can present challenges, teachers often have the means to get online through personal or school computers or devices, and even in migrant communities access to the internet, while unstable and constantly under threat (Gibon, 2022), has still been possible.

Of course, this is not the only, or most typical, way that digital education is thought to help in these circumstances. In many of the most challenging environments for teaching and learning, claims are increasingly made about how digital education can facilitate access to learning, enhance curriculum content, support educators, and increase the wider social and psychological benefits of learning. However, digital education is often viewed uncritically, taking the form of tools, platforms or programmes imported from vastly different contexts, often from the Global North, to improve opportunities for those who have little access to education, often located in the Global South. Moreover, the digital 'solutions' are often provided without the involvement of local teachers. Yet, the learners in these settings are those who need the support of caring and sensitive teachers even more than their better resourced counterparts. Teachers are closest to their learners and their families, and their knowledge and understanding is vital to develop appropriate and effective digital education initiatives. This means that all these teachers need access to professional development to help them respond to the needs of vulnerable children in situations with few resources and which are constantly under stress, *and* they need to understand how digital technologies could help in these contexts.

These dual needs led us to co-design the *Transforming Education in Challenging Environments* CoMOOC with a group of teachers, teacher-educators and education stakeholders in Lebanon, as one of the most challenging education contexts across the world. We wanted to learn to what extent digital access to TPD could help them.

The rest of this chapter sets out the vision of online, collaborative teacher professional development in the CoMOOC, along with the approach to using technology for the education of children and young people in challenging environments that we embedded within it. We use this initiative and its outcomes as an evidential basis to propose a similar approach in other professional contexts.

Co-designing 'Transforming Education in Challenging Environments'

We took a 'co-design' approach, explained in Chapter 6, to create a CoMOOC to support teachers working in challenging environments. The co-design approach moved through five stages described below: engage; develop; extend; embed and sustain. These five stages come from our co-design theory of change presented more fully in Chapter 9. The *Transforming Education in Challenging*

Environments CoMOOC is used as a detailed case study here to show how this process works in practice.

Engaging the main stakeholders (Engage)

The first stage of our co-design process is Engage, where stakeholders are brought together to begin the co-design of the CoMOOC. The engage stage of co-designing *Transforming Education in Challenging Environments* was conducted through a series of consultation meetings and workshops with a wide range of stakeholders from the education sector in Lebanon. In Lebanon, refugees make up over a quarter of the population (around 1.5 million), the majority from Syria, and nine out of ten live in extreme poverty (UNHCR, 2022). Around 600,000 refugees are of school age, but 30 per cent have never attended school (UNHCR, UNICEF, & World Food Programme, 2021). The public school system was smaller and less privileged compared to the private school sector, but the refugee crisis expanded its remit, offering an additional 'second shift' school day to accommodate Syrian refugees. NGOs run their own schools, but are permitted to educate children only at the primary level. The COVID-19 pandemic and the economic crisis have exacerbated the challenges facing refugee children's access to education (HRW, 2021). These conditions are not unique in the world. The hope of the research team was that if we could find a way to support teachers in Lebanon, there would be transferable lessons for other crisis contexts.

To create a CoMOOC that would bring together the different sectors of the Lebanese system and encourage dialogue that would produce shared knowledge outcomes, we needed to adopt a participatory approach with stakeholders drawn from government and the official teacher training bodies, universities, local and international NGOs, and teachers themselves. We sought the input of teachers from across the public/private and charitable/NGO sectors, including from teachers who were refugees themselves. Meetings and workshops took place in minister's offices, university campuses, conference rooms and INGO offices in Beirut, and NGO headquarters within the Bequa'a refugee community. Outcomes from the workshops were reported in Kennedy & Laurillard (2019).

As part of the co-design process, we invited representatives from across the education landscape in Lebanon to attend three days of collaborative workshops in London. During the three days we constructed a curriculum together and began to develop the learning design for the CoMOOC. Representational artefacts (objects such as maps, diagrams, pictures) have been proposed as a valuable method to support workshop participants to adopt a shared language and achieve meaningful collaborative knowledge production (Morrison & Dearden, 2013). For this purpose, we adapted the ABC module planning workshop developed at UCL which uses cards printed with the six learning types developed for the Learning Designer from the Conversational Framework (Laurillard, 2012). The cards operate as a kind of 'boundary object' (Star & Griesemer, 1989) because the learning types (see Chapter 2) are recognizable across all education environments, but are flexible enough to be applied differently in specific contexts. For example, the stakeholders understood the types of learning from their different face-to-face practices, and were therefore able to translate this knowledge to the context of a CoMOOC.

Developing the Co-MOOC (Develop)

The face-to-face workshops promoted ideation and group bonding, which was perhaps especially important due to the divergent politics of Lebanon. Taking the participants to London, away from their daily contexts in Lebanon seemed to help this process. For the second co-design stage, 'develop', the paper-based outputs from the workshops were digitized and further refined in the Learning Designer tool. As the digital representation of the CoCMOOC developed, it was shared online for comment and revision with the workshop team.

This part of the co-design process resulted in a four-week, three hours per week CoMOOC with the following outline, taking participants from reflecting on their available resources, through alternative approaches to understanding their learners, to new ways of working with learners, and to the extension of this to digital methods.

WEEK 1 Educators changing learning environments
Educators imagining and creating change with limited resource
Educators responding to challenges in the social environment
Approaches to changing the learning space
Moving forward with ideas for change

WEEK 2 Understanding learners in context
The wider contexts that influence teaching and learning
Understanding learner perspectives
Teaching controversial issues

WEEK 3 Transforming learning for an unknowable future
Responding to students' needs and aspirations

Transformative teaching and learning
Collaborating on transformative education
Understanding and working within limitations

WEEK 4 Digital networks for change
Digital tools to help learners
Digital tools to help teachers
Sharing our best ideas

For each activity, short documentary-style videos of teachers on location in Lebanon discussing the issues were followed by written texts, collaborative exercises and discussions. Week 1 focused on empowering educators in low-resourced environments to create supportive learning environments based on values. Week 2 introduced Bronfenbrenner's (1979) ecological systems theory and invited teachers to use the concepts to make sense of their current teaching strategies and how these could adapt in the future. Week 3 focused on the concept of the teacher as a transformative intellectual, and encouraged teachers to analyse and critically reflect on their pedagogy and practice. Digital education was featured throughout the course and the final week focused on how digital tools could help both teachers and learners, and support the sharing of practice. These activities foregrounded the importance of learning design for using technology in challenging environments.

An equivalent educational experience was designed on two platforms: Edraak in Arabic and FutureLearn in English, to reach as many teachers as possible in Lebanon and elsewhere. Since the launch of the CoMOOC, there have been three runs on both platforms, which as a result have attracted over 25,000 enrolments from educators in Lebanon and around the world.

Giving voice to the teacher community (Extend)

The Extend stage of the co-design process was to launch the CoMOOC, attracting participation from 167 countries, including 102 Low and Middle Income Countries (LMICs). This was supported by running the CoMOOC in two languages, as the Arabic version reached countries in the MENA region, while the English version also recruited from North and South America, East and South East Asia, Europe and Africa.

The discussion and collaboration activities that we designed into the CoMOOC provided a mechanism for giving voice to the teachers on the course. We designed activities for participants to reflect on the teaching ideas presented in the videos and written case studies, and apply them to their own contexts, suggesting the modifications that would be necessary. We created exercises where teachers would add one idea – e.g. a teaching principle or a technology tool – to a word cloud generator or a Padlet, and see the results as accumulated ideas from all other participants. We also added a peer review activity, where participants gave feedback on their peers' lesson plans. In this way, we opened up the collaboration process at the heart of the CoMOOC to the participants that enrolled. This allowed us to evaluate what value the teachers were gaining from the CoMOOC (see evaluation below).

Establishing the approach (Embed)

Co-design is essential if we are ever to address the threat that stakeholders see a CoMOOC as coming from outside, even as a competitor to their own activities. This is why multiple stakeholders were involved in the co-design process from the beginning. To consolidate the sense of co-ownership of the CoMOOC, and to pave the way for sustainability, we worked with stakeholders to embed the CoMOOC into established TPD provision in Lebanon. For example, with colleagues at Lebanese American University (LAU) we created a *Blended Learning Summer School for Teachers Working with Vulnerable Children* around the first run of the CoMOOC as part of their Continuing Professional Development programme for teachers. The Summer School enabled teachers from NGO schools and trainee teachers at Lebanese University to meet at LAU for campus-based classes which extended the discussion and activities from the CoMOOC and helped to build a community.

All the resources from the CoMOOC were accessible for use offline, so the education NGOs Jusoor and MAPS used these in workshops for their teachers both to extend access to the CoMOOC beyond those enrolled (e.g. because of limited availability of internet and digital devices), and to create a community of teachers at the NGOs. Evidence of the impact of these embedded activities is presented in the *'Elevating the teacher'* section below.

Going beyond the funded project (Sustain)

For the CoMOOC to sustain itself beyond the funding period, the co-design process has to continue during the run. Embedding the CoMOOC into stakeholders' own professional development activities elicits a long-term commitment to it, while the ideas and suggestions supplied by participants revitalize the content. For example, the value creation stories provided by Mariam Khalaf and Lea George Elias (see below) became a video in the CoMOOC, accompanied by an activity where others could add examples of value gained from participation.

Since this collaboration, other conflicts and crisis situations have arisen, for example, the military coup in Myanmar which has created extremely challenging conditions for teachers, who often lack physical classrooms and must teach under trees. By embedding the CoMOOC into the TPD activities of new communities like this, a route to sustainability can be established. In particular, if those new communities add case studies from their own context, the CoMOOC can be reimagined for a changing world. Supporting teacher communities to embed CoMOOCs into their practice is therefore a new focus for our research. The quotation from a participant in Myanmar indicates the potential of this approach:

> I found it valuable to see how educators in a different part of the world (Lebanon) were meeting challenges. These insights can transfer to the country I work on, Myanmar. I am also involved in an international advisory group to a political group in Myanmar, and I will suggest that they take the course.
>
> (Khin, FutureLearn)

Sustainability is also dependent on whether the CoMOOC can achieve positive changes in practice for the participants. The following section therefore presents an evaluation of the Extend stage – identifying the value of participation in the CoMOOC and its impact on practice.

Evidence from the evaluation

In order to identify the value to the participants of taking part in the CoMOOC, we used a hybrid inductive-deductive approach (Fereday & Muir-Cochrane, 2006) to analyse post-course surveys (722 responses) and interviews (with 22 participants). For this we created a template using *a priori* codes from the Value Creation Framework (VCF) (Wenger, Trayner, & De Laat, 2011) outlined in Chapter 7 and also discussed in Chapter 9. The VCF identifies five possible cycles of value creation for teacher professional development networks or communities. These range from the **immediate value** derived from engaging in the community or network (i.e. social presence from being with like-minded others), through **potential value** (or learning), **applied value** (application of learning to one's professional context), **realized value** (e.g. benefits to student learning outcomes) and **reframing value** (rethinking at an individual or institutional level). We used the five cycles of value to code the survey responses and interviews, whilst also noting themes and patterns within these broad categories. The results of this analysis are available in Kennedy, Masuda, Moussaoui, Chase, & Laurillard (2022) and provide evidence of the effectiveness of the Extend stage of the Theory of Change in terms of all five forms of value.

Responses from the end of course surveys indicated that participants valued the experience, with 81 per cent reporting that the course met or exceeded their expectations. The participants gained immediate value from learning in a social environment with inputs from fellow teachers (pseudonyms have been provided):

> Particularly how involved and passionate the other participants are and the involvement of those running the course. It is brilliant to hear from teachers in the field as well as students too.
>
> (Alice, FutureLearn)

> I liked sharing experiences between teachers from different places and different cultures.
>
> (Aisha, Edraak)

> I liked seeing the comments of experiences others have had.
>
> (Bennett, FutureLearn)

> I liked not only the lecturers but the teachers who are involved in the educational process.
>
> (Zein, Edraak)

Participants reported the potential value they gained from both the videos and the discussion pointing to the theoretical frameworks such as Bronfenbrenner's ecological systems theory, the Transformative Education approach, creative teaching with limited resources and the importance of collaboration with others:

> [I learnt to] Pay more attention to the learner's social conditions and how they relate at the learning level.
>
> (Rayan, Edraak)

> Using the skills of communication, dialogue and consultation with students.
>
> (Jamal, Edraak)

> Transformative is paramount and the need to share a passion in education to collaborate [with] like-minded people and the emphasis on teamwork.
>
> (Robin, FutureLearn)

> I will be more aware of the issues some of our more challenging pupils have. I will be using some of the techniques to help the children. Transformative technique is the one thing I really want to work on. Going the extra mile for the pupils when they need it.
>
> (Jordan, FutureLearn)

Many of the participants specifically mentioned the potential value of learning about the use of digital technologies – including through experiencing them as useful for their own learning during the course:

> Digital tools to interact with students and discuss with them to reach the goal.
>
> (Majd, Edraak)

> I can use Padlet with students to show their participation, responses like you used in this course and can be used in the professional development trainings of the teachers.
>
> (Ehsan, Edraak)

Like Ehsan, many of the participants reported sharing the digital tools they encountered with their colleagues and teacher trainees, demonstrating evidence of embedding the resources into the practice of teacher professional development, and showing that the reach of the CoMOOC extended beyond enrolments.

In addition to highlighting concepts and techniques they learnt, participants were also able to show that they could apply these to their practice. Participants gave examples of the applied value of using the six learning types and the Learning Designer tool to help them plan teaching with technology:

> I like using the Learning Designer to help me cover all 6 types of learning.
>
> (Avery, FutureLearn)

> The 6 steps of learning was particularly interesting and I shall be more aware of these in my future planning.
>
> (Haven, FutureLearn)

> [I liked] Methods of designing learning and student participation ... the Learning Designer.
>
> (Farah, Edraak)

How to use the available tools in the education process, how to build relationships with students, how to make a lesson plan.

(Nour, Edraak)

In the second week of the course, an activity asked students to apply Bronfenbrenner's ecological systems theory to a situation that they had encountered. Participants were invited to share an example of a difficult situation they had encountered and describe what they did to improve things, identifying which system from the ecological systems theory was involved. The participants shared stories from their experience of teaching in the discussion, demonstrating that they not only understood the theory, but were able to apply it in their practice. For example:

> One participant gave an example from her teaching with Syrian refugee women, describing how, one day, only half the class turned up. The teacher discovered that the women were under pressure from men in the community to stay home rather than attend school, and correctly identified that this involved intervening in the macrosystem to change beliefs about gender in society, and potentially laws too.

The discussions enabled the team to learn a lot about the challenges that teachers and parents face:

> Another participant provided an example from her practice, where a child was exhibiting challenging behaviour. The teacher met with his mother, and discovered the mother was under pressure because her husband was rarely at home and had been taking it out on the child. The participant correctly identified that she acted in the mesosystem by talking to the parent, and then in the exosystem to address the problem, as she called on the services of a psychologist to help.

There were many other examples from the discussion, including participants' applications of the theory to situations and locations all around the world, involving children suffering bullying or abusive behaviour, or enacting this themselves, children running away from home, children coming to school unfed, children staying away from school. Many of the participants that shared their stories were also able to suggest further ways they could have responded by pointing to additional systems in which they could make a change. For example, in responding to tiredness among children at school, a participant suggested they could work within the exosystem to start a community-wide campaign to raise awareness of the importance of rest for children, and another suggested school-wide training for teachers from NGOs specializing in psychosocial support to deal with violence. As a result, the discussion provided not only evidence of potential and applied learning, but also indications of reframing value as the participants used the theory to re-evaluate their practice and plan new approaches. This kind of discussion shows how participants in a CoMOOC can contribute to community knowledge building and create a rich resource of examples of transformative practice.

The surveys and discussion contributions provided evidence of immediate, potential, applied and reframing values. However, realized value is more difficult to capture. This is the value of the improved practice for others, such as the students in the classes taught by the participants, or their colleagues at school, or for the students' families or communities. It is challenging to provide evidence of realized value during the CoMOOC, because this value necessarily occurs later and relies on participants reporting back the evidence of the impact. Yet, it is critical to know how participation in the CoMOOC could be of benefit to others, and knowing that potential value accrued by teachers in the CoMOOC could become realized value for others is a strong motivator to participate.

For these reasons, we conducted follow-up interviews with participants to explore the CoMOOC's impact on their own practice and on the practices of others they encounter in their professional work. With their permission we presented these in subsequent runs of the course to encourage more participants to share their evidence of realized and reframed values to further enhance the co-designed contributions to the course.

Mariam Khalaf is a former participant who shared her story on video. Mariam is Operations Manager at the Lebanese NGO Thaki, which recycles digital devices (such as laptops donated by commercial companies), loads them with educational content and distributes them to educational centres who work with refugees and other vulnerable Lebanese children and young people. Thaki provide training to teachers to help them use the content and devices effectively. Mariam explained that during the CoMOOC, she discovered a range of digital technologies, like Padlet, Mentimeter, word cloud generators, and how to use them in an educational context, and she was able to pass this knowledge onto the teachers she works with:

> On one occasion a teacher shared with me that she had shy students in her class. I suggested she use a word cloud. This tool helped the students break the fear barrier and express their thoughts – first electronically, then it encouraged them to express their thoughts and speak about it. (Mariam Khalaf in El Moussaoui, 2020)

Another participant, Lea Georges Elias, an English teacher in Lebanon, also described her use of technologies she learnt about in the CoMOOC and the positive effect on her students: 'They were very interactive, they enjoyed it.'

> Lea also described the impact of her engagement with the theory and concepts from Bronfenbrenner, which helped her understand how to communicate with students and the effect that had on their learning. Lea recounted an experience she had with a student who was struggling in class, and with whom all the teachers were struggling. Lea described how Bronfenbrenner's theory taught her to think 'outside the box' and find out more about the child from his parents and community: 'and it really helped get through to him, and right now, he's amazing in class'. (Lea Georges Elias in El Moussaoui, 2020)

These examples demonstrate the realized value from participants implementing the ideas, tools and concepts into their practice. We have collected value creation stories like these from further participants (Kennedy et al., 2022) and each demonstrates the specific value to both the teacher and those they work with.

The contributions of participants to surveys and to the CoMOOCs themselves demonstrate that *Transforming Education in Challenging Environments* was effective in supporting teachers to teach vulnerable learners in challenging settings like those caused by conflict and crisis, as well as to integrate technology into that teaching.

So what does this tell us about how technology can best support learners and teachers in any type of challenging environment? What are the lessons for governments, organizations and companies advocating educational technology for emergency situations? The next section argues that a focus on learning design should be central to the use of technology in crisis contexts.

Transformative education with technology in crisis contexts

Teachers as learning designers

Throughout *Transforming Education in Challenging Environments* we introduced teachers to learning design with digital technologies. We did this in three ways.

First, we modelled good learning design by embedding external tools to support interactive and collaborative learning within the CoMOOC, such as Padlet and Mentimeter. As mentioned earlier, we also added a link to the learning design for each week in the introduction steps. This is one important way of introducing teachers to effective methods for online learning by modelling the use of them in TPD courses, so that they experience learning in this new way.

Secondly, we added videos to weeks 1 and 2 that de-emphasized using technologies for acquisition, which can be many teachers and developers' sole focus. Instead the video introduced ways of using technologies for interaction and communication, drawing on case studies from practice. This shifted teachers towards designing for students' active learning with technology rather than using technology as digital resources. We discussed ways that technologies could be used even in low-resourced environments. For example, some of the teachers in the videos said that they only had access to one shared laptop and a projector, and had no internet connection in the school. For these situations, we shared PowerPoint templates adapted from files uploaded to the teachers' sharing repository TES.com which modelled how to create fun quizzes for the class using slide animations. In addition, we showed how teachers could use tools both inside and outside of the classroom to support their students to communicate with them and, crucially, with each other. These practical tools enabled the teachers to start using them immediately in their practice, for example:

> I have already used some of the resources in my work – the quiz PowerPoints and Mentimeter being just 2.
>
> (Oma, FutureLearn)

Thirdly, in the final week, we brought this learning together with a focus on digital technologies for supporting learners and teachers. We invited teachers to share both their excitement about technologies and their stories of the barriers they face. We used a Padlet to orchestrate participants' solutions to the three main challenges that the teachers we interviewed for the video case studies told us that they had encountered when using technologies in the classroom:

- technical,
- personal knowledge and skills,
- leadership and organizational issues.

The purpose of this was to leverage the experience of teachers to help each other respond to the obstacles in positive ways. We then introduced the Conversational Framework and the six learning types, and asked participants to map the technologies they use against the six learning types. We managed to build up an extensive database of tools mapped to learning types this way.

Having equipped teachers with an understanding of learning design and the tools they could design into their teaching, we invited teachers to adapt or create learning designs in the Learning Designer tool and share them with the other participants. This approach was effective in supporting teachers to use the Learning Designer to create lesson plans and share them with each other, which the participants' comments above indicate. Moreover, it is the kind of teacher knowledge sharing practice which is necessary in challenging environments, such as crisis or conflict settings, since teachers need access to the expertise of other teachers working on the ground in such contexts.

We argue that taking a learning design approach to deploying technologies in challenging environments is vital for effective use of digital technologies for learning. In such environments, teachers work with learners every day, trying out ideas to help them learn, looking and listening for feedback to judge whether they have been successful, and using this information to adjust their approach. The classroom – whether it is online or face-to-face – is a living laboratory where the teacher conducts repeated experiments. This capacity for teachers to incorporate research into their practice has enormous potential for understanding how technology could support learners, as Laurillard (2008, p. 140) explained:

> If we problematize teaching and learning, confront the need for innovation, and turn the teaching community into a profession capable of being experimental innovators and reflective practitioners, then we release a huge resource of energy and imagination for tackling the core educational problem of enabling what it takes to learn.

The teacher's role in transformative education

In emergency settings, teachers' practical wisdom gained from experimenting as they work is critical to understanding how technologies could be used to support vulnerable learners.

Conflicts and environmental and other crises disrupt children's education, often for years, while also causing trauma and reducing the resources available to support them. In terms of Bronfenner's (1979) ecological systems, when a child experiences a war, for example, this is a major life event that occurs within the chronosystem. Teachers need to understand its impact on the child in order to understand what the child brings to the learning environment. Teachers also need to consider how prevalent discourses and value systems within the wider society construct those events – for example, how does society's view of refugees affect the children being taught? Are there differences in the way society views girls' and boys' needs for and rights to education? Are disabled children guaranteed access?

These macrosystem considerations are central to understanding the role for the teacher and the school in creating a supportive place to learn. In order to secure the support of the child's parents and wider community, the teacher must work outside of the classroom, in the exosystem, to understand and influence local attitudes and policies. Practically, the teacher needs to engage in the mesosystem as a matter of course to engage with other professionals, such as child psychologists, social services, parents and community leaders. Teachers need to consider and take account of this wider context in the way they design the learning experience for children in the microsystem, because if they do not, the child may unable to learn. As such the design of learning with technology needs to be highly specific to this context and cannot be done by others, such as policymakers or education programme designers, at a distance. For example, teachers need to know what learning the child has missed, how they will respond to new learning and about the conditions for learning at home. Only then can they design a mobile learning programme to help them catch up. They need this depth of understanding to integrate an activity like a digital learning game into their classroom teaching so that it will motivate the children and be effective for learning. To understand children's behaviours, for example, why they might be coming late to school, means understanding the pressures on a child's parents or caregivers. Understanding the everyday technologies that are used within the community and the way they fit with a child's parents' languages, digital (and other) literacies and routines are central to the choices that teachers need to make when they set activities for outside class, or need to communicate with parents.

Digital technologies cannot be parachuted into crisis contexts without this knowledge – the teachers' everyday knowledge gathering activity in the classroom is necessary to understand what and how technology is needed. This is why teachers deserve so much more online community support than they currently receive.

Learning design for transformative education

The Conversational Framework introduced in Chapter 2 is a theoretical approach to defining the elements that an effective teaching strategy requires for any educational context, in any sector, including crisis contexts. The Conversational Framework helps to demonstrate how to get the best from technologies because it first identifies the form of learning that the technologies must support. This is fundamental to using digital technologies in crisis contexts – the *precise pedagogical* need for the technologies must be established *before* the technology is deployed to help. Teachers who interact with learners on a daily basis are the only professionals in a good enough position to discover these needs and design learning with technology in response. Therefore, teachers in crisis contexts must be considered as researchers, collecting evidence from observations and communication with learners, parents and the wider community, which they can then use to design an effective digitally enhanced learning environment. To do this, it is a priority to develop teachers' competency in learning design, i.e. a learner-oriented, teacher-constructed methodology for planning effective teaching with technology. Moreover, because digital tools like the Learning Designer enable teachers to represent their learning designs as boundary objects, able to transcend disciplines and contexts, this vital, practical knowledge that teachers accrue when teaching in challenging environments can be shared with others in different contexts, and easily adapted.

Learning design is, therefore, a practice that depends on teachers-as-researchers and supports them to develop creative designs for their own tailored response to students' needs with a sophisticated understanding of the role that digital technologies can play in relation to supporting the six learning types.

This approach puts teachers at the centre of practice and enables them to use their considerable knowledge to respond precisely to the contextualized needs of their learners. Through using the Learning Designer tool, it also enables them to articulate and share this knowledge with other teachers in similar settings.

A learning design can be adapted much more easily than a de-contextualized resource since it is the teaching idea that is being articulated and shared. In the next section, we demonstrate how important it is that teachers were enabled to implement this approach following their participation in the *Transforming Education in Challenging Environments* CoMOOC.

Elevating the teacher in challenging environments

Design and content contributions and support from two education-focused NGOs in Lebanon, Jusoor and MAPs, were critical to developing the CoMOOC on *Transforming Education in Challenging Environments*. Both NGOs run schools and education programmes for Syrian refugee communities in Lebanon, and were willing to share their expertise in supporting teachers (who were themselves refugees) to teach in the challenging environments of refugee camps, and generously facilitated the video team's recording of interviews with teachers at the NGOs' schools. Teachers at Jusoor and MAPs were influential in the co-design of the project by helping to define two key strands to the work that were becoming established within their communities: they believed in the concept of teachers-as-researchers, and they were optimistic about the potential of digital technology for learning in the context of displacement.

Teachers at Jusoor and MAPs took part in the CoMOOC if they were able to, and the NGOs used the videos in blended workshops for those who found it difficult to participate because of poor internet or lack of devices, thereby taking the value of the CoMOOC beyond its initial instantiation online. Teachers who participated were also able to mentor others. Interviews with a group of seven NGO teachers conducted immediately after the first run of *Transforming Education in Challenging Environments* also highlighted their use of WhatsApp as a supplement to the CoMOOC to discuss the issues being raised. During the course, the teachers told us they could use the ideas in the CoMOOC in their teaching, but the extent to which the knowledge gained created realized value for their learners, and even their learners' families, only became apparent later, at the beginning of the pandemic.

In Lebanon, as elsewhere around the world, the COVID-19 pandemic led to a lockdown and school closures. This exacerbated many of the challenges facing the refugee population, and the NGO schools had to be creative in their approach to continue the education of children and young people. For example, Jusoor were able to build on teachers' prior experience of digital learning to develop the *Azima: Determined to Learn* programme, which redesigned the curriculum to be easily accessible online in the context of the low-resourced environment in which the children and their families were living. At the heart of the Azima programme was communication between teachers and parents using WhatsApp. WhatsApp is a very familiar technology in Lebanon which operates in low internet bandwidth conditions, so the choice of this tool over other dedicated educational software, for example, Microsoft Teams, was informed by Jusoor teachers' understanding of the local context. In addition to this knowledge, the teachers' understanding of learning design and the role of technology for supporting communication enabled them to see how a simple tool like WhatsApp could function perfectly well to keep learners in touch with the school if they designed the learning experience around it. Jusoor did this by creating short videos accompanied by activities so that the children could engage with the video content. They also sent physical learning packs to families so children could participate when the internet or energy supply was interrupted, which is a regular occurrence in Lebanon. Jusoor teachers effectively designed a multimodal communication channel between teachers and learners, enabling children to engage with teaching and learning activities in whichever way suited them. For example, children could complete their work digitally or on paper, then take a photo to send back to the teacher for feedback. In addition, a counsellor was available to provide psychosocial support. The Azima programme was pedagogy-led, the technology simply mediated teachers' communication with learners. The teachers created learning designs that could be implemented on technology like WhatsApp as well as workarounds for when even that technology failed. They could do this because they had confidence with designing online learning and they had an informed understanding of the context of their learners' lives. This meant they were able to understand what technology would work for the children and their families and what the challenges might be. This programme needed to be designed by these teachers, not by external EdTech experts, because the teachers were the ones with the relevant pedagogical and contextual knowledge. This is an example, of why we should be trusting teachers in these contexts, investing in teachers, and elevating the status of the teacher, because it is through their expertise that solutions will be found.

Jusoor (2022) reported successful impact of the Azima programme on children's learning outcomes between March and December 2020 for 58 per cent of the 900 children who regularly participated in the project. While it would be even better if all children were able to benefit, the teachers' knowledge of learning design and the most appropriate technology to use to support the learning meant that at least some children who would otherwise have missed out on learning could continue with their education.

This is an excellent example of how technology can help in crisis contexts. It is significant that the technology that helped was simple and readily available. While cutting-edge technological developments, like Augmented Reality, can appear exciting, with the promise of bringing distant learning environments into a user's home, any technology that requires high internet bandwidth and sophisticated or expensive devices will only ever work for the most highly resourced learners – and even then, everyone suffers technological failure sometimes! Teachers know this and if they have confidence in their learning design skills, then they are best able to choose what will work for their learners.

In 2021 the director of Jusoor, Suha Tutunji and the director of MAPS, Dr Fadi Al Halabi, participated in a RELIEF Conference panel. Suha Tutunji explained that Jusoor's participation in the RELIEF CoMOOC project supported them to design their innovative solution:

> [The CoMOOCs] put us a step ahead of other NGOs so when Covid-19 hit Lebanon, our teachers were ready, they were ready, they knew exactly how to research, how to use the links, how to use videos, how to use questions, how to use discussions and in 3 weeks we were off and we had started with our online learning using WhatsApp because this is the easiest form that the students and the teachers can relate to, and they can use it easily and they are familiar with it. So we used all that information that we had learnt to create a curriculum that condensed ... an integrated curriculum that was used on the phone itself.
> (Tutunji in Akle, Al Halabi, Tutunji, & Zeitoun, 2021)

This provides compelling evidence that developing teachers' learning design knowledge and research skills is the key to using technology most effectively in crisis contexts and emergency situations. Dr Fadi Al Halabi endorsed the importance of 'changing the mindset' of teachers so that they began to see themselves as researchers: 'because they are in the field, they are seeing new challenges' (Al Halabi in Akle et al., 2021). Al Halabi acknowledged that online learning had been difficult during the pandemic, with many families having only one device among many family members who all needed access, but MAPS also saw possibilities and opportunities. One such opportunity was a new initiative for family learning, since parents had started learning through online content sent via WhatsApp, and were in a stronger position to support their children.

A further development was the capacity to create online communities for teachers themselves to share the knowledge they had created at MAPs and Jusoor, inspired by the Conversational Framework:

> When the teachers went through the learning types, especially the collaboration and the discussion types, we created a teacher learning community between our three centres. So the teachers would meet once a month or once a fortnight, depending on their time, and they would discuss together and collaborate on issues they were facing when they were inside the classrooms and now they do it for challenges they are facing online.
> (Tutunji in Akle, Al Halabi, Tutunji, & Zeitoun, 2021)

The online practices at Jusoor and MAPs demonstrate that developing teachers-as-researchers, capable of responding to the unique and contextualized challenges facing children and their communities, is the key to using technology impactfully in crisis contexts. Learning design knowledge enables them to design appropriate responses with technology, and put in place a thoughtful programme of learning within which technologies can play a part. This is the key to meaningful use of technologies for learning – that they are integrated in a responsive learning design which takes account of the learning needs and their contexts of learning. If we are to realize the potential of learning technology then we must elevate teachers to a new role as *teacher-researchers* who research their learners needs, build on the work of other teachers to create learning designs in response, test these in class, adapt and share the outcomes. Online communities enable this knowledge to pass from teacher to teacher, lessening the load, refining the designs, and in the process developing digital pedagogic knowledge.

Developers of technologies or digital learning packages also need to put the teacher at the centre of their work. The focus of anyone developing a digital learning solution should first understand how the teacher will use or adapt their products to create a balanced learning experience and make it their aim to work with teachers. Too often the ambition of digital learning developers is to become a replacement for teachers, particularly where demand exceeds supply. Yet the solution can never be to sidestep teachers, but to train more, using CoMOOCs to extend high-quality professional development to all those who cannot currently access it. This is the best use of technology in challenging circumstances. If we elevate the status of teachers in these circumstances, then they will do the rest.

Conclusion

This chapter set out to explore the potential for technology to support teachers in challenging environments, such as within the contexts of mass displacement in Lebanon. The value of transformative education in the context of mass displacement and other crises is that it supports teachers to build on their considerable knowledge of education, the local community and the needs of their learners, and bring about positive changes for vulnerable children and young people (Pherali et al., 2020). Envisaged this way, teachers are no longer passively waiting for external organizations such as humanitarian agencies or EdTech providers, to provide the solution, but can take meaningful action themselves. Teachers can become learning designers and teacher-researchers to design ways of using technology to support learners and then reporting back to the teacher community with evidence of what works.

We have demonstrated that CoMOOCs can provide the support that helps teachers play this transformative role, by providing access to a knowledge-sharing community of peers whose ideas they can adapt to their own contexts, and feedback to help others. By following the stages of the co-design process it is possible to *engage* co-designers, *develop* a CoMOOC together, *extend* local, community knowledge on a global scale, *embed* the CoMOOC into community practice and thereby *sustain* the collaborations long term. These steps are the building blocks for a co-design theory of change that we will formalize in Chapter 9.

This chapter also provided evidence that the CoMOOC model does indeed work because (a) its collaborative design and development identifies the priorities for these teachers, and creates immediate, potential and applied value, often transforming their whole approach; and (b) the collaborative activities among the participants build the shared knowledge they need for the realized and reframing value that advances their practice.

But why stop there? We need also need all professional developers to adopt a learning design approach to online learning futures. The CoMOOC model can be applied not just to teaching but to many other professional areas. If we hope to address the challenges represented by the SDGs, we need to scale up this kind of contextualized, practical professional development across a range of professions: medicine and health care, biosciences, engineering, architecture, planning, construction, business, law and many others. In our work we have created CoMOOCs with sustainable energy practitioners and community-based researchers as well as teachers, and so we can show that the CoMOOC model works across professions.

We argue that the practitioner's applied wisdom is necessary to understand the needs of crisis contexts, and they are best placed to teach other professionals about what works on the ground. This chapter demonstrated how this worked in one case study, where a CoMOOC was able to help elevate the teachers so that they can lead the innovative technological response. In challenging environments, more so than ever, universities and other tertiary institutions, backed by governments and transnational organizations, need to reach out to all professionals through CoMOOCs, so that we can start to tackle the many challenges that we can no longer avoid.

Questions and activities

To consolidate the ideas and issues discussed in this chapter, here are some questions or activities that might help to reinterpret them for your own teaching-learning context. How would you

1. Use a learning design approach to tackle an important education challenge in your own context?
2. Support teachers to become teacher-researchers and share evidence of how their classroom innovations impact their learners, using digital tools?
3. Apply the five stages of the co-design approach (engage, develop, extend, embed and sustain) in a professional area you are familiar with, linking it to one of the SDGs? For example:
   - Who are the stakeholders that could be invited to become co-designers?
   - Who are the practitioners that could be identified to help **develop** the CoMOOC by appearing in the videos – what knowledge could they share?
   - What platform would you choose to launch the CoMOOC to **extend** the involvement of participants around the world? Who would it reach? Are there design issues to consider (e.g. language or user experience)?
   - What kind of professional development organization could **embed** the CoMOOC in their activities? Were they among your list of stakeholders for 'engage'?
   - What is the likelihood that the CoMOOCs would **sustain** themselves? How could this be managed?

9

Planning for an Evidence-Based Approach to Co-designed Massive Open Online Collaborations (CoMOOCs)

Introduction

This chapter presents a guide for educators in all areas of tertiary education that takes an evidence-based approach to co-designing online learning, whether for students or for professional development. This means designing with evidence of impact in mind – that is, creating online learning that is both informed by evidence of what works and designed to collect further evidence of impact.

The chapter draws together the insights into collaborative learning design and evaluation presented in previous chapters, and translates these into practical ways that an online educator can design for impact.

We begin by formalizing the way in which the Value Creation Framework (VCF) can be used to guide the learning design, and the data collection and analysis for evaluating online learning. The point is to find out how well the course works, and how we can keep improving it. The evaluation provides evidence of the value we hope to provide, but we also need a plan for how to achieve that. A 'Theory of Change' (ToC) is now widely accepted as a good way to plan for impact, and there are many examples now of how such a tool is used (Davies, 2018). We present our approach to developing a ToC that represents the co-design methodology we have shown to be so essential to making online learning work for professional development. Essential, because professionals already know a great deal about their work, and it would be perverse not to build in that extraordinary advantage to the way we set about enabling their further learning. With that explicit foundation we can then see how it is possible for professionals across the world to collaborate on building community knowledge, just as scientists and scholars do. We have the technology. This chapter sets out to provide the means to harness it to this endeavour.

An evaluation framework for online learning

Existing methods of online evaluation focus primarily on course satisfaction surveys and engagement analytics, for the good reason that they are easy and efficient to collect and process. These measures often tell us little about the different types of value a course has for its learners or, even more importantly, its second-order success in terms of what the learners do with what they have learnt. In this chapter, we use the idea of a 'value creation framework' illustrated in Chapters 7 and 8, to formalize a more robust way of evaluating online learning, and propose an approach to the learning design that sets out from the start to collect evidence of value in online participation, online learning, application of that learning, its realization as value for others and its transformational potential for enabling a reframing of professional practice.

The VCF is a very useful evaluation framework for initiatives where impact is important because it identifies five critical types of value to the participants. Chapters 7 and 8 have illustrated the methods of data collection and analysis relevant to them in terms of initiatives for the teaching profession. Now we want to generalize that experience and formalize the framework for application in any professional field to clarify how the framework enables us to design for impact.

Chapter 7 defined the *immediate* value generated by participation at any level in the course, the *potential* value of what they learn, the *applied* value that derives from using this in their own digital pedagogy, the *realized* value of discovering better outcomes from using the Learning Designer, and the *reframing* value of re-assessing their current approach. Chapter 8 used the same definitions of value to analyse survey responses and interviews about participants' experience of the *Transforming Education in Challenging Environments* CoMOOC.

We know the VCF is a useful guide to designing CoMOOCs in the context of TPD. Can this generalize to other professional fields? Each type of value requires a different learning design feature and data collection, so we now set out to build on the experience from TPD to devise a general formulation for the design features of a CoMOOC that can be expected to achieve these different types of value. Table 9.1 maps the different types of value to the various design features developed and tested in our CoMOOCs, expressed in a generic form. They could all be interpreted for use in a wide range of professional development initiatives.

Table 9.1 The Value Creation Framework as a guide to learning designs for a CoMOOC

Value	The nature of the value	Design features that elicit or enable this value
Immediate	Engaging in the community or network; social presence from being with like-minded others	Video case studies from trusted peers, access to new useful tools and techniques, access to relevant data and information, sources of new ideas and guidance, social activities in discussions, polls, word clouds, games and online pinboards, particularly those that communicate a sense of studying with many others, friendly and inviting language e.g. in discussion prompts and activities.
Potential	Building human, social, tangible, and learning capital as knowledge and skills	Experiencing new ways of learning and new tools, videos, texts explaining theoretical concepts and contextual articles, and new approaches they could use with their own communities; reflective quizzes and discussions inviting participants to articulate their understanding.
Applied	Taking the Potential value into actual application	Exercises on learning how to apply principles or use tools in practice, interpret theory in their own local contexts and act on it, peer feedback on their ideas for application, discussions, and activities for exchanging local practices and possible solutions, curating participants' own contributions.
Realized	The outcome of Applied value, changes that are of value to end-users or a local community	Exercises to monitor the adaptation of ideas and practices to their own context, and interpretation of generic concepts in local contexts, support for creating blended learning for communities and groups from course resources for social and practical benefit, activities to collect feedback and reports on implementing adaptations to local practice.

Value	The nature of the value	Design features that elicit or enable this value
Reframing	New ways of thinking or planning local practices, reassessing, or re-evaluating current practices for improvements	Engaging with new ideas in new ways, having the opportunity to experiment and rethink in a safe context, and to critique existing approaches from a new perspective, being able to build on the work of their peers as a scaffolding for redeveloping their own thinking, encouragement to test their own voice in exchanges with peers.

Being able to scaffold the progression from Immediate and Potential value through exercises that develop the Applied value of new ideas, concepts, skills and practice provides a crucial foundation for participants to build their confidence in taking what they have learned beyond the course.

The follow-through to the Realized value of that new capability in practice is crucial for impact, so the course must support participants by modelling implementation practice, such as lesson plans in the case study in Chapter 7, or by interpreting theory as plans, actions or designs in their own context – such as using the concept of the 'exosystem' to design a community campaign in the evaluation study in Chapter 8. Supporting their own contributions creates the chance to hear from them, support the peer conversations that report back on their explorations, and empower them to take new ideas and practices into their own environments and communities to make an effective difference.

These are the kinds of activities that can lead to the impact of the Reframing value. As we have reported, this can happen within the duration of the course, but a post-course survey picks up more evidence as it gives time for their ideas to develop. Again, the sharing of practice and the exchange of stories of barriers and solutions helps to empower that process of developmental change for professionals, who may often find themselves without many allies, having to forge their own pathways to change.

One key reason for advocating the use of CoMOOCs is the scale of the reach. In the field of health and medicine, for example, there has been Immediate value from UCL MOOCs due simply to this access to high-quality professional development, well-targeted for those working in the most challenging environments (Laurillard & Kennedy, 2020):

A course created and run three times as a rapid solution to the Ebola crisis engaged 12,000 health professionals with the most critical research findings, primarily from the five countries most affected and >180 Low and Middle Income Countries (LMICs).

For a course on global blindness a post-course survey showed that 94 per cent were healthcare professionals, with 82 per cent living in LMICs. Eighty-five per cent applied their learning at work, and many had gained career advantage from the MOOC.

Critically, 70 per cent had re-used the course resources to guide proposal writing, and 65 per cent were guiding others about eye care, further scaling up the impact of the MOOC.

A course on perioperative medicine generated £94,000 of income in seven runs, showing the value accorded to certification when it is locally endorsed, and enabling the course to cover the development and running costs to be self-sustaining. 36 per cent of active learners were from forty-five LMICs, i.e. targeting most of the key groups.

Wenger's VCF is important because it identifies for an online course initiative the most important forms of value that are likely to have a positive impact on professional practice. The value to participants is the focus. With the addition of our analysis of the generic design features needed for impact the enhanced framework provides a useful tool to both design the course and evaluate its impact, because it can be interpreted and adapted to guide a wide range of professional development initiatives.

The argument here is for a new departure for TPD and other forms of professional development. A recent review of online TPD studies revealed how difficult it has been to develop successful and impactful models for these initiatives (Macia & García, 2016).

A similar review recognizes the value to teachers of informal communities exchanging ideas, but notes also the common finding that 'these communities were often sites for "superficial" sharing of information, quick exchanges and a "smash-and-grab" approach to becoming informed' (Lantz-Andersson, Lundin, & Selwyn, 2018, p. 311).

Our approach contrasts with those reviewed because it neither confines the teacher to a one-way development of their personal capability via experts, nor relies on teacher communities to support their own learning via communities of practice with their rather onerous expectation of 'technology stewardship' (Wenger, White, & Smith, 2009), or the even more onerous expectations of 'collaborative professionalism', involving the write-up of 10,000-word case studies (Hargreaves, 2019). Stewardship is indeed important as communities do not function without that, but teachers have no spare time to offer. The alternative model of the CoMOOC hands that responsibility to an originating university, college or partner of a MOOC platform. The plan for ensuring impact therefore resides with them, as we discuss in the next section.

Using a Theory of Change for accountable impact

Establishing a ToC for an education initiative was originally introduced by researchers in the 1980s to show that an evaluation could find out not only whether it achieved the intended outcomes, but also how it did so. Understanding how the process led to the outcomes was as important as achieving them. The idea was to

> build and test a theory regarding the more general causal mechanisms responsible for the outcome behavior ... generalize the results ... to other settings, populations, and treatments ... [and] better predict whether they [the results] will be produced in other contexts.
>
> (Judd & Kenny, 1981, p. 603)

The original medical context could expect precision in data collection and analysis of the kind needed to establish cause and effect. Similarly, within the social sciences we also begin an initiative with an expectation that it will produce impact of value. In her later critical review of the field, Carol Weiss argues

> that the beliefs and assumptions underlying an intervention can be expressed in terms of a phased sequence of causes and effects ... [which] offers a way in which evaluation can tell not only how much change has occurred but also, if the sequence of steps appears as expected, how the change occurred.
>
> (Weiss, 1997, p. 501)

At the start of an initiative, the sequence of planned activities is based on experience from the literature and previous relevant research studies in a way the researchers believe to be optimized to achieve the intended outcomes. These assumptions should be explicit, i.e. the researchers should have a theory of the change process they are attempting to achieve with the initiative. Each stage should provide the grounding and information to guide the next, feeding back to adjust the initial assumptions, until they are able to judge the success or not in terms of the evaluation framework for the principal activity, and so deduce the extent to which it vindicates their initial theory of how the intended change would come about. This is close to what we mean by 'designing with evidence of impact in mind'. For an online learning initiative our approach should be both informed by evidence of what works and designed to collect further evidence of impact. And in the expectation that it will not necessarily produce all the intended outcomes, we should be able to explain why, and what aspects of the approach we need to revise.

To see how this would work for professional development we use our experience with working on TPD drawing on the previous two chapters.

Teachers should be doing it for themselves

In the context of developing initiatives for TPD there is a long history of unmet outcomes, as discussed in Chapter 7, 'Collaborative knowledge building for the teaching community', where we concluded that it was time to support teachers to test and share their own practice, and so build the community professional knowledge of digital pedagogy. Our proposal is that CoMOOCs provide the means for teachers to do this at scale.

The top-down, cascade and centre-periphery models of TPD preferred by policymakers (Bett, 2016; Kennedy, 2005; Marginson & Xu, 2021) fail because the knowledge being disseminated has not been built from the many and varied contexts of teaching, but from small local pilots, typically in Western countries, which are then scaled up for everyone else to follow, across the nation and across the world. For conventional HE research on the practice of teaching, we have to recognize that the hegemonic effects of Western-dominated research will impose inappropriate assumptions on most of the research outcomes that are meant to 'scale'.

In his coruscating critique of his own earlier policy aims, Richard Elmore ('a recovering political scientist' at Harvard) uses his long experience of educational policy in practice to demonstrate that any policy to implement best practices at scale cannot work because it is 'an irresponsibly simplistic and schematic view of human learning and development' (Elmore, 2016, p. 530). It is not feasible for policymakers to ask teachers in any sector to 'implement best practice', because this would be mere recipe-following, not professional development, and because 'best' practice cannot be generalized across so many wide-ranging contexts. Instead he proposes that we move on from the conventional approaches to more open methods, as shown in the first two columns of Table 9.2 (Elmore,

Table 9.2 From conventional to open methods of TPD and how to achieve them

From	to	by
a) basing new learning designs on received ideas that are "'feasible'" in existing institutions	basing learning designs on the theory and science of how humans learn	using the Learning Designer to create, share and build new knowledge of effective learning designs from a wide range of sources (Chapter 2)
b) focusing on "'universal'" prescriptions for organization and practice	the processes required to adjust powerful ideas to diverse contexts	working to a ToC (this chapter) that begins with engagement in diverse contexts
c) universal prescriptions for learning	multiple, diverse, and promising adaptations to diverse populations	localising shared learning design ideas for change (Chapter 2)
d) complex, technical expressions of expert knowledge	simple, transparent expressions, accessible to adults and children alike	generic versions of learning designs that represent local knowledge, enabling innovation (Chapter 5)
e) a focus on producing predictable effects across many settings	a focus on expecting to be surprised by effects and patterns that emerge from divergent thinking and practices	inviting practitioners to share their experiences of localizing and improving the generic versions in CoMOOCs (Chapter 6)

2016), where the final column represents our interpretations of how the new approaches might be achieved.

But even this generous recognition of the failing of a centralizing policy does not envisage the engagement of the teaching community itself in the discovery of new pedagogic knowledge. There is no explicit practice recommended that would enable either policymakers or teachers to act in a significantly different way. By adding our interpretation of each part of the new approach in Table 9.2, we take it beyond the imagined idea of a more open approach, to a practical instantiation of it.

We have discussed the value of developing 'scalable' professional development throughout this book, so we have to be clear about the meaning of 'operating at scale'. The 'at scale' process criticized by Elmore is akin to the cascade model, where a small national group disseminate good ideas widely through a top-down hierarchy of national to regional to local groups to achieve impact at scale, as in Figure 9.1a. The process we advocate flattens the hierarchy to a two-way communication network, orchestrated by an operational engine that creates and

Planning for an Evidence-Based Approach to CoMOOCs 187

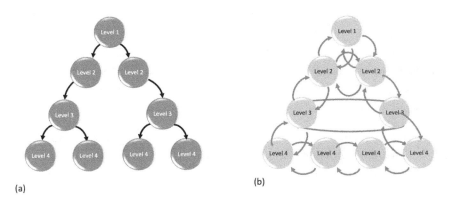

Figure 9.1 The contrast in value between (a) a top-down hierarchy with no internal feedback and (b) a hierarchical network of two-way communication in which the top of the hierarchy can learn from the lower levels.

fuels the exchanges within it. Scale is achieved because the centre links directly to all the localities, each of which also conducts its own local engagement network and sends its messages back to the rest of the network, as in Figure 9.1b.

The orchestrated network of knowledge exchange, enabled technologically by a CoMOOC (see Chapter 6), brings the individual teacher's voice into the knowledge-building and testing process directly. They have the opportunity to access the case studies and stories from their peers, contribute to the debate, test the ideas in their practice and report back to the community with their findings, and to make their own innovative contribution if they wish.

We have a mountain to climb to discover how to use digital methods effectively in teaching and learning. Teachers, in all sectors and discipline areas, should be in the vanguard of this knowledge development. They are with their students, designing for them and learning from them, every day. They know a lot and they have the opportunity to learn and discover a lot. The CoMOOC is a means to orchestrate and curate that process of dynamic knowledge development. In the next section we look at how well this works for TPD, and need to consider whether it could also work for other professional groups.

Applying a Theory of Change to a professional development initiative

In Chapters 7 and 8 we showed how the VCF has been applied in TPD courses to establish the different types of value they offer to participants. Here we take a step back from the detail of participants' engagement with the course design to look at how we get to the point of being able to achieve the value of impact on both participants and their communities. For this we need a ToC that guides the whole initiative from inception through to the long-term impact that is the whole point of research.

Four factors defined the basic requirements for our own ToC, which are sufficiently generic to be applicable to any professional field:

1. The focus is online learning for professional development, meaning that we are working with knowledgeable professionals.
2. The model must work at scale across diverse countries and cultures to meet the needs of professionals everywhere.
3. Aiming to work at scale entails a wide variation in local contexts, so the process must be participatory and contributory, rather than imposing a prior perspective.
4. Any external initiative must plan to be sustainable by the participants themselves, beyond the short-term funding period.

Chapters 6–8 have documented the evidence for the ways in which a co-design methodology can work well for professional development. Requirements (a) and (b) effectively made that decision. The question was, how to enact those intentions, given the scale required by (c)? The final requirement is to guide the research process from its endpoint back, to influence each of the earlier stages. Therefore: we begin by engaging with the professionals who are working in the most challenging contexts, because whatever works for them will be of broader relevance to all; we end by ensuring that enough has been done to sustain the continuing value of the initiative; we bridge the two by collaborating to find out how best to do this; and develop an ongoing formalization of the stages of sharing and collaboration.

ToCs can be extremely complex, as documented in a recent review of the many different representations of ToCs (Davies, 2018). The point of them is to explain 'how and why an initiative works' and to 'define the connection between activities and outcomes' which leads to problems of usability as well as interpretability if they are too complex.

Our concern was to capture the key stages of a CoMOOC initiative in its essential aspects, of being: *co-designed, scaled up, participatory* and *sustainable*, and to formalize this as simply as possible. We therefore developed it as a 'co-design' ToC consisting of five steps: *engage* collaborators, *develop* learning content together, *extend* practice through scaling up online, *embed* the shared ideas in participants' own blended courses and *sustain* the initiative through collaborators' ongoing practices. Each stage had to generate its own data to establish the progress made through iterative cycles of change as the course was developed and redeveloped over several runs.

One problem in the more complex ToCs is the absence of annotation of what the arrows between boxes mean in the diagrams, another is the absence of feedback loops, whether positive or negative (Davies, 2018). In our case, our programme of work is conceived as a much simpler iterative sequential process, which avoids the complexities, and gives meaning to all the arrows. There are also feedback loops, although these are either positive or negative, depending on the outcomes of the later stages, because they are all adaptive revisions, correcting or enhancing the earlier stages in the light of their outcomes. Figure 9.2 represents the Co-Design ToC quite simply, clarifying the influences and feedback for each stage, and instantiating each stage in terms of its activities, actors, and the types of impact each creates.

For each successive stage the arrow can be interpreted in terms of how it contributes to the next stage:

Engage – **defines the needs** to be addressed in the intended learning outcomes and curricula for the course;

Develop – collaboratively **creates the course** as a CoMOOC with those outcomes and curriculum topics to elicit feedback from participants in terms of their ideas, experiences and contributions;

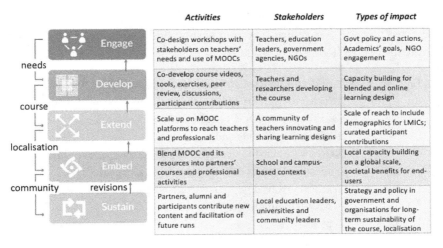

Figure 9.2 An iterative co-design Theory of Change for TPD.

Extend – publishes the course on a platform that broadens its reach to a wide range of teachers now able to **localize the ideas** and solutions to their own contexts;

Embed – uses the activities in the course that foster embedding of the course ideas, tools and materials enabling each **community to develop** their ideas, concepts, and skills;

Sustain – builds on the communities generated and those invited to rejoin the course to continue as mentors and educators, who then create the **revisions** for each stage in the light of ongoing feedback.

These definitions clarify the meaning of the arrows and how the iterative workflow proceeds as the project develops, and they specify the type of data to be collected in order to show evidence of the intended impact.

How does this help to plan the evidence gathering for each stage? We consider each in turn.

Engage and Develop

The first two columns in Figure 9.1 describe what is done with whom at each stage. The final column identifies the types of impact to be achieved, which can be characterized in terms of the values in the VCF. The collection of data is relatively straightforward in the first two stages of Engage and Develop because the stakeholders are known to the researchers, and can testify to the nature of the value they experienced. For the *Transforming Education in Challenging Environments* CoMOOC, discussed in Chapter 8, that originated in a research collaboration with universities in Lebanon, stakeholders provided feedback on the types of value they gained that went beyond fulfilling their original need to create the course (Kennedy et al., 2022) for example:

Engage	Workshops on teachers' needs and the use of MOOCs for TPD led to Ministry of Education officials running their own workshops on MOOCs (Realized Value)
	Teachers from public and private schools, universities and NGOs were able to interact on educational issues of mutual interest for the first time (Potential Social capital value)
Develop	Teachers involved requested workshops on the detailed design of MOOC activities (Applied value)
	Lebanese academics extended the CoMOOCs through a funded research project to collect online learning designs from Arabic/Francophone universities (Realized value)

Data collection on these two stages has relied on surveys from the participants in the workshops, and anecdotal feedback from collaborators during and after the course development process, which will not be a complete account of all that might have been achieved without our knowledge. A more formal opportunity to express the impact of these stages came after the first complete run of the course when we invited individual partner representatives to give verbal reports on their experience of working on the collaboration. Their presentations to the RELIEF Conference 2021 are quoted in Chapter 8, 'Elevating the teacher in challenging environment', as evidence of the value they found in the new learning design knowledge they developed through the CoMOOC.

Extend

The Extend stage takes the collaboration beyond stakeholders, who are known to the researchers, to the participants recruited to the CoMOOC. The point of extending the initiative by using a MOOC is to achieve a large-scale impact, potentially commensurate with the scale of the education challenges we are facing across the world. We may count them only in the 10,000s or 100,000s occasionally, while the need is to reach the 10,000,000s. However, the model is scalable. It costs as much to develop and run a CoMOOC for 10,000 as for 10,000,000. The use of MOOCs transforms the potential reach of educational initiatives when they are aimed at professionals (i.e. not undergraduate students, who need labour-intensive personal nurturing).

The MOOC platforms themselves collect the data needed for evidence of scale (numbers who enrol, engage and complete), or of reach to relatively disadvantaged groups (nationality). The value of hearing the teacher's voice from a wide range of experience is further enhanced if their contributions can be curated as collections, enabling the true ongoing development of knowledge, akin to an academic journal. This would be a good example of achieving the Realized value of the course. MOOC platforms cannot host such collections, so this has to be arranged by the educator team – for example, we have done this in the case of new pedagogies, by linking to a tool like the Learning Designer. For many areas a simple structured case study may be the optimal representation of a contribution, and this could be held on any university website if they choose to host such a collection. Multimedia resources would be more costly, but still may be of value to a particular discipline if they defined a particular area of growing practical professional knowledge.

Embed

The Embed stage requires evidence of embedding from the participants. The CoMOOC design must encourage participants to use the course and its resources within their own communities, with colleagues, managers, students, employees, as appropriate, and report back. Here the type of impact we intend is the Realized value that has a positive effect on participants' own communities.

Chapters 4, 7 and 8 illustrate examples of data collection techniques for this stage: interviews with alumni, in-course and post-course surveys with quantitative and qualitative questions, analysis of discussions and participant contributions, and the participant reviews made public on the site. It is difficult to control the selection of participants, as GDPR[1] rules make this very difficult, and those who respond are generally those who have completed or engaged a lot with the course. These are not techniques that are likely to collect and test the negative opinions. The FutureLearn platform does what it can to address this issue by collecting 'why did you leave?' data on specific likely reasons, the great majority of which seem to be 'lack of time', or 'not what I expected', rather than quality issues. Suggestions for improvements are most likely to be found in the discussions, where participants take seriously any invitations to comment on what they have seen in the videos, or on how useful the ideas are in their personal context.

For these reasons, the evidence we set out to collect is necessarily the 'proof of concept' or 'existence proof' as evidence that demonstrates the volume of intended outcomes achieved, and not the proportion of the cohort who achieved them. The proportion will be important when numbers in a pilot are as small as 10s of participants, and a statistical analysis is necessary for predicting the potential large-scale impact. If the active cohort is numbered in the 10,000s, as in a CoMOOC, the total volume itself is reliable testimony to the actual large-scale impact.

Sustain

Sustaining the long-term future of any initiative is difficult because project funding itself is short term. The conditions for sustainability have to be created during the project but funding will not endure long enough to ensure it. The aim, therefore, is to produce evidence that some organization or individuals will be able to take responsibility for maintaining the initiative. This is most likely to happen when there is evidence of Reframing value, when individuals, organizations and community leaders change the way their perceive the issue and their own responsibility for it.

For the case of TPD there is in every country a government ministry with responsibility for TPD, and the national education policy and strategy can be seen as the most secure option. However, governments and enthusiastic ministers come and go, and such initiatives can be wiped from the record within weeks. The same applies to every other professional area where government has an interest. Even successful science projects have known the cold dismissal when it does not suit a particular government line. So we must look beyond government to organizations that would benefit and would be sympathetic, such as NGOs and INGOs, institutions (schools, universities and education associations in the context of TPD), and individual leaders and influencers. For evidence of individuals, organizations and influencers changing their approach to TPD, we look for examples of Reframing such as these testimonies from stakeholders in Lebanon and MENA:

- A MOOC-based workshop at LAU on online learning for their Innovative Learning Faculty Fellows stimulated the people who became 'the champions who carried the day' by training their colleagues in how to design good quality online courses during the COVID-19 lockdown (LAU Associate Provost, Barbar Akle in Akle, Al Halabi, Tutunji, & Zeitoun, 2021)
- Changing the learning design orientation of the Edraak platform to incorporate social and collaborative learning into the platform[2] later adopted across all their MOOCs, with >2m learners.
- An official at CERD, the body responsible for teacher training in Lebanon, kindly provided a video endorsement of our Teaching Online course, included in the first step. They are now conducting their own training of teachers in and through online methods.
- One course is listed on the Jordan Ministry of Education website of recommended courses for teachers.[3]

The tasks involved in sustaining a CoMOOC are principally hosting, updating, marketing and engaging in discussions.

For hosting, a CoMOOC has the advantage of having built an engaged group of professionals from the start, who will be good candidates to take responsibility for the continual running of the course.

Updating is more onerous because it involves collecting and implementing new material in response to ongoing developments in the field, and participant feedback. This should be a small and manageable amount of time for one person, but must be an agreed contribution from the host or other partners. The cost can be balanced by income from participants buying the upgrade certificate. The endorsement of ministries or professional organizations can make the upgrade certificate a highly valuable asset for the individual participant.

This became clear in an interesting comparison between two UCL MOOCs on health. The *Peri-Operative Medicine in Action* MOOC is endorsed by the Royal College of Anaesthetists and the World Federation of Societies of Anaesthesiologists. The *Global Blindness* MOOC had no such professional endorsement. The comparison is stark: 20 per cent of participants in the former generated £94,000 from upgrades to acquire the certificate, compared to 7 per cent paying for upgrades for the latter (Laurillard & Kennedy, 2020). Professional bodies are key influencers.

The value of required assignments with scores has also been demonstrated, for example, by a national MOOC in China, where a five-week course on project-based learning for teachers attracted a 90 per cent completion rate on these formative assessment activities, which is an unusually high completion rate for activities within a MOOC (Ma, Li, Guo, Laurillard, & Yang, 2022). An upgrade certificate that depends on required assignment completion, where the certificates are valued, could lead to much higher completion and uptake.

Marketing is the most expensive cost, and also the most important if the course is to achieve its true ongoing value at scale. University marketing departments are geared to the recruitment of students to more traditional courses, and are unlikely to have either the reach or the techniques to help niche professional development courses. The host partner will need to develop networks and communications for the specific ministries, organizations and influencers to reach the target audiences for a CoMOOC. If the embedding activities in the course work well, it will continue to recruit new participants from these influencers.

Supporting discussions is critical to developing a sense of community on a CoMOOC. One especially important action here is to invite alumni to apply to become mentors in future runs. The invitation is placed in the final steps, and the applicant's engagement and completion can be checked in the platform data, as well as the nature of their contributions to activities such as Padlets,[4] discussions and peer reviews. On the BOLD course, for example, this has created a group of over forty mentors from across the world, twenty-five of whom have returned to engage in the discussions for several runs. They are a valuable group of collaborators who also offer advice and guidance to the educator team on improvements. Their contributions help to keep the discussions always fresh and responsive to the current cohort. This is one critical aspect of making sustainability feasible.

The five stages each have their own distinct role to play in the Co-Design ToC, and the data collection needed has to be foreseen and planned in from the beginning of the project, depending on the aims for its ultimate impact. Our own research has not been in place for long enough to discover how difficult the *Sustain* stage will be in the long term. At least the planning and data collection has begun.

Building community knowledge

A viable means of building community knowledge among professionals is important for developing effective practice in a constantly changing world. For the worlds of scientific and scholarly knowledge academics of all disciplines have developed an enduring system, being '*organised* in *global epistemic communities* that *codify their knowledge* in *peer-reviewed articles published* in *specialist journals*' (Wuestman, Hoekman, & Frenken, 2019, p. 1772, our italics). That is a very concise description of all the key features that afford both the quality and reach of the knowledge being developed. It captures all the aims outlined in Chapter 2, of finding ways to communicate innovative teaching practices so that by sharing learning designs teachers can build on each other's work. Could the development of professional knowledge use the same model, even though its members are so many and so widely distributed across different types of organization?

The model of academic knowledge building

To a great extent we can already interpret each of those features in terms of what the CoMOOC model offers:

Organized	by the course running continuously on a large-scale platform
Global	MOOC platforms have a global reach
Epistemic	the focus is on exchanging and developing practice knowledge
Communities	the persistence of the course, interactive exercises, discussions, and exchanges creates a sense of community for each course

Codify knowledge	with tools such as the Learning Designer participants are able to codify their knowledge so that others can build on their work
Peer-reviewed Article	the course conducts the process of peer review the mode of communication is not common to all topic areas, as it depends on the tool used for codifying the knowledge
Journal	the persistence of the codified knowledge is not provided by MOOC platforms, but depends on the repository of codifications collected by the tool chosen for the topic area.

Our CoMOOCs on learning design have been able to fulfil all these features. We use the Learning Designer tool and website we created to provide the codifying, the article and the journal. For other topics, such as community-based research, sustainable energy and health we have used case study formats, although not all those courses have established permanent sites for curating the contributions made.

The representation of the full knowledge development process for professional knowledge in general is in its very early stages. We are not there yet. It took the scientific world a century or two to establish its now high-quality process, but we can expect that the rapid and widespread communications and storage technologies we now have would present no great delay in our emulating that model. The barriers are all human. What it takes to shape the leadership and innovation needed to put this in place remains to be seen.

Marginson has identified four elements that comprise the global science system:

> (1) a common pool of knowledge in the natural science-based disciplines, defined by two bibliometric collections of papers, Web of Science and Scopus; (2) scientists, who produce and exchange knowledge; (3) their structure of communications between them and (4) practices and protocols that govern their work.
>
> (Marginson, 2021, p. 2)

For professional practice knowledge, most areas will work to a common core of generic concepts and practical knowledge validated through their prior education, but by no means captured through any such central system. The people are there, in their millions, practising and building their knowledge of their field every day. There is no formal structure of communications between professionals as they develop, only the informal local communications through everyday practice, but this is where the CoMOOC can offer a simulacrum of science communications through journals and conferences. How else can professionals share the burden of innovation in effective practice on the large scale that makes a truly global impact? With tertiary institutions leading the way, we can rise above the concerns of commercial competition for the sake of the SDGs. The practices and protocols that govern professionals' work reside in the foundational learning acquired through their normal local practice and experience. The video case studies in a CoMOOC demonstrate that personal codified knowledge, and the activities use the appropriate mediating tools and boundary objects of their field. We seek to formalize the CoMOOC as communication and sharing, the process that builds on practitioners' foundational knowledge to create a dynamic and responsive professional field, in any area.

The Citizen Science model

There is another source of distributed learning. The idea of Citizen Science (CS) projects has been growing rapidly over the last decade, to the point where it can be seen as a potential solution to the urgent need for knowledge development for the UN SDGs (Fritz, See, Carlson, & al., 2019). One report is centred around the environmental sciences and defines CS as 'as the practice of engaging the public in a scientific project – a project that produces reliable data and information usable by scientists, decisionmakers, or the public and that is open to the same system of peer review that applies to conventional science' (McKinley, Miller-Rushing, Ballard, & al., 2017, p. 4). The idea casts the net wider than we have done in attempting to embrace the world of working professionals, so is even more ambitious in terms of scope and reach. McKinley et al. have investigated the way these projects run in terms of both building scientific knowledge and using this to inform policy and encourage public action. Like CoMOOCs, CS projects need investment in staff to organize and run the projects, volunteers to carry out the exploration, experimentation, and evaluation, and a qualified leader to assure the quality of the project. However, although the ambition is to operate at scale, across global, national and local projects, there is no clear mechanism to foster the integration of project work on such a scale.

Another recent analysis of the CS approach provides a model for comparing with what a CoMOOC offers. The authors developed an extensive roadmap at global, national and local levels to set out what is needed for a fully functioning

CS programme, targeted on, in this case, some of the UN SDGs also focused on environmental issues (Fritz et al., 2019). Figure 9.2 shows the elements of the roadmap in terms of the global and national activities needed to organize the experimental and data gathering processes. The scale is massive: global to national to local, across several SDGs. However, the plan is very extensive over time as well as space, from initial identification of the indicators needed through to the evaluation of pilots, even before attempting to scale up.

At the global level, comparing the plan with what a CoMOOC could offer, the initial three preparatory Global activities (see Figure 9.3) are similar to the preparations done in the Engage stage of the Co-Design ToC to work with stakeholders such as professionals, agencies and NGOs and to source video case studies from existing CS projects. The Develop stage then workshops the methods, data collection and protocols to be practised in exercises during the course, with peer review to assist the quality, and curation of selected contributions managed by the educator team. There is no pilot stage. The course goes directly to roll-out at the Extend stage, upscaling across any and all countries that are interested, via the platform. The timeline can usually be achieved within six months, and the mechanism for scaling up is already actioned.

At the national level, the mapping and inventory activities depend upon the codifying tools being used, and the curation of contributions by a central

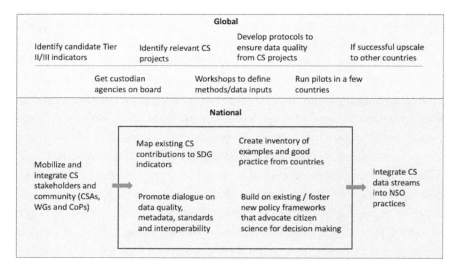

Figure 9.3 Roadmap of activities for integrating citizen science into SDG reporting. Upper box, global activities, where 'Tier II/III' refers to quality of data sources. Lower box, national activities (redrawn from Fritz et al., 2019).

team on a central site, as in a CoMOOC. The promotion of dialogues is part of the social learning within a CoMOOC, and fostering new policy frameworks would be a suitable collaborative exercise for professionals drawn from the intended participant stakeholders. The Embed stage would be important here for seeding and guiding the kind of localization activity needed at both national and local levels. Finally the Sustain stage would need to employ all the techniques of following up on the engagement with stakeholders and participants as alumni in order to ensure the hosting and updating of the various courses involved.

The focus of the whole end-to-end Co-Design ToC for CoMOOCs is to enable professionals to build their own tested and shared community knowledge of effective practice, and in a way that addresses the massive scale on which we must now act to meet the UN SDGs. We have shown the model can work for TPD, and have created two further examples of *Community-Based Research* for citizen scientists and *Sustainable Energy Access for Communities* for local authority, energy and engineering professionals. The model can work for other professional areas. Both are available on large-scale platforms, where the only limit on numbers is the resource available for promotion.

Affordability

The affordability of a model for knowledge building is an essential consideration. For academic knowledge building university research budgets fund the academic time needed to publish, and library budgets fund access to the products, while the publishers maintain their own workable model. CS projects are typically run by charities or research organizations that do not expect a financial return. However, our proposed knowledge building model for professional development will only flourish if it is affordable for both educators and participants.

The costing approach we propose in Chapter 5 shows the relatively high cost of developing a MOOC, while the running and support costs are low, especially on a per participant basis, as illustrated in the first case study in Chapter 7. The CoMOOC was running on Edraak, which does not offer any upgrade or charge any fee, so there is no financial return, and its sustainability depends on university partners being prepared to bear the costs of continuing to update and run it. The second case study was running on FutureLearn, which offers an upgrade for a certificate of completion, and permanent access to the course. This showed a net cost to the university per active participant, not covered by the total income from fees. If there is a strong incentive for the participants to acquire a certificate as part of their require professional development, which in turn requires careful attention to the social and peer learning and review activities offered completion rates can be relatively high at around 45 per cent of participants (Ma et al., 2022), whereas typically MOOCs achieve rates of less than 10 per cent. Most MOOCs are unlikely to break even, therefore. Affordability will depend crucially on three main parameters: enrolments, completion rates and percentage who pay an upgrade fee. Enrolments depend on an attractive course title, trusted educators, but most of all on a well-targeted promotional campaign. Universities know very little about how to achieve this. Completion rates of course depend on the perceived value and enjoyment of the course, and for professional development, especially, on the social and peer learning that is built in. The affordability of the fee itself depends crucially on the participant's own circumstances. Professional incomes for the same job vary by orders of magnitude across countries, so a localized pricing strategy will be essential. The motivation to pay it will then depend most on the perceived value of the certificate, which in turn depends on local professional development policy.

Affordability therefore involves many dependencies that are not in the control of the educator. For this reason we return to the issue in Chapter 10 and the responsibilities of leadership.

Conclusions

The chapter has demonstrated a way of planning for an evidence-based approach to developing CoMOOCs that will inspire professionals to develop their own to build a shared community of knowledge.

To have an impact they must be effective for the intended audience, so the Value Creation Framework is an essential tool for designing with evidence in mind, and discovering just what kind of value they achieve.

That process will assure the quality of the CoMOOC, but an effective collaborative course is not enough on its own. To reach the scale we need it must be developed within the overall plan from engagement with intended participants through to its extension to the large-scale participatory exercise in collaborative knowledge building, and ultimately to its long-term sustainability. The Co-Design Theory of Change is the plan that assures the ultimate goals of large-scale professional development can be achieved. 'Quality at scale' is the vision: we need both quality *and* scale.

The CoMOOC is undoubtedly an ambitious model, but it does have the benefit of evidence that it works on a scale and within a timeframe that is commensurate with the needs of the massive task of building a global professional development and citizen science network.

Questions and activities

This chapter is about building the evidence of how well interventions in the style of CoMOOCs work for their stakeholder professionals. We have applied some of the conceptual tools you might use for developing your own version of a CoMOOC. So it could be useful to consider: how would you

1. Adapt Table 9.1 with ways of eliciting each value type for your context?
2. Change your local hierarchy to operate as a network of knowledge exchange rather than a command-and-control structure of information flow?
3. Adapt the cells in Figure 9.2 to represent a Co-Design process for your own project?
4. Identify one or more SDGs that would act as useful overall framings for the work you are doing?

10

Harnessing the Potential of Online Learning to Democratize Knowledge Exchange

Introduction

We began the book with the ambition to address the global challenges of the UN SDGs. The intervening chapters set out to show the potential for online learning to be harnessed for the greater good – IF we use the digital tools we now have. They enable us to create an affordable new system for the global professional development the tertiary sector needs to adopt if we are to contribute on the massive scale that the SDGs demand.

Now we attempt to summarize the main points of the argument, the evidence we have in support of this vision and how the futures of online learning might now progress.

Knowledge exchange and the future of tertiary education

In Chapter 1 we noted the dire effects of the COVID-19 pandemic on achieving the UN SDGs. Decades of progress have been halted or reversed (United Nations, 2021). Now more than ever, there is a global need for professionals capable of driving the innovations that will put us back on the path to implementing the SDGs. This requires a commitment from universities and other tertiary institutions to engage professionals by democratizing knowledge exchange so that we can speed up the process of translating knowledge into action.

What professionals bring to the dialogue

There are many ways of understanding what is meant by knowledge exchange. In one view, knowledge exchange is no more than a 'top down' dissemination of research to the public. This can amount to the provision of information on university websites or articles in the press. However, as Murunga notes,

> It is now common wisdom that communicating about pressing issues to the public, particularly involving our planet or human wellbeing, is not only about raising awareness, informing, persuading, or changing behaviors. Instead, it is also about listening to and exploring alternative perspectives.
>
> (Murunga, 2022, p. 238)

Knowledge exchange can go further even than this. When we communicate our research ideas to professionals who are highly skilled and well educated, and are immersed in the practical activities that researchers are studying and theorizing about, those professionals are in a position to contribute to the development of knowledge. Knowledge exchange can become a genuine *exchange*, a two-way conversation, involving a process of active collaboration, where both professionals *and* researchers learn something they can use.

Networks or communities of practice for knowledge exchange have the most potential for moving knowledge into action effectively because they connect people who otherwise would not interact (Gagnon, 2011).

However, networks and communities of practice rarely organize themselves, and may easily wane over time. They need all three of the essential features for a community of practice: meaningful, shared and coordinated activity (Akkerman, Petter, & De Laat, 2008). From Chapter 6 onwards, we have demonstrated that the CoMOOC model is well designed for orchestrating such a network because it engages professionals in dialogue with other professionals to derive what is meaningful for them, and fosters the exchange and sharing of their developing knowledge. Crucially, they not only exchange and build on what works in different cultural locations, but they also dialogue with researchers/experts, to feed back their practical knowledge of what does and does not work well. This shift from 'disseminating' research knowledge to 'knowledge exchange' between researchers and practising professionals will democratize the development of new professional knowledge to the benefit of all.

What professionals need

We saw in Chapters 4 and 6 that professionals have particular learning needs, especially the rapid and responsive education that supports the urgent decisions they are making in their daily working activities. They are confident and capable learners, but they are immersed in complex personal and professional worlds that press heavily on their available time. They need online learning environments that have the flexibility to accommodate this. When they do allocate their time for learning, professionals want deep professional learning experiences with opportunities for interactivity and collaboration, so that they can learn from each other, not just educators.

As we saw in Chapter 3 there are many professionals in every field who had to discover how to manage online learning, both in education and in wider professional training. They learned a lot. They certainly discovered that online learning has a future, given its many advantages. And they will certainly bring their own expertise to an online discussion and collaboration. For education professionals we have tools such as the Learning Designer, discussed in Chapter 2 as an illustration of how we can instantiate, share and build on each other's pedagogic knowledge through digital means. The tool for knowledge exchange is critical to the process because it enables the professional to instantiate what they know in a formalized way, just as we do in science and scholarship through the format of a journal paper. It serves as a boundary object for the communities it serves, a kind of standard form, in the way that (Star & Griesemer, 1989, p. 411) describe: 'boundary objects devised as methods of common communication across dispersed work groups'. Other professions will need their own specialized tools for sharing and exchanging knowledge.

Embedding this kind of tool enables the representation and sharing of professional knowledge within a CoMOOC. The tertiary sector could be orchestrating professional knowledge exchange to brings this vital, practical knowledge to shape our research, and give us a way of engaging in dialogue with users of that research. This kind of Continuing Professional Development (CPD) is a rich and rewarding form of collaborative learning that could help the tertiary sector serve society more effectively.

But universities in particular do not focus on CPD and find it difficult to engage with professionals who are not formally enrolled on a degree course. CPD should play a major part in online learning futures, but it has barely even begun, as we saw in Chapter 1. This is an opportunity for the sector to deliver on its mission for social impact. The development of the MOOC platform has made it possible to provide CPD at scale, driving equity and sustainability. The interactive, social and collaborative pedagogy of the CoMOOC is the driver of quality. So we now have the means to accelerate our contribution to the SDGs. Using the tools and techniques presented here, the sector can deliver on the global challenges, and at the same time strengthen the impact of university research on end-users, and the CPD of the professions.

What makes a CoMOOC an important model for the UN SDGs?

The CoMOOC is a new model of online professional development – a vehicle for Co-designed, Massive, Open, Online Collaboration. Its importance for the future of online learning is that it aligns so well with the future demand for lifelong education to update professionals' skills in fast-changing, digitalized economies (Comyn, 2018), and because the digital tools and platforms available can now support it. The CoMOOC represents a synthesis of technology and pedagogy to create quality online learning designed around professionals' needs.

The CoMOOC is based on an evidence-based approach to design and evaluation. Evidence is used in several ways. In Chapter 2 we build on evidence from pedagogic research to establish the principles of quality learning. In Chapters 3 and 4 we collect new evidence from professionals, and in Chapter 5 develop a new tool for managing workload, to instantiate those principles in ways that support equitable, sustainable, quality professional development in the form of the CoMOOC. Finally, we design the CoMOOCs in ways that enables us to collect evidence of the effectiveness of the model and its instantiations.

The CoMOOC suits the needs of professionals because the co-design process

- enables the model to present case studies drawn from practices of professionals on the ground
- brings together stakeholders who are also the target end-users of the CoMOOC, either as participants or as educators who will embed the CoMOOC in the courses they offer
- identifies the stakeholders and professionals who can explain how they are responding to changing contexts, develop case studies of their practices, and feature in videos.

The CoMOOC educators are then able to embed these case studies in a social learning design:

- creating activities for CoMOOC participants to practice concepts, reflect on the applicability to their own contexts and contribute to community knowledge building
- providing the situated learning approach that professionals need

- practical video or written case studies start the conversation, mirroring the process that professionals use to learn by creating and exchanging in stories from practice, as discussed in Chapter 6
- participants exchange their own experience and discuss ways of applying the knowledge to their own contexts.

This helps to build community knowledge, and when we embed a tool like the Learning Designer in the CoMOOC – or another way of representing the community knowledge appropriate to professional area of the participants – then a community resource is created for everyone to use.

A more equitable future for CoMOOCs

The emphasis on co-design in the CoMOOC model means that it achieves greater equity than most MOOCs, because it explicitly enables the Global South-to-South knowledge exchange now needed to decentre the hegemony of the Global North. One of our first CoMOOCs, *Community-Based Research: Getting Started* shows what can be achieved. Researchers in Lebanon provided video case studies demonstrating how and why they conducted community-based research, including the voices of Syrian refugees. By building these into a CoMOOC, we shared this practical knowledge from the Global South with other community-based researchers in the Global South by recruiting participants from eighty LMIC countries. Reviews of the CoMOOC show that participants find the experience of learning from practising researchers extremely valuable because it is the practical – but also as one reviewer put it, innovative – knowledge they need:

> This course examines and advises on research in parts of the world that experience real hardships. As such it demonstrates practical as well as innovative ways of carrying out research in demanding circumstances. Highly recommended for anyone commencing research.
> (Diane R. review, FutureLearn)

> Studies in Community Based Research was impactful and instrumental to my short and long-term goal in working with a team of people to foster community development. This experience has honed my ability for strategic and practical community based research that I would leverage on when working with local and international organizations.
> (Amos O. review, FutureLearn)[1]

The CoMOOC model can thus support professionals to transcend the North/South and West/East hierarchies that Marginson and Xu argue are still being reproduced in global science, share their expertise directly with each other via digital platforms (Marginson & Xu, 2021), and so begin to democratize knowledge exchange.

In digital education the North/South divide persists because English is still the universal language. This is not equitable, so to facilitate genuine North/South and West/East knowledge exchange, we must move away from the hegemony of English as the language for MOOCs. Platforms resist translation because they prefer to guarantee a quality user experience, even if that means excluding those for whom the chosen language is a barrier. This issue is at the heart of equality, and we have worked with both English and Arabic platforms to address it. However, working in two languages required us to adapt and translate the design and content of the CoMOOCs for different platforms, which was a lengthy and costly process. A far more efficient and sustainable approach would make more use of automatic translation software that is now widely available. We need to find ways of embedding it in the design of CoMOOCs and persuading MOOC platforms to support its use as part of a more equitable future for online learning. We will be working on this issue in our next projects.

Roles and responsibilities for tertiary education in a global digital world

The tertiary sector across the world has a unique responsibility for working towards the goals of SDG4. We have the means to develop the teachers needed for the universal basic education goal, and to achieve the second goal of universal lifelong learning. Do we have the will?

The urgency of meeting the first goal is well established. A recent report on the global economics of developing 'universal basic skills' demonstrates how critical it is to make progress towards this aim:

> Ensuring that all of the world's youth have at least basic skills is a prime development goal by itself, but reaching such a goal also has immense importance for inclusive and sustainable world development.
> (Gust, Hanushek, & Woessmann, 2022, p. 1)

Despite the market-facing logic of the report, the wide-ranging analysis of the global economic gain from universal basic education shows that the value to the lower-middle-income countries would be the greatest, at over half the improved world GDP, because they are the largest group. And yet:

> Our results suggest that the world is incredibly short of meeting the goal of universal quality education, and this leaves many in the world short of the basic skills needed to participate in modern economies.
> (Gust, Hanushek, & Woessmann, 2022, p. 32)

There is a very long way to go, therefore, to meet the goals for 2030. And, as we have argued:

> Because of the fundamental importance of education for economic development and, by implication, for meeting the other 16 SDGs, education is actually the cornerstone to the entire effort.
> (Gust, Hanushek, & Woessmann, 2022, p. 32)

So what is the solution? For the economists, the solution is to measure 'what would it mean for world development to reach global universal basic skills?'. So the action recommended in the report is to develop and fund 'assessment instruments benchmarked to international educational standards' which, they contend,

> are likely to have much more long-run payoff than much of the current development aid.
> (Gust, Hanushek, & Woessmann, 2022, p. 34)

But redirecting investment towards measurement and away from action cannot be the right thing to do. We have questioned the kinds of small-scale practical action by global agencies in Chapter 7, to propose investment in more effective, large-scale action. Our Theory of Change (ToC) guides the way for the tertiary sector to act to deliver both the teachers needed and the professional development needed to make significant progress on SDG4 and the wider SDGs. This form of *development investment* would generate immediate and lasting value to the recipients and their beneficiaries.

This means that the role of tertiary institution leaders and governance is critical to enabling the world economy to achieve its potential. Across the world this is a large sector of powerful institutions engaged already with both innovative knowledge development through research, and individual knowledge development through teaching. It is a unique responsibility.

A recent analysis of the principal barriers to the adoption of blended and online learning in HE identified two main failures in overall governance in the tertiary sector (Laurillard, 2023):

- to organize sufficient teacher professional development (TPD) in digital methods for teaching staff and professional development for administrative staff, and
- to scrutinize, understand and reform the business modelling used for the teaching costs and learning benefits of our academic programmes of study.

The attention to TPD has increased dramatically across the world since the COVID-19 pandemic, so that institutional governance bodies are now beginning to negotiate and ensure TPD to engage their teaching staff across all disciplines in effective innovation in digital pedagogy. But they plan on only their own local scale. There is not yet the will to do it as either a national or international intervention.

There is always an anxiety over costs, especially when the levels of inequality of access are at such a high level. The solutions will tend to involve expansion of access to tertiary education at a time of reducing government funding, and increasing private poverty. Understanding how to achieve growth in student numbers, of a kind that achieves greater equity against the productivity of different teaching/study models in a digital/hybrid world is critical. However, Chapter 5 and the examples in Chapters 7 and 9 show that the costs do work out if they are carefully modelled to optimize the learning benefits of digital methods and represent accurately the medium-term costs of innovative digital teaching. The crucial point is to understand the economies of scale that online learning and hybrid models can offer, as discussed in Chapter 5. Once that happens the sector could be running CoMOOCs effectively, with the cost-benefit ratio sufficiently well-balanced to help universities direct the will to improve the world, expressed in their mission statements, towards action on helping professionals learn.

Are CoMOOCs sustainable?

Our Co-Design ToC is a method for ensuring that a CoMOOC will achieve sustainability if the design team plans for engagement, embedding and sustainability partners from the start. We have had some success by doing precisely this. For example,

Community-Based Research was embedded as part of MAPS[2] higher education provision

Transforming Education in Challenging Environments was embedded as part of a blended learning course for teachers, and in the *Education During Emergency Situations* MA at UCL, and as part of Jusoor and MAPs teacher training

Teaching Online was embedded as part of the teacher training provision at the Lebanese University

The collaborative activities within *Blended and Online Learning Design* encouraged many alumni to apply to act as Mentors in the later runs of the course, helping to sustain it over time.

These collaborative opportunities during engagement and embedding mean that participants are more likely to adopt, adapt and sustain the CoMOOC for the longer term.

But if we orchestrate the development of community knowledge, we have to sustain that output as well. How can we maintain this new community knowledge? MOOCs do not currently have a sharing platform, and are unlikely to provide this expensive resource, so we use tools like Padlet and Menti in the course. But can we make this developing shared knowledge available beyond the course? The next section proposes how we might use digital platforms for collaborative knowledge building.

How professional knowledge can travel in a digital world

The curation of the products of collaboration, as the collection of knowledge in the form of digital outputs, is possible on digital sites such as Wikimedia for mixed media, or on the sites maintained for professional organizations, such as the TES site for teachers.[3] However, these do not come with the expectation of adaptation and testing by others to build pedagogic knowledge.

We need the right model for exchanging ideas. In Figure 9.1, we flattened the usual top-down hierarchy with no internal feedback into a hierarchical network of two-way communication. This model makes it easier to move knowledge through a network in a productive way: the local, specific design for a particular outcome is turned into a generic design available at the national level, and is thereby made available for adaptation to a range of new local and specific contexts. Further testing and sharing follow. This is a powerful alternative to the classic pilot-rollout-dissipate model, the failing 'cascade' model (Kennedy, 2005).

The Learning Designer instantiates an early version of a curated site for collaborative knowledge development, using educator reviews of peer reviews, described in Chapter 2, 'A quality process for improving the learning experience'. This is a labour-intensive process, as it requires an hour or so to do the high-level review. In time this could be run as a community-sourced process, as we do for journals once we know how to make it as light-touch as possible. Much of the review process could eventually be automated, where corrections relate to the way the parameters for a design are used, which the program can discern as likely errors, leaving human reviewers to evaluate, for example, the pedagogic flow and internal alignment between outcomes, activities and assessment methods. Other professional areas will have their own rubrics for quality assurance.

These are early days for testing the viability of this process, but the academic community has its own well-established model of curated knowledge development in the academic journal model. We now have to imagine the equivalent for practical professional knowledge of impactful action in the world.

Over to you

This is how we have been inviting the participants to engage in discussions on the CoMOOC. A book cannot match that social dimension, so all we can do is suggest some next steps depending on your own context. They are quite simply described.

Next steps

For governments, supranational bodies (e.g. UN, World Bank, INGOs) and business organizations:

Invest in CoMOOCs for professional education

Utilize the large-scale features of MOOC platforms to go beyond the small numbers in pilot studies, and harness the capability of professionals for learning with peer feedback that avoids the need for personal nurturing

Promote the use of CoMOOCs for impactful professional collaboration on achieving sustainability goals

Promote the value of the certification of online professional development

Encourage a country-specific pricing strategy for large-scale online professional development courses

For research funders and leaders of tertiary institutions:

> Promote the ways in which CoMOOCs could help make the most impact with the research you support

For educators and researchers

> Design a CoMOOC into every research project or educational intervention as a means of maximising the value of the research impact or the teaching intervention.

Why is the expansion of professional development and knowledge exchange so important? Because the stated missions of universities require this level of ambition, and the tertiary sector has the responsibility to lead on the quality of teaching. Quality is not something to be led by government, we know how to work together, we can do this ourselves and collaborate.

If we harness the potential of online learning to democratize knowledge exchange, we thereby harness the knowledge and practice of millions of professionals to the cause of sustainability.

Questions and activities

We have included questions for you as the reader at the end of each chapter. Could you join in the next steps we have proposed? How would you

1. Use your position to build these ideas into your own practice?
2. Use the assets and tools in the book to encourage your colleagues to be involved in this new approach to professional development in your field?

There could be questions for the authors, of course. The website for the book has a place for posing questions and comments where we can regularly offer responses. Ideally, we would continue this otherwise one-sided conversation with you there. Please join us ...

Appendices

Appendix A: CoMOOCs referred to in this book

Community-based research: Getting started
Three weeks – three hours per week

- Co-designed with community-based researchers from Lebanon.
- Introduces the skills needed to carry out research in the community using the 'citizen science' approach of PROCOL Lebanon.
- Available on demand at FutureLearn:
  https://www.futurelearn.com/courses/community-based-research

Transforming education in challenging environments
Four weeks – Four hours per week

- Co-designed with teachers and teacher-educators in Lebanon.
- Introduces practical ways teachers can transform the education of children and young people living in conflict-affected contexts, including digital education.
- Available on demand at FutureLearn:
  https://www.futurelearn.com/courses/transforming-education

Sustainable energy access for communities
Three weeks – three hours per week

- Co-designed with researchers and professionals in sustainable energy working in the Middle East and Africa.
- Introduces energy access options to help communities move towards a renewable energy future with examples from Scotland, Lebanon, Kenya and more.
- Available on demand at FutureLearn:
  https://www.futurelearn.com/courses/sustainable-energy-access-for-communities

Blended and online learning design
Three weeks – four hours per week

- Co-designed with teacher-educators from IOE, UCL's Faculty of Education and Society and teachers from the community
- Supports participants to develop and share the best pedagogy for their students using blended and online learning methods.
- Available on demand at FutureLearn: https://www.futurelearn.com/courses/blended-and-online-learning-design

The new era of teaching and learning (formerly Teaching online: Be ready now!)
Three weeks – four hours per week

- Co-designed with teachers and students at Lebanese University.
- Introduces learning design for online and blended learning, focusing on support for learners, teachers and parents.
- Re-designed to provide ongoing support for teachers since its initial presentation during the first months of the COVID-19 pandemic.
- Available on demand at Edraak https://www.edraak.org/en/programs/course/ucl-mooc1-v1/

Appendix B: Definitions of 'learning types' in terms of typical technologies used

Learning type	Conventional technology	Digital technology
Acquisition	Reading books, papers; Listening to teacher presentations face-to-face, lectures; Watching demonstrations, master classes.	Reading multimedia resources, websites, digital documents and resources; Listening to podcasts, webcasts; Watching animations, videos.
Collaboration	Small group project, discussing other students' outputs, creating a joint output.	Small group project, using online forums, wikis, chat rooms, etc. for discussing other students' outputs, creating a joint digital output.

Learning type	Conventional technology	Digital technology
Discussion	Tutorials, tutor groups, student seminars (students leading discussion), discussion groups, class discussions.	Online tutorials, tutor groups and seminars, email discussions, discussion forums, web-conferencing tools (synchronous and asynchronous).
Investigation	Using text-based study guides; Analysing the ideas and information in a range of materials and resources; Using books, people, field trips, to collect data for analysis; Comparing texts, searching and evaluating information and ideas.	Using online advice and guidance; Analysing the ideas and information in a range of digital resources; Using digital tools to collect and analyse data; Comparing digital texts, using digital tools for searching and evaluating information and ideas.
Practice	Doing practice exercises; using tools; doing practice-based projects, labs, field trips, face-to-face role-play activities.	Using digital tools, models, simulations, digital games, microworlds, virtual labs and field trips, online role-play activities.
Production	Producing their own representations of what they have learned, using statements, essays, reports, accounts, designs, performances, artefacts, animations, models, videos.	Producing and storing digital documents, representations of designs, performances, artefacts, animations, models, resources, slideshows, photos, videos, blogs, e-portfolios.

Definitions are taken from Chapters 6–11 in Laurillard, D. (2012). *Teaching as a Design Science: Building Pedagogical Patterns for Learning and Technology*. New York and London: Routledge.

Appendix C: Rubric for evaluating a learning design

———

Comments on the learning design 'Title'
Designer: Name
These comments are organized according to the numbered rubric for curated designs.

1. Clear learning outcomes
   [Answer]

2. Appropriate use of pedagogic choices
   [Answer]

3. Sufficient guidance in text for students to follow
   [Answer]

4. Use of digital resources
   [Answer]

5. Balance of learning types
   [Answer]

6. Feedback to students
   [Answer]

7. Alignment between intended outcomes, activities and assessable activities
   [Answer]

8. Is this a learning design that other teachers would value?
   [Answer]

Overall,

There are only three evaluations:

1. Good (e.g. This is ready to publish …)
2. Good but edit (e.g. This is not quite ready, but with the few edits suggested it would certainly be of interest to other teachers)
3. No, not yet ready

Thank you very much for your submission.
Diana Laurillard
Professor of Learning with Digital Technology

Appendix D: Learning designs for understanding [the Topic]

Both learning designs displayed here have been exported from the Learning Designer to Word.

The face-to-face lecture (https://v.gd/B8BpuP)

Context

Topic: The Topic

Total learning time: One hour

Designed learning time: One hour

Size of class: 25

Description: This is a design for a class using classroom-based methods.

It is a generic version for [the Topic], where [the Topic] could be replaced by any specific topic for which this approach would be relevant

Mode of delivery: Classroom based

Aims

This session introduces [the Topic] and invites students to apply it to a context they are familiar with.

Outcomes
Knowledge: Be able to explain [the Topic]
Application: Be able to apply [the Topic] to a specific context
Analysis: Be able to analyse a specific context in the light of [the Topic] and identify how it might change future actions

Teaching-learning activities

Introduction to [the Topic]

| *Read Watch Listen* | *20 minutes* | *25 Students* | *Teacher present* | *F2F* |

Listen to the presentation about [the Topic].
It explains why … how … what …

Does [the Topic] make sense to you? Please note any questions you have.

| *Discuss* | *5 minutes* | *25 Students* | *Teacher present* | *F2F* |

Join the class discussion by asking the questions you noted or making a comment in response to the teacher.

Applying [the Topic]

| *Read Watch Listen* | *25 minutes* | *25 Students* | *Teacher present* | *F2F* |

Watch the demonstration of how [the Topic] can be applied to a specific context. Think about other contexts you might apply it to. Note the questions you need to ask.

| *Discuss* | *5 minutes* | *25 Students* | *Teacher present* | *F2F* |

Join the class discussion by raising your question and noting what comes up in the discussion.

| *Read Watch Listen* | *5 minutes* | *25 Students* | *Teacher present* | *F2F* |

Learning through	minutes	%
Acquisition (Read, Watch, Listen)	50	83
Investigation	0	0
Discussion	10	17
Practice	0	0
Collaboration	0	0
Production	0	0

Figure D.1 Representation of the learning experience (f2f).

Listen to the teacher's summary of [the Topic] and how it can be applied in a range of contexts.

The online version (https://v.gd/x9s0mv)

Context

Topic: Correlation

Total learning time: One hour 40 minutes

Designed learning time: One hour and 40 minutes

Size of class: 25

Description: This is a design for a class using wholly online methods.

Mode of delivery: Wholly online
Aims

This session introduces [the Topic] and invites students to apply it to a context they are familiar with.

Outcomes
Knowledge: Be able to explain [the Topic]
Application: Be able to apply [the Topic] to a specific context
Analysis: Be able to analyse a specific context in the light of [the Topic] and identify how it might change future actions

Teaching-learning activities

Introduction to [the Topic]

Read Watch Listen   10 minutes   1 Student   Teacher not present   Online

Watch the video about [the Topic].

It explains why … how … what …

Does [the Topic] make sense to you? Please pause the video to note any questions you have.

Linked resources: Screencast or video

Practice   5 minutes   1 Student   Teacher not present   Online

Work through the quiz questions, to check on your understanding. Repeat the quiz if necessary, until you score 100 per cent – this will help you remember what you have learned.

Linked resources: Provide link to quiz

Discuss   10 minutes   25 Students Teacher present   Online

Post your questions to [the Discussion site] by [date, time]. Click 'Like' for any other questions you would like to know the answers to. Check the site on [date, time] when the teacher will show the answers to all the questions posted.

Applying [the Topic]

Read Watch Listen   20 minutes   1 Student   Teacher not present   Online

Read the article on how [the Topic] can be applied to a specific context. Think about other contexts you might apply it to.

Practice   5 minutes   1 Student   Teacher not present   Online

Work through the quiz questions, to check on your understanding. Repeat the quiz if necessary, until you score 100 per cent – this will help you remember what you have learned.

Linked resources: Provide link to the quiz

Practice   10 minutes   1 Student   Teacher not present   Online

Think of an example of a situation that is relevant to [the Topic] in your context, and how you could make use of it.

Make notes to share with your group.

Arrange a time when you will meet with your group online.

Collaborate   15 minutes   3 Students   Teacher not present   Online

In your group, take turns to share your ideas of how you would use [the Topic] in each of the three contexts.

Decide on your best example, and what you will post to the class site.

Post a brief description of how you would use [the Topic] in which context.

Linked resources: Sharing site for class, e.g. Googledoc, discussion forum in Moodle, etc.

Analysing how [the Topic] could guide your future practice

Read Watch Listen   5 minutes   1 Student   Teacher not present   Online

Read through the other groups' posts to the class site and make notes on what you will contribute to the discussion.

Linked resources: Sharing site for class, e.g. Googledoc, discussion forum in Moodle, etc.

Discuss   20 minutes   25 Students   Teacher present   Online

The class discussion of [the Topic] is on [date, time].

Discuss with the teacher, using the audio and the chat, the examples the groups have posted to the class site, and how you might change your actions in future by applying [the Topic].

Linked resources: Sharing site for class, e.g. Googledoc, discussion forum in Moodle, etc.

Figure D.2 Representation of the learning experience (online).

Notes

Series editor's foreword

* The initials ESRC/OFSRE stand for the Economic and Social Research Council/ Office for Students and Research England. Part of the original ESRC funding that supported the Centre for Global Higher Education's research work was sourced from the Higher Education Funding Council for England, the ancestor body to the OFS and RE. Research England continues to provide financial support for the research.

Chapter 1

1. https://unstats.un.org/sdgs/report/2021/The-Sustainable-Development-Goals-Report-2021.pdf
2. Tertiary education builds on secondary education, providing learning activities in specialized fields of education. It aims at learning at a high level of complexity and specialization. Tertiary education includes what is commonly understood as academic education but also includes advanced vocational or professional education. http://uis.unesco.org/sites/default/files/documents/international-standard-classification-of-education-isced-2011-en.pdf
3. http://www.un.org/sustainabledevelopment
4. https://www.hesa.ac.uk/data-and-analysis/providers/business-community/table-2b
5. https://www.timeshighereducation.com/world-university-rankings/2022/world-ranking#!/page/0/length/25/sort_by/rank/sort_order/asc/cols/stats
6. https://www.timeshighereducation.com/rankings/impact/2022/overall#!/page/0/length/25/sort_by/rank/sort_order/asc/cols/undefined
7. 2013–14 'Building community knowledge about learning and teaching through technology', ES/K005545/1; 2015–23 Centre for Global Higher Education, ES/M010082/1; ES/M010082/2; ES/T014768/12017–22 RELIEF Centre, ES/P008003/1.
8. https://www.bera.ac.uk/publication/ethical-guidelines-for-educational-research-2018
9. http://www.un.org/sustainabledevelopment

Chapter 2

1. 40 hours per week for 40 weeks a year is 1600 hours per year. So in 7 years they have well more than the 10,000 hours of practice it takes to be an expert.
2. learningdesigner.org – the tool is free and open to all on registration. The website gives access to video tutorials and text resources on ways of using the tool as an individual or member of a community.
3. E.g. using Quizlet.
4. E.g. using Mentimeter.
5. https://www.futurelearn.com/courses/blended-and-online-learning-design
6. https://padlet.com/d_laurillard2/x4nug4b5dn0xh490
7. Participants in the Blended and Online Learning Design course were invited to consent to their comments being quoted.
8. Post Graduate certificate of Education, a qualification for teachers in the UK.

Chapter 3

1. The project was funded by the British Council and led by Pauline Ngimwa, PASGR, with Eileen Kennedy, Allison Littlejohn and Collins Odote.
2. The MOTH research was led by Allison Littlejohn with Lesley Gourlay, Martin Oliver, John Potter, Jennifer Rode, Eileen Kennedy, Tim Neumann and Kit Logan.

Chapter 5

1. Originally developed within the Building Community Knowledge project (https://buildingcommunityknowledge.wordpress.com/cram/). Now available at http://web.lkldev.ioe.ac.uk/cram/index.html
2. Formative assessment is a form of learning, and low risk. It is very different from summative assessment, which simply tests what has been learned, is high risk, and in most cases is very difficult to automate.
3. For an extended description, see Laurillard (2007b).
4. The two designs can be found at https://v.gd/oEnWMp and (f2f), https://v.gd/b5bVYg (blended).
5. One solution could be MOOCs on blended learning, of which there are many on FutureLearn and similar platforms, e.g. https://www.futurelearn.com/courses/blended-and-online-learning-design; https://www.futurelearn.com/experttracks/blended-learning

Chapter 6

1. https://www.futurelearn.com/courses/blended-and-online-learning-design

Chapter 7

1. https://web.mit.edu/about/mission-statement/
2. https://english.pku.edu.cn/about.html
3. https://www.ox.ac.uk/about/organisation/strategic-plan-2018-24
4. https://www.ucl.ac.uk/about/what/vision-aims-values
5. UNESCO 2016. The world needs almost 69 m new teachers to reach the 2030 education goals. UNESCO Institute for Statistics http://www.uis.unesco.org/Education/Documents/FS39-teachers-2016-en.pdf
6. https://reliefweb.int/report/world/20-reasons-why-2020-there-are-still-260m-children-out-school
7. https://en.unesco.org/news/mobile-technology-key-bringing-education-all-says-broadband-commission
8. https://www.timeshighereducation.com/world-university-rankings/2022/world-ranking#!/page/0/length/25/sort_by/rank/sort_order/asc/cols/stats
9. https://www.timeshighereducation.com/rankings/impact/2022/overall#!/page/0/length/25/sort_by/rank/sort_order/asc/cols/undefined
10. Geographic Information System.
11. https://padlet.com/edraak/onlineteaching

Chapter 8

1. http://tpdatscalecoalition.org
2. UNESCO 2016. The world needs almost 69 m new teachers to reach the 2030 education goals. UNESCO Institute for Statistics http://www.uis.unesco.org/Education/Documents/FS39-teachers-2016-en.pdf United_Nations (2022). The Sustainable Development Goals Report, https://unstats.un.org/sdgs/report/2022/The-Sustainable-Development-Goals-Report-2022.pdf

Chapter 9

1. General Data Protection Regulation.

2   https://ioelondonblog.wordpress.com/2020/02/20/a-more-collaborative-learning-design-is-transforming-arabic-moocs/
3   https://www.edraak.org/en/course/course-v1:UCL_LU+TO101+2020_Darsak/
4   Padlet is a free, open, online pinboard for sharing text, images and links.

Chapter 10

1   Reviewers publish their names on the FutureLearn website.
2   Multi-Aid Programs.
3   https://www.tes.com/teaching-resources

References

Akkerman, S., & Bakker, A. (2011). Boundary crossing and boundary objects. *Review of Educational Research*, 81(2), 132–69.

Akkerman, S., Petter, C., & De Laat, M. (2008). Organising communities-of-practice: Facilitating emergence. *Journal of Workplace Learning*, 20(6), 383–99. doi:10.1108/13665620810892067.

Akle, B., Al Halabi, F., Tutunji, S., & Zeitoun, S. (2021). Transformative education panel. In *Presentation at Working through Crisis RELIEF Conference 2021*. Online.

Alexander, C., Ishikawa, S., & Silverstein, M. (1977). *A Pattern Language: Towns, Buildings, Construction*. New York: Oxford University Press. Retrieved from http://books.google.com/books?id=hwAHmktpk5IC&pgis=1.

Anderson, T., and Shattuck, J. (2012). "Design-based research: A decade of progress in education research?" *Educational Researcher*, 41(1), 16–25. http://edr.sagepub.com/cgi/doi/10.3102/0013189X11428813 (July 21, 2014).

Ausubel, D. P. (1980). Schemata, cognitive structure, and advance organizers: A reply to Anderson, Spiro, and Anderson. *American Educational Research Journal*, 17(3), 400–4.

Avalos, B. (2011). Teacher professional development in teaching and teacher education over ten years. *Teaching and Teacher Education*, 27, 10–20.

Barros-Lane, L., Smith, D. S., McCarty, D., Perez, S., & Sirrianni, L. (2021). Assessing a trauma-informed approach to the COVID-19 pandemic in higher education: A mixed methods study. *Journal of Social Work Education*, 57(1), S66–S81. doi:10.1080/10437797.2021.1939825.

Bett, H. K. (2016). The cascade model of teachers' continuing professional development in Kenya: A time for change? *Cogent Education*, 3(1). doi:10.1080/2331186X.2016.1139439.

Biggs, J. (2003). *Aligning teaching and assessing to course objectives*. Paper presented at the International Conference on Teaching and Learning in Higher Education: New Trends and Innovations, University of Aveiro, Portugal.

Bloom, B. S. (Ed.) (1956). *Taxonomy of Educational Objectives: The Classification of Educational Goals, Handbook 1 Cognitive Domain*. New York: David MvKay Co. Inc.

Bodenheimer, G., & Shuster, S. M. (2020). Emotional labour, teaching and burnout: Investigating complex relationships. *Educational Research*, 62(1), 63–76. https://doi.org/10.1080/00131881.2019.1705868.

Bonal, X., & González, S. (2020). The impact of lockdown on the learning gap: Family and school divisions in times of crisis. *International Review of Education*, 66(5–6), 635–55. https://doi.org/10.1007/s11159-020-09860-z.

Bond, M., Bedenlier, S., Marín, V. I., & Händel, M. (2021). Emergency remote teaching in higher education: Mapping the first global online semester. *International Journal of Educational Technology in Higher Education*, 18(1). https://doi.org/10.1186/s41239-021-00282-x.

Brandi, U., & Thomassen, M. L. (2021). Sustainable organizational learning and corporate entrepreneurship: A conceptual model of sustainability practices in organizations. *Journal of Workplace Learning*, 33(3), 212–28. Retrieved from https://www.emerald.com/insight/1366-5626.htm.

Braun, V., & Clarke, V. (2020). One size fits all? What counts as quality practice in (reflexive) thematic analysis? *Qualitative Research in Psychology*, 18(3), 328–352. https://doi.org/10.1080/14780887.2020.1769238.

Bronfenbrenner, U. (1979). *The Ecology of Human Development – Experiments by Nature and Design*. Cambridge, MA: Harvard University Press.

Brown, J. S., & Duguid, P. (1991). Organizational learning and communities-of-practice: Toward a unified view of working, learning, and innovation. *Organization Science*, 2(1), 40–57.

Burns, M., & Lawrie, J. (2015). *Where It's Needed Most: Quality Professional Development for All*. New York: INEE. Retrieved from http://toolkit.ineesite.org/toolkit/INEEcms/uploads/1162/Teacher_Professional_Development_v1.0_LowRes.pdf.

Chandra, Y. (2018). New narratives of development work? Making sense of social entrepreneurs' development narratives across time and economies. *World Development*, 107, 306–26. https://doi.org/10.1016/J.WORLDDEV.2018.02.033.

Christensen, G., Steinmetz, A., Alcorn, B., Bennett, A., Woods, D., & Emanuel, E. J. (2013). The MOOC phenomenon: Who takes massive open online courses and why? *SSRN*, 6, 1–14. https://doi.org/10.2139/ssrn.2350964.

Coman, C., Țîru, L. G., Meseșan-Schmitz, L., Stanciu, C., & Bularca, M. C. (2020). Online teaching and learning in higher education during the coronavirus pandemic: Students' perspective. *Sustainability*, 12(24), 10367. https://doi.org/10.3390/su122410367.

Comyn, P. J. (2018). Skills, employability and lifelong learning in the Sustainable Development Goals and the 2030 labour market. *International Journal of Training Research*, 16(3), 200–17. doi:10.1080/14480220.2018.1576311.

Conole, G. (2016). MOOCs as disruptive technologies: Strategies for enhancing the learner experience and quality of MOOCs Los MOOC como tecnologías disruptivas: estrategias para mejorar la experiencia de aprendizaje y la calidad de los MOOC. *Revista de Educación a Distancia*, (50), Art 2. https://doi.org/http://dx.doi.org/10.6018/red/50/2.

Crilly, N., Blackwell, A. F., & Clarkson, P. J. (2006). Graphic elicitation: Using research diagrams as interview stimuli. *Qualitative Research*, 6(3), 341–66. https://doi.org/10.1177/1468794106065007.

Cross, N. (2011). *Design Thinking: Understanding How Designers Think and Work*. Oxford: Berg.

Dachner, A. M., Ellingson, J. E., Noe, R. A., & Saxton, B. M. (2021). The future of employee development. *Human Resource Management Review*, 31(2). doi:10.1016/j.hrmr.2019.100732.

Dalziel, J. (Ed.) (2016). *Learning Design: Conceptualising a Framework for Teaching and Learning Online*. New York: Routledge.

Darling-Hammond, L., Hyler, M. E., & Gardner, M. (2017). *Effective Teacher Professional Development*. Retrieved from Palo Alto, CA: https://learningpolicyinstitute.org/product/teacher-prof-dev.

Davies, R. (2018). Representing theories of change: Technical challenges with evaluation consequences. *Journal of Development Effectiveness*, 10(4), 438–61. doi:10.1080/19439342.2018.1526202.

DeSantis, N. (2012, May 2). Wired campus: Harvard and MIT put $60-Million into new platform for free online courses. *The Chronicle of Higher Education*. Retrieved from https://www.chronicle.com/blogs/wiredcampus/harvard-and-mit-put-60-million-into-new-platform-for-free-online-courses.

Dingyloudi, F., Strijbos, J. W., & de Laat, M. (2019). Value creation: What matters most in communities of learning practice in higher education. *Studies in Educational Evaluation*, 62(September), 209–23.

Disabled Students UK (2020). *Impact of the Pandemic on Disabled Students and Recommended Measures*. Retrieved from https://disabledstudents.co.uk/DSUK_Impact_of_Pandemic.pdf.

Ehrmann, S., & Milam, J. H. (2003). *Flashlight™ Cost Analysis Handbook: Modeling Resource Use in Teaching and Learning with Technology*. Retrieved from https://eric.ed.gov/?q=technology+in+teaching+and+learning&ff1=pubGuides+-+Non-Classroom&ff2=souOnline+Submission&id=ED557064.

El Moussaoui, R. (2020). *How Teachers Are Using This MOOC*. Lebanon: RELIEF Centre. Retrieved from https://youtu.be/pe7gmvdfTM4.

El Moussaoui, R. (2022). *Collaborative Learning in MOOCs*. Retrieved 27 October 2022, from https://www.relief-centre.org/blog/collaborative-learning-in-moocs.

Elmer, G., Neville, S. J., Burton, A., & Ward-Kimola, S. (2021). Zoombombing during a global pandemic. *Social Media and Society*, 7(3). https://doi.org/10.1177/20563051211035356.

Elmore, R. F. (2016). 'Getting to scale …' it seemed like a good idea at the time. *Journal of Educational Change*, 17(4), 529–37. doi:10.1007/s10833-016-9290-8.

Entwistle, N. (2018). *Student Learning and Academic Understanding: A Research Perspective with Implications for Teaching*. London: Academic Press. https://doi.org/10.1016/B978-0-12-805359-1/00004-8.

Ericsson, K. A. (2008). Deliberate practice and acquisition of expert performance: A general overview. *Academic Emergency Medicine*, 15, 988–94. doi:10.1111/j.1553-2712.2008.00227.x.

Eteläpelto, A., Vähäsantanen, K., Hökkä, P., & Paloniemi, S. (2013). What is agency? Conceptualizing professional agency at work. *Educational Research Review*, 10, 45–65.

Fenwick, T., & Nerland, M. (2014). Sociomaterial knowing, work arrangements and responsibility: New times, new concepts? In T. Fenwick & M. Nerland (Eds.), *Reconceptualising Professional Learning*, 1–8. Abingdon: Routledge.

Fereday, J., & Muir-Cochrane, E. (2006). Demonstrating rigor using thematic analysis: A hybrid approach of inductive and deductive coding and theme development. *International Journal of Qualitative Methods*, 5(March), 1–13.

Ferguson, R., & Clow, D. (2015). Examining engagement: Analysing learner subpopulations in massive open online courses (MOOCs). *Proceedings of the Fifth International Conference on Learning Analytics and Knowledge – LAK '15*. https://doi.org/10.1145/2723576.2723606.

Fransella, F., Bell, R., & Bannister, D. (2004). *A Manual for Repertory Grid Technique*. London: John Wiley & Sons.

Fransson, A. (1977). On qualitative differences in learning: IV – effects of intrinsic motivation and extrinsic test anxiety on process and outcome. *The British Journal of Educational Psychology*, 47(3), 244–57. https://doi.org/10.1111/J.2044-8279.1977.TB02353.X.

Fritz, S., See, L., Carlson, T., & al. (2019). Citizen science and the United Nations Sustainable Development Goals. *Nature Sustainability*, 2(October), 922–30. doi:10.1038/s41893-019-0390-3.

Gagnon, M. L. (2011). Moving knowledge to action through dissemination and exchange. *Journal of Clinical Epidemiology*, 64, 25–31. doi: https://doi.org/10.1016/j.jclinepi.2009.08.013.

Gibon, C. (2022, July 26). In crisis-hit Lebanon, mobile and broadband are for the rich. *The New Arab*. Retrieved from https://english.alaraby.co.uk/features/crisis-hit-lebanon-mobile-and-broadband-are-rich.

Gourlay, L., Campbell, K., Clark, L., Crisan, C., Katsapi, E., Riding, K., & Warwick, I. (2021). 'Engagement' discourses and the student voice: Connectedness, questioning and inclusion in post-Covid digital Practices. *Journal of Interactive Media in Education*, 2021(1). https://doi.org/10.5334/jime.655.

Grandinetti, J. (2022). 'From the classroom to the cloud': Zoom and the platformization of higher education. *First Monday*, 27. https://doi.org/10.5210/fm.v27i2.11655.

Gu, M. M., & Huang, C. F. (2022). Transforming habitus and recalibrating capital: University students' experiences in online learning and communication during the COVID-19 pandemic. *Linguistics and Education*, 69, 101057. https://doi.org/10.1016/j.linged.2022.101057.

Guo, P. J., Kim, J., & Rubin, R. (2014). How video production affects student engagement. In *Proceedings of the First ACM Conference on Learning @ Scale Conference* (pp. 41–50). New York: ACM. https://doi.org/10.1145/2556325.2566239.

Gust, S., Hanushek, E. A., & Woessmann, L. (2022). *Global Universal Basic Skills: Current Deficits and Implications for World Development* (10029). Retrieved from Munich: https://www.cesifo.org/en/wp.

Hager, P. (2004). The conceptualization and measurement of learning at work. In H. Rainbird, A. Fuller, & A. Munro (Eds.), *Workplace Learning in Context* (pp. 242–58). London: Routledge. https://doi.org/10.4324/9780203571644.

Hamori, M. (2018). Can MOOCs solve your training problem? *Harvard Business Review*, 96(1), 70–6. Retrieved from https://hbr.org/2018/01/can-moocs-solve-your-training-problem.

Hargreaves, A. (2019). Teacher collaboration: 30 years of research on its nature, forms, limitations and effects. *Teachers and Teaching*. doi:10.1080/13540602.2019.1639499.

Hattie, J., & Timperley, H. (2007). The Power of Feedback. *Review of Educational Research*, 77(1), 81–112.

Hettick, L. (2014). Blackboard using WebRTC to reinvent educational collaboration. Retrieved 21 July 2022, from https://www.networkworld.com/article/2688823/blackboard-using-webrtc-to-reinvent-educational-collaboration.html.

Hill, C., & Lawton, W. (2018). Universities, the digital divide and global inequality. *Journal of Higher Education Policy and Management*, 40(6), 598–610. doi:10.1080/1360080X.2018.1531211.

Hochschild, A. R. (1983). *The Managed Heart: The Commercialization of Human Feeling*. Berkeley: University of California Press.

Hökkä, P., & Eteläpelto, A. (2014). Seeking new perspectives on the development of teacher education: A study of the Finnish context. *Journal of Teacher Education*, 65(1), 39–52.

HRW (2021). Lebanon: Syrian refugee children blocked from school. Retrieved from https://www.hrw.org/news/2021/12/03/lebanon-syrian-refugee-children-blocked-school.

Hunzicker, J. (2011). Effective professional development for teachers: A checklist. *Professional Development in Education*, 37(2), 177–9. doi:10.1080/19415257.2010.523955.

Idoiaga, N., Legorburu, I., Ozamiz-Etxebarria, N., Lipnicki, D. M., Villagrasa, B., & Santabárbara, J. (2022). Prevalence of Post-Traumatic Stress Disorder (PTSD) in university students during the COVID-19 pandemic: A meta-analysis attending SDG 3 and 4 of the 2030 agenda. *Sustainability Science*, 14(13). doi:10.3390/su14137914.

Isenbarger, L., & Zembylas, M. (2006). The emotional labour of caring in teaching. *Teaching and Teacher Education*, 22(1), 120–34. https://doi.org/10.1016/j.tate.2005.07.002.

Ismail, M. H. (2019). *What Is the Relationship between Learning Design and User Interface/User Experience in MOOC Virtual Learning Environments?* Unpublished Masters Dissertation, UCL.

Jaggars, S. S. (2011). Online learning: Does it help low-income and underprepared students? CCRC Working Paper No. 26. Assessment of Evidence Series. *Community College Research Center, Columbia University* (26). Retrieved from http://proxying.lib.ncsu.edu/index.php?url=http://search.ebscohost.com/login.aspx?direct=true&db=eric&AN=ED515135&site=ehost-live&scope=site.

Jaggars, S. S. (2014). Choosing between online and face-to-face courses: Community college student voices. *American Journal of Distance Education*, 28(1), 27–38. https://doi.org/10.1080/08923647.2014.867697.

Jones, D. (2004). *Technology Costing Methodology Handbook, Version 2.0*. Retrieved from Boulder, CO, USA: https://wcet.wiche.edu/wp-content/uploads/sites/11/2021/07/TCM-Handbook-1.pdf.

Jones, L., & Cunliffe, P. (2020). *Saving Britain's Universities: Academic Freedom, Democracy and Renewal*. Retrieved from https://www.cieo.org.uk/research/saving-universities/.

Judd, C. M., & Kenny, D. A. (1981). Process analysis: Estimating mediation in treatment evaluations. *Evaluation Review*, 5(5), 602–19.

Jusoor (2022). Azima: Determined to learn. Retrieved from https://jusoor.ngo/Program-page/refugee/62/Azima:-Determined-to-Learn.

Kaplan, R. S., & Anderson, S. S. (2004). Time-driven activity-based costing. *Harvard Business Review*, 1–9.

Ke, Z., & Ng, V. (2019). *Automated Essay Scoring: A Survey of the State of the Art*. Paper presented at the Twenty-Eighth International Joint Conference on Artificial Intelligence (IJCAI-19).

Kelly, G. (1955). *The Psychology of Personal Constructs Vol.1, A Theory of Personality*. New York: Norton.

Kennedy, A. (2005). Models of continuing professional development: A framework for analysis. *Journal of In-Service Education*, 31(2), 235–50.

Kennedy, A. (2014). Understanding continuing professional development: The need for theory to impact on policy and practice. *Professional Development in Education*, 40(5), 688–97. doi:10.1080/19415257.2014.955122.

Kennedy, E., & Laurillard, D. (2019). The potential of MOOCs for large-scale teacher professional development in contexts of mass displacement. *London Review of Education*, 17(2), 141–58. https://doi.org/10.18546/LRE.17.2.04.

Kennedy, E., Laurillard, D., Horan, B., & Charlton, P. (2015). Making meaningful decisions about time, workload and pedagogy in the digital age: The course resource appraisal model. *Distance Education*, 36(2), 177–95.

Kennedy, E., Masuda, C., El Moussaoui, R., Chase, E. & Laurillard, D. (2022) Creating value from co-designing CoMOOCs with teachers in challenging environments, *London Review of Education*, 20(1), 1–15. https://doi.org/10.14324/LRE.20.1.45.

Kennedy, E., Oliver, M., & Littlejohn, A. (2022). 'You make yourself entirely available': Emotional labour in a caring approach to online teaching. *Italian Journal of Educational Technology*, 30(1), 30–48. doi:10.17471/2499-4324/1237.

Khalid, M. S., & Strange, M. H. (2016). *School Teacher Professional Development in Online Communities of Practice: A Systematic Literature Review*. Paper presented at the 15th European Conference on e-Learning, Aalborg University.

Kita, Y., Yasuda, S., & Gherghel, C. (2022). Online education and the mental health of faculty during the COVID-19 pandemic in Japan. *Scientific Reports*, 12(1). https://doi.org/10.1038/s41598-022-12841-x.

Kolowich, S. (2012, January 24). Stanford open course instructors spin off for-profit company. *Inside Higher Ed*. Retrieved from https://www.insidehighered.com/news/2012/01/24/stanford-open-course-instructors-spin-profit-company.

Krathwohl, D. R. (2002). A revision of Bloom's taxonomy: An overview. *Theory into Practice*, 41(4), 212–18.

La Velle, L., & Flores, M. A. (2018). Perspectives on evidence-based knowledge for teachers: Acquisition, mobilisation and utilisation. *Journal of Education for Teaching*, 44(5), 524–38. doi: https://doi.org/10.1080/02607476.2018.1516345.

Lantz-Andersson, A., Lundin, M., & Selwyn, N. (2018). Twenty years of online teacher communities: A systematic review of formally-organized and informally-developed professional learning groups. *Teaching and Teacher Education*, 75, 302–15. doi:10.1016/j.tate.2018.07.008.

Laurillard, D. (1979). The processes of student learning. *Higher Education*, 8(1), 395–409.

Laurillard, D. (2002). *Rethinking University Teaching*. London: Routledge.

Laurillard, D. (2007). Pedagogical forms of mobile learning: Framing research questions. In N. Pachler (Ed.), *Mobile Learning: Towards a Research Agenda* (Vol. 1, pp. 153–75). London: Occasional Papers in Work-based Learning, WLE Centre, Institute of Education.

Laurillard, D. (2007a). Modelling benefits-oriented costs for technology enhanced learning. *Higher Education*, 54, 21–39. Retrieved from http://www.springerlink.com/content/c176t337h7381n51/.

Laurillard, D. (2007b). Pedagogical forms of mobile learning: Framing research questions. In N. Pachler (Ed.), *Mobile Learning: Towards a Research Agenda* (Vol. 1, pp. 153–75). London: Occasional Papers in Work-based Learning, WLE Centre, Institute of Education.

Laurillard, D. (2008). The teacher as action researcher: Using technology to capture pedagogic form. *Studies in Higher Education*, 33(2), 139–54. https://doi.org/10.1080/03075070801915908.

Laurillard, D. (2012). *Teaching as a Design Science: Building Pedagogical Patterns for Learning and Technology*. New York and London: Routledge.

Laurillard, D. (2016). Foreword. In J. Dalziel (Ed.), *Learning Design: Conceptualising a Framework for Teaching and Learning Online*. New York: Routledge.

Laurillard, D. (2022). Foreword. In M. Smith & J. Traxler (Eds.), *Digital Learning in Higher Education: COVID-19 and Beyond*. Cheltenham, UK: Edward Elgar Publishing Ltd.

Laurillard, D. (2023). The role of governance in opening up digital innovation in teaching and learning. In P. Shroff, J. Sheth, J. Garrison, & S. R. Mehta (Eds.), *Global Governance Futures: Digital Transformation and Democratic Reform*. Delhi, India: Routledge.

Laurillard, D., & Kennedy, E. (2020). MOOCs and Professional Development. In Claire Callender, William Locke and Simon Marginson (Eds.), *Changing Higher Education for a Changing World* (pp. 157–170). London: Bloomsbury Publishing Plc.

Laurillard, D., Kennedy, E., & Wang, T. (2018). *Learning at Scale for the Global South*. Quezon City, Philippines. Retrieved from http://dl4d.org/portfolio-items/learning-at-scale-for-the-global-south/.

Laurillard, D., Charlton, P., Craft, B., Dimakopoulos, D., Ljubojevic, D., Magoulas, G., … Whittlestone, K. (2013). A constructionist learning environment for teachers to model learning designs. *Journal of Computer Assisted Learning*, 29(1), 15–30. doi:https://doi.org/10.1111/j.1365-2729.2011.00458.x.

Levin, B. (2013). To know is not enough: Research knowledge and its use. *Review of Education*, 1(1), 2–31. doi:10.1002/rev3.3001.

Levis, J. (2007). Computer technology in teaching and researching pronunciation. *Annual Review of Applied Linguistics*, 27, 184–202. doi:10.1017/S0267190508070098.

List, J. A. (2022). *The Voltage Effect: How to Make Good Ideas Great and Great Ideas Scale*. London: Penguin Random House.

Littlejohn, A. (2020). Seeking and sending signals: Remodelling teaching practice during the Covid-19 crisis. *ACCESS: Contemporary Issues in Education*, 40(1), 56–62. https://doi.org/10.46786/ac20.8253.

Littlejohn, A., & Hood, N. (2018). *Reconceptualising Learning in the Digital Age: The [Un]democratising Potential of MOOCs*. Singapore: Springer. https://doi.org/10.1007/978-981-10-8893-3.

Littlejohn, A., Gourlay, L., Kennedy, E., Logan, K., Neumann, T., Oliver, M., … Rode, J. A. (2021). Moving teaching online: Cultural barriers experienced by university teachers during Covid-19. *Journal of Interactive Media in Education*, 2021(1):7, 1–15. https://doi.org/10.5334/jime.631.

Liyanagunawardena, T. R., Kennedy, E., & Cuffe, P. (2015). Design patterns for promoting peer interaction in discussion forums in MOOCs | Open Education Europa. *ELearning Papers* 42(7), 1–16. Retrieved from http://openeducationeuropa.eu/en/article/Design-Patterns-for-Open-Online-Teaching-and-Learning-Design-Paper-42-7?paper=170920.

Lo, M. N., Marton, F., Pang, M. F., & Pong, W. Y. (2004). Toward a pedagogy of learning. In F. Marton & A. B. M. Tsui (Eds.), *Classroom Discourse and the Space of Learning*. Mahwah, NJ: Lawrence Erlbaum Associates.

London, M. (2020). *The Oxford Handbook of Lifelong Learning, 2nd edition*. Oxford, UK: Oxford University Press.

Ma, N., Li, Y.-M., Guo, J., Laurillard, D., & Yang, M. (2022). A learning model for improving in-service teachers' course completion in MOOCs. *Interactive Learning Environments*. doi:10.1080/10494820.2021.2025405.

Macgilchrist, F. (2020, June). Three stories about edtech after the corona pandemic. *TECHLASH*. Retrieved from http://der.monash.edu.au/lnm/wp-content/uploads/2020/06/TECHLASH-01-COVID-education.pdf.

Macia, M., & García, I. (2016). Informal online communities and networks as a source of teacher professional development: A review. *Teaching and Teacher Education*, 55, 291–307.

Malee Bassett, R. (2020). Sustaining the Values of Tertiary Education during the COVID-19 Crisis. *International Higher Education, Special Issue*, 102, 5–7. Retrieved from https://www.internationalhighereducation.net/.

Malee Bassett, R., & Anderson, J. (2021). *Tertiary Education Systems and Diversification: Adapting the Wisdom of Burton Clark to the World Bank's Support for Effective and Inclusive Reforms*. Centre for Global Higher Education working paper series. University of Oxford. Retrieved from https://www.researchcghe.org/publications/.

Marginson, S. (2021a). Global science and national comparisons: Beyond bibliometrics and scientometrics. *Comparative Education*, 58(2), 125–46. doi:10.1080/03050068.2021.1981725.

Marginson, S. (2021b). *Heterogeneous Systems and Common Objects: The Relation Between Global and National Science*. Retrieved from Centre for Global Higher Education, https://www.researchcghe.org/.

Marginson, S., & Xu, X. (2021). *Moving Beyond Centre-periphery Science: Towards an Ecology of Knowledge, Working paper No. 63*. Retrieved from Centre for Global Higher Education, Department of Education University of Oxford, https://www.researchcghe.org/publications/.

Marton, F. (1994). Phenomenography. In T. Husen, & T. N. Postlethwaite (Eds.), *International Encyclopedia of Education* (2nd). Oxford: Pergamon.

McAndrew, P., & Weller, M. (2005). Applying learning design to supported open learning. In R. Koper, & C. Tattersall (Eds.), *Learning Design: A Handbook on Modelling and Delivering Networked Education and Training*, 281–91. New York: Springer.

McKinley, D. C., Miller-Rushing, A. J., Ballard, H. L., & al. (2017). Citizen science can improve conservation science, natural resource management, and environmental protection. *Biological Conservation*, 208(April), 15–28. doi:10.1016/j.biocon.2016.05.015.

McVitty, D., Jackson, A., & Hutchens, B. (2021). Students' experiences of study during Covid-19 and hopes for future learning and teaching. Retrieved from https://wonkhe.com/wp-content/wonkhe-uploads/2021/02/Wonkhe-Pearson-expectation-gap-II-Feb-2021.pdf.

Mikołajczyk, K. (2022). Changes in the approach to employee development in organisations as a result of the COVID-19 pandemic. *European Journal of Training and Development*, 46(5/6), 544–62. doi:10.1108/EJTD-12-2020-0171.

Milligan, C., & Littlejohn, A. (2014). Supporting professional learning in a massive open online course. *The International Review of Research in Open and Distributed Learning*, 15(5). https://doi.org/10.19173/irrodl.v15i5.1855.

Mintchev, N., Baumann, H., Moore, H. L., Rigon, A., & Dabaj, J. (2019). Towards a shared prosperity: Co-designing solutions in Lebanon's spaces of displacement. *Journal of the British Academy*, 7(2), 109–35. Retrieved from https://doi.org/10.5871/jba/007s2.109.

Moore, H. L. (2015). Global Prosperity and Sustainable Development Goals. https://doi.org/10.1002/jid.3114.

Morrison, C., & Dearden, A. (2013). Beyond tokenistic participation: Using representational artefacts to enable meaningful public participation in health service design. *Health Policy*, 112(3), 179–86. https://doi.org/10.1016/j.healthpol.2013.05.008.

Murunga, M. (2022). Public engagement for social transformation: Informing or Empowering? *Environmental Science and Policy*, 132, 237–46. doi:10.1016/j.envsci.2022.02.03.

Nanda, V. P. (2016). The journey from the millennium development goals to the sustainable development goals. *Denver Journal of International Law and Policy*, 44(3), 389–412.

NCIHE (1997). *Higher Education in the Learning Society* (NCIHE/97/850). Retrieved from London: http://www.educationengland.org.uk/documents/dearing1997/dearing1997.html.

Nicholls, A. (2010). The legitimacy of social entrepreneurship: Reflexive isomorphism in a pre-paradigmatic field. *Entrepreneurship Theory and Practice*, 34(4), 611–33. https://doi.org/10.1111/j.1540-6520.2010.00397.x.

Nicolini, D., & Roe, B. (2014). Surfacing the Multiple. In T. Fenwick, & M. Nerland (Eds.), *Reconceptualising Professional Learning*, 67–81. Abingdon: Routledge.

Noddings, N. (1999). Caring. *Counterpoints* (Vol. 70, pp. 42–55). Bern, Switzerland: Peter Lang AG.

Noddings, N. (2012). The caring relation in teaching. *Oxford Review of Education*, 38(6), 771–81. https://doi.org/10.1080/03054985.2012.745047.

OCDE (2018). *The Future of Education and Skills: Education 2030. OECD Education Working Papers*. Retrieved from http://www.oecd.org/education/2030/E2030 Position Paper (05.04.2018).pdf.

OECD (2021). Micro-credential innovations in higher education: Who, what and why? *OECD Education Policy Perspectives*, No. 39. Paris: OECD Publishing. doi:10.1787/f14ef041-en.

OfS (2021). *Office for Students: Consultation on Our Strategy for 2022-25*. Retrieved from https://www.officeforstudents.org.uk/publications/consultation-on-ofs-strategy-for-2022-25/.

Oliveira, G., Grenha Teixeira, J., Torres, A., & Morais, C. (2021). An exploratory study on the emergency remote education experience of higher education students and teachers during the COVID-19 pandemic. *British Journal of Educational Technology*, 52(4), 1357–76. https://doi.org/10.1111/bjet.13112.

Owens, T. L. (2017). Higher education in the sustainable development goals framework. *European Journal of Education*, 52(4), 414–20. https://doi.org/10.1111/ejed.12237.

Pang, F. P., & Marton, F. (2003). Beyond "lesson study": Comparing two ways of facilitating the grasp of some economic concepts. *Instructional Science* (31), 175–94.

Parker, N. (2008). The Quality Dilemma in Online Education Revisited. In T. Anderson (Ed.), *The Theory and Practice of Online Learning* (pp. 307–32). Edmonton, Canada: AU Press, Athabasca University.

Pask, G. (1976). *Conversation Theory: Applications in Education and Epistemology*. Amsterdam: Elsevier.

Peel, K. L. (2020). Professional dialogue in researcher-teacher collaborations: Exploring practices for effective student learning. *Journal of Education for Teaching*, 47(2), 201–19. doi:org/10.1080/02607476.2020.1855061.

Perry, W. G. (1970). *Forms of Intellectual and Ethical Development in the College Years*. New York: Holt Rhinehart and Winston.

Pherali, T., Moghli, M. A., & Chase, E. (2020). Educators for change: Supporting the transformative role of teachers in contexts of mass displacement. *Journal on Education in Emergencies*, 5(2), 147–75. https://doi.org/10.33682/gtx6-u5q8.

Phipps, L. (2021). Learning from students and staff during the pandemic: A talk for #ESLTIS21. Retrieved 14 July 2022, from https://lawriephipps.co.uk/learning-from-students-and-staff-during-the-pandemic-a-talk-for-esltis21/.

Picton, C. (2022, May 6). King's College London ditches online-only classes following student anger – as government threatens universities with massive financial penalties. *Mail Online*. Retrieved from https://www.dailymail.co.uk/news/article-10788957/Kings-College-London-ditches-online-classes-announces-return-face-face-lessons.html.

Pipa, T., Rasmussen, a., & Pendrak, K. (2022). *The State of the Sustainable Development Goals in the United States*. Retrieved from Washington, US: https://www.brookings.edu/wp-content/uploads/2022/03/2022_Brookings_State-of-SDGs-in-the-US.pdf.

Powell, K., Helm, J. S., Layne, M., & Ice, P. (2012). Quantifying online learning contact hours. *Administrative Issues Journal: Education, Practice, and Research*, 2(2), 80–93. *Administrative Issues Journal: Education, Practice, and Research*, 2(2), 0–93. Retrieved from https://dc.swosu.edu/cgi/viewcontent.cgi?article=1054&context=aij.

Ria, S., Cox, M. J., Quinn, B. F., San Diego, J. P., Bakir, A., & Woolford, M. J. (2018). A scoring system for assessing learning progression of dental students' clinical skills using haptic virtual workstations. *Journal of Dental Education*, 82(3), 277–85. doi:10.21815/JDE.018.028.

Richardson, E., Macewen, L., & Naylor, R. (2018). *Teachers of refugees: A review of the literature*. Retrieved from https://www.educationdevelopmenttrust.com/EducationDevelopmentTrust/files/8e/8ebcf77f-4fff-4bba-9635-f40123598f22.pdf.

Robinson, J. P., Winthrop, R., & McGivney, E. (2016). *Millions learning: Scaling up quality education in developing countries.* Retrieved from Washington, DC, USA: https://papers.ssrn.com/sol3/papers.cfm?abstract_id=3956210.

Rode, J., Kennedy, E., & Littlejohn, A. (2022). Gender and the lived body experience of academic work during COVID-19. *Learning, Media and Technology,* 47(1), 109–24. https://doi.org/10.1080/17439884.2022.2031214.

Rosati, F., & Faria, L. G. D. (2018). Business contribution to the sustainable development agenda: Organizational factors related to early adoption of SDG reporting. *Corporate Social Responsibility and Environmental Management,* 26, 588–97. doi:10.1002/csr.1705.

Rosendale, J., & Wilkie, L. (2021). Scaling workforce development: Using MOOCs to reduce costs and narrow the skills gap. *Development and Learning in Organizations: An International Journal,* 35(2), 18–21. doi:10.1108/DLO-11-2019-0258.

Rowe, A. D., Fitness, J., & Wood, L. N. (2015). University student and lecturer perceptions of positive emotions in learning. *International Journal of Qualitative Studies in Educational Evaluation,* 28(1), 1–20. doi:10.1080/09518398.2013.847506.

Scardamalia, M., & Bereiter, C. (2006). Knowledge building: Theory, pedagogy and technology. In K. Sawyer (Ed.), *Cambridge Handbook of the Learning Sciences* (pp. 97–118). Cambridge, UK: Cambridge University Press.

Scheyvens, R., Banks, G., & Hughes, E. (2016). The private sector and the SDGs: The need to move beyond 'business as usual'. *Sustainable Development,* 24(6), 371–82. https://doi.org/10.1002/sd.1623.

Schmidt, D. A., Baran, E., Thompson, A. D., Mishra, P., Koehler, M. J., & Shin, T. S. (2009). Technological pedagogical content knowledge (TPACK). *Journal of Research on Technology in Education,* 42(2), 123–49. doi:10.1080/15391523.2009.10782544.

Schwartz, D., Bransford, J., & Sears, D. (2005). Efficiency and innovation in transfer. In J. P. Mestre (Ed.), *Transfer of Learning from a Modern Multidisciplinary Perspective* (pp. 1–51). Greenwich, CT: Information Age Publishing.

Seeber, M., Barberio, V., Huisman, J., & Mampaey, J. (2017). Studies in higher education factors affecting the content of universities' mission statements: An analysis of the United Kingdom higher education system factors affecting the content of universities' mission statements: An analysis of the United Kingdom. https://doi.org/10.1080/03075079.2017.1349743.

Selwyn, N. (2020, June). Digital education in the aftermath of COVID-19: Critical concerns & hopes. *TECHLASH.* Retrieved from http://der.monash.edu.au/lnm/wp-content/uploads/2020/06/TECHLASH-01-COVID-education.pdf.

Shah, D. (2020). *Capturing the Hype: Year of the MOOC Timeline Explained. Class Central.* Retrieved from https://www.classcentral.com/report/mooc-hype-year-1/.

Sharples, M., & Ferguson, R. (2019). *Pedagogy-informed Design of Conversational Learning at Scale.* Paper presented at the CEUR Workshop Proceedings, 2437.

Sherman, N. (2020, June 2). Zoom sees sales boom amid pandemic. *BBC News.* Retrieved from https://www.bbc.co.uk/news/business-52884782.

Shulman, L. S. (2005). Signature pedagogies in the professions. *Daedalus*, 134(3), 52–9.
Smith, M., & Traxler, J. (Eds.). (2022). *Digital Learning in Higher Education: Covid-19 and Beyond*. Cheltenham, UK: Edward Elgar Publishing Ltd.
Sorros, J., Karagiorgos, A., & Mpelesis, N. (2017). Adoption of activity-based costing: A survey of the education sector of Greece. *International Atlantic Economic Society*, 23, 309–20. doi:10.1007/s11294-017-9640-1.
Star, S. L. (1989). The structure of ill-structured solutions: Boundary objects and heterogeneous distributed problem solving. In L. Gasser, & M. Huhns (Eds.), *Distributed Artificial Intelligence* (pp. 37–54). San Mateo, CA: Morgan Kaufmann.
Star, S., & Griesemer, J. (1989). Institutional ecology, 'translations' and boundary objects: Amateurs and professionals in Berkeley's Museum of Vertebrate Zoology, 1907–39. *Social Studies of Science*, 19(3), 387–420. doi:10.1177/030631289019003001.
Stegeager, N., & Thomassen, A. O. (2021). Guest editorial: Sustainable organisational development. *Journal of Workplace Learning*, 33(3), 149–54. doi:10.1108/JWL-04-2021-195.
Taylor, R., & Watson, D. (1998). *Lifelong Learning and the University*. London: Routledge.
Tett, L., Cree, V. E., & Christie, H. (2017). From further to higher education: Transition as an on-going process. *Higher Education*, 73, 389–406. doi: 10.1007/s10734-016-0101-1.
UNESCO-ICHEI (2022). *Research Report on Digital Transformation of Higher Education Teaching and Learning*. Beijing: UNESCO-ICHEI. Retrieved from https://en.ichei.org/Uploads/Download/2022-05-16/62820a2a9bceb.pdf.
UNESCO (2020). *Education for Sustainable Development: A Roadmap*.
UNHCR, UNICEF, & World Food Programme (2021). Vulnerability Assessment of Syrian Refugees in Lebanon. Retrieved from https://data2.unhcr.org/en/documents/details/90589.
UNHCR (2022). Lebanon Fact Sheet. Retrieved 17 May 2022, from www.unhcr.org.
UNICEF (2016). In war-torn Syria, three million children out of school or at risk of dropping out. Retrieved 31 October 2022, from https://news.un.org/en/story/2016/10/543542.
United Nations (2013a). *Corporate Sustainability and the United Nations Post-2015 Development Agenda*. Retrieved from www.unglobalcompact.org.
United Nations (2013b). *An Action Agenda for Sustainable Development*. Retrieved from https://sdgs.un.org/publications/action-agenda-sustainable-development-17672.
United Nations (2021). *The Sustainable Development Goals Report*. Retrieved from https://unstats.un.org/sdgs/report/2021/The-Sustainable-Development-Goals-Report-2021.pdf.
USDoE (2014). *The Future Ready District: Professional Learning through Online Communities*. Retrieved from Washington, DC.
Walji, S., Deacon, A., Jawitz, J., Small, J., & Jaffer, T. (2018). Understanding how participants use open online courses for transitions. Paper presented at the

International Conference on e-Learning, Kidmore End. https://www.proquest.com/conference-papers-proceedings/understanding-how-participants-use-open-online/docview/2081756392/se-2?accountid=14511.

Weiss, C. (1997). How can theory-based evaluation make greater headway? *Evaluation Review* 21(4), 501–24.

Wenger, E., Trayner, B., & De Laat, M. (2011). *Promoting and assessing value creation in communities and networks: A conceptual framework Rapport 18.* Heerlen: Dutch Ministry of Education, Culture and Science.

Wenger, E., White, N., & Smith, J. D. (2009). *Digital habitats: Stewarding technology for communities.* Portland, OR: CPsquare.

White, D., Warren, N., Faughnan, S., & Manton, M. (2010). Study of UK online learning (October), 82. Retrieved from: http://www.hefce.ac.uk/media/hefce/content/pubs/2010/rd1710/rd17_10.pdf.

Williams, J. R. (2021). Designing for the margins: Addressing inequities in digital learning starts with hearing and engaging the student voice. *Change: The Magazine of Higher Learning.* https://doi.org/10.1080/00091383.2021.1850118.

World_Bank (2020). *The World Bank Group Partnership Fund for the Sustainable Development Goals. Annual Report 2020.* Retrieved from https://documents1.worldbank.org/curated/en/654371599038705862/pdf/World-Bank-Group-Partnership-Fund-for-the-Sustainable-Development-Goals-Annual-Report-2020.pdf.

Wuestman, M. L., Hoekman, J., & Frenken, K. (2019). The geography of scientific citations. *Research Policy*, 48, 1771–80. doi:10.1016/j.respol.2019.04.004.

Yang, J., Schneller, C., & Roche, S. (2015). *The Role of Higher Education in Promoting Lifelong Learning* (ISBN 978-92-820-1194-2). Retrieved from https://uil.unesco.org/lifelong-learning/policies-database/role-higher-education-promoting-lifelong-learning.

Young, C., & Perović, N. (2016). Rapid and creative course design: As easy as ABC? *Procedia – Social and Behavioral Sciences*, 228(June), 390–5. https://doi.org/10.1016/j.sbspro.2016.07.058.

Zaidi, A., & Beadle, S. (2018). Review of the online learning and artificial intelligence education market, (July).

Zarb, M., Alshaigy, B., Bouvier, D., Glassey, R., Hughes, J., & Riedesel, C. (2018). An international investigation into student concerns Regarding transition into higher education computing. Paper presented at the ITiCSE '18 Companion, Larnaca, Cyprus.

Zimmerman, B. J. (2000). Attaining self-regulation: A social cognitive perspective. *Handbook of Self-Regulation*, 13–39. https://doi.org/10.1016/B978-012109890-2/50031-7.

Index

Abu Moghli, Mai 141, 155, 239
accessibility 54, 79, 173, 186 (*see also* disabled students)
acquisition (in learning) 17, 18, 20, 96, 168, 216 (*see also* teachers' concepts)
active learning 17, 20, 28, 91, 92
   professionals 65, 78
   multiple choice questions 93
   student workload 84, 96
   teacher workload 85
   cost-benefits 99–100
activity-based costing 87–9
Africa 9, 39, 40, 142, 160, 215
Akkerman, Sanne 141, 204, 229
Anderson, Terry 8, 229, 239
anxieties
   student 49, 53, 84
   teacher 43–4, 47
applied learning 67–9, 72, 81, 115
applied value 144, 146, 162, 164, 180–2, 190
assessment 3, 62, 65–7, 93, 149, 194
Azima programme 173

basic skills 208–9
blended learning 38–40, 84, 113, 146, 161, 181
boundary objects 141, 159, 205
Bronfenbrenner, Urie 155, 160, 163, 165, 167

cameras on/off 45–6
caring pedagogy 44–6, 48–9, 58, 84, 116, 157
cascade model 144, 185–6, 211
case studies
   in CoMOOCs 116–7, 121, 129, 161, 162, 168–9, 181, 197–198
   online learning during pandemic 38, 127
   professional learning 111–2, 187, 206–207
   impact 142–148, 150

Chase, Elaine 141, 155, 163, 234, 239
chat 46, 62, 216, 224
China 38, 194
chronosystem 155–6, 170
citizen science 113, 197–9, 201, 215
classroom 16, 27, 32, 41, 49, 92, 156
   extending learning beyond 90, 94, 140, 168
   lack of 162
   sharing practice 125, 175
co-design 107, 109–117, 121, 127–9, 156–7
   equity 207
   process 159–162, 176
   SDGs 206
   Theory of Change 179–201
   video 122
collaboration
   community 34, 127, 138, 175, 204–5
   definition 216
   learning 19, 22, 32–3, 91–2, 96, 107, 110, 114, 117–9, 128, 163
   professional development 3, 5, 13, 139
   researchers and professionals 8, 116, 141, 143, 150, 154, 160–1, 191
   universities 6, 38, 39, 142, 190
community
   learning 2, 53, 77, 80, 93, 161
   learner's 165–7, 170, 176
   participatory research 113
   stakeholders 113, 115, 122, 193
   teaching 1, 13, 25, 30, 39, 84, 144–9, 160, 169, 171, 175, 185
   knowledge building 25, 33–4, 102, 116, 121, 126–8, 136–49, 176, 179, 195–200
Community Based Research: Getting Started 118, 207, 215
CoMOOC
   critical design features 121, 140–1
   case study examples 142–3, 145–8, 157–167

compassion 47, 53–5
computers 16, 42, 156
Conversational Framework 16, 18, 20–9, 79, 117, 142
    ABC workshop 159
cost-benefits balance 11, 49, 84–106, 210
Course Resource Appraisal Modeller (CRAM) 90–3, 97, 101, 102
Coursera 76, 108
crisis contexts 6, 48, 54, 115, 127, 134, 151–2, 158, 162, 167–177, 183

Dalziel, James 24–25, 231
deep learning 10, 64, 79, 81
deep professional learning 107, 121, 123, 126, 129, 205
design science 9, 35, 121
digital devices 28, 39, 132, 166, 174
    professionals 127, 156, 172
    limited access 142, 161, 172
digital engagement 73, 77, 79, 107, 115, 121
digital infrastructure 58, 102, 113, 156
disabled students 54–5
discussion (in learning) 19, 23, 69–77, 107–9, 117, 123–129
    evidence of learning 165–6, 181
    structured 79, 118–21
    mentors 194

ecological systems theory 155, 160, 163, 165
EdTech industry 58, 173, 176
EdX 108
Edraak 97, 117–8, 121, 126, 142, 160, 193, 199
Egypt 38
El Moussaoui, Rym 114, 167, 231, 234
emergency situations 102, 107, 127, 132, 151, 170
    professional development 72, 109–10, 115, 154
    technology and learning design 154–7, 167, 174
emotion 22–3, 44, 54
emotional labour 43, 48–50, 58
employee 2, 3–6, 132, 192
employer 3–6, 20
Entwistle, Noel 59–60
Equity 7, 10–13, 141, 149, 205, 207, 210
evaluation see Value Creation Framework
excitement 22, 23, 83, 168

face-to-face teaching 37, 43, 49
family 40, 48, 76, 155–7, 166, 172–4
feedback
    in learning 17–20, 22, 25, 29–30, 54, 62, 93–4, 98, 173, 181
    in MOOCs 66, 79, 84, 120, 132, 145, 161, 212
    on learning designs 26–8, 34, 92
    in teaching 50, 52, 169
fees 4, 76, 90, 98, 148, 199
Ferguson, Rebecca 117, 142, 232, 240
flexibility 42, 54, 55, 57, 84, 112, 205
formal learning 15
FutureLearn 33, 69, 76, 80, 117, 118, 121, 124–5, 145–7, 160, 192, 199, 215–6

gender 132, 134, 153, 165, 170
global challenges 6, 7, 107, 136, 153, 203, 205
Global North 157, 207
Global South 38–9, 76, 127, 152, 157, 207

health 3, 6, 39, 108, 115, 133–4, 176, 182–3, 194, 196
    mental 42, 75
human capital 3–4, 181

immediate value 144, 162, 163, 182
In-house training 7
    compliance 73, 75
inclusive learning 39, 64, 77 (see also accessibility)
Indonesia 38
Inquiry (in learning) 18, 21, 33, 94, 146
institutional support 25, 50, 83, 97, 101, 105
    support services 40, 85, 105, 152, 170
interaction online 17–20, 29, 39, 50, 57, 73, 80, 167, 168, 195, 205
    lack of 42, 54, 109
    teachers' needs 43, 45–6, 50, 52
    learners' needs 44, 53, 62, 73, 78, 79, 114, 119
internet bandwidth 41, 43, 112, 173, 174

Japan 42
Jusoor 116, 161, 172–5, 211

Kennedy, Eileen 42, 44, 48, 80, 83, 90, 113, 141, 154, 158, 163, 167, 182, 190, 194, 226, 234–6, 240

Index

Kenya 9, 39–40, 215
knowledge exchange 107, 139, 154, 187, 203–5, 208, 213

labour 4, 6, 43, 47, 49, 50, 149, 191, 212
   (*see also* emotional labour)
language 76, 77, 80, 113, 153, 160, 170
   discussion prompts 120, 181
   auto-translation 76, 208
   hegemony of English 208
Laurillard, Diana 9, 16, 21, 24–31, 35, 48, 59, 83, 88–90, 105, 113, 141, 149, 152–159, 163, 169, 182, 194, 209, 217, 219, 226, 234–237
learner-centred 34, 39
learners' experiences 46, 47, 49, 53–80
learners' needs 46–7, 50, 54, 59, 77, 111, 157, 175–6, 204
learning design
   concept 20, 24–5
   in crisis contexts 171–4
   examples 23, 30–32, 219–24
   rubric 29, 217
   workshops 27–28, 114, 158–9
Learning Designer (tool) 9, 25–35, 96–7, 101, 114–5, 128–9, 186, 219
   in CoMOOCs 141–8, 169, 191, 196, 205, 207, 211
Learning Management System (LMS) 83, 85, 93, 96
learning outcomes 29, 30, 89, 140, 162, 173, 189, 218
learning types 25, 29, 32, 119, 159, 164, 169, 171, 175
   definitions 18–23, 216
   in benefit-cost modelling 90–6
Lebanon 8, 12, 37, 56, 80, 107, 109, 113, 122, 142–3, 157–62, 167, 172–6, 190, 193, 207, 215
lifelong learning 2, 13, 111
   SDGs 38, 132, 135, 153, 208
Littlejohn, Allison 41–43, 71, 83, 111, 226, 234, 236, 238, 240
Lower Middle Income Countries (LMIC) 160, 183, 207

Ma, Ning 194, 200, 237
Malaysia 38
Marginson, Simon 6, 138, 143, 185, 196, 208, 237

MAPs (Muti-Aid Programs) 116, 161, 172, 174–5, 210–11
Marton, Ference 29, 60, 236, 237, 239
Mentimeter 166, 168, 226
mentors 72, 79, 103, 116, 125, 128, 146, 190, 194, 211
micro-credential 4, 38, 148
Middle East and North Africa (MENA) 37, 56, 142, 160, 193
Morocco 38
Moving to Online Teaching and Homeworking (MOTH) project 40, 42, 226
motivation 22, 70, 71, 109, 118, 200
multimedia 74, 77, 191, 216
music 74–5
Myanmar 12, 162

narrative structure 77, 79, 114, 117
Non-governmental organization (NGO) 113, 116, 158, 161, 166, 172, 174, 193, 198
Noddings, Nell 44–6
North America 63, 160

online teaching 42, 44, 45, 93, 121
   infrastructure 37
   emotional labour 47–53
   support for 55, 142, 145
Organization for Economic Cooperation and Development (OECD) 4, 238

Padlet 33, 80, 118–21, 126, 142–3, 147, 161, 164, 166, 168–9, 194, 211
Pask, Gordon 18
passive learning 59, 100
peer review 25–7, 30, 33, 66, 67, 88, 93, 98, 116, 121, 145, 147, 165, 196–8
Peru 38
phenomenography 60
Pherali, Tejendra 141, 155, 156, 176, 239
Pinterest 74
polling tools 114, 119, 142
postgraduates 40, 57, 70, 86
potential value 144, 146, 162–4, 180, 181
practice (in learning) 16–7, 19, 20, 22, 23, 24–6, 27, 31–2, 92–4, 97, 217, 222
production (in learning) 19, 21, 23, 66, 91, 95, 217

quiz 46, 66–7, 73, 94, 95, 99, 100, 108, 109, 118, 168, 181, 222
   concealed multiple choice questions (CMCQs) 93

rankings (university) 5, 136
realized value 144, 146, 162, 166–7, 172, 180, 182, 190, 191–2
reframing value 144, 147, 162, 166, 176, 180, 182, 192
refugees 137, 151–2, 158, 166, 170, 172, 207
RELIEF Centre 8, 80–1, 113, 117

self-regulated learning 55, 65, 70–1, 84–5, 96, 111, 156
signature pedagogy 20
situated learning 111, 206
social learning 10, 92, 112, 139, 156, 199, 206
   demand for 64, 69, 72, 77, 84
   challenge for teachers 50, 57
   digital support for 107, 114, 117, 126
social presence 121, 162, 181
Star, Susan Leigh 141, 159, 205, 241
stories 165, 168, 182, 187, 207
   value creation 162, 167
Sustainable Development Goals (SDGs) 1–2, 7–8, 12–3, 38–9, 131–150, 154, 176, 197–9, 203–8
   SDG 4 (education) 132, 135, 151, 153, 208–9
Sustainable Energy Access for Communities 116, 199, 215
synchronous learning 57
Syria 77, 151, 158

teachers' concepts 16–17, 128, 160
Teaching Online: Get Ready Now! 57, 142, 193, 211, 216
Thaki 166
Theory of Change 10, 13, 150, 157, 163, 176, 179, 184, 187, 189, 200, 209

transformative education 160, 170–1, 176
Transforming Education in Challenging Environments 116, 121, 157–172, 180, 190, 211, 215
Tutunji, Suha 174, 175, 193, 229

Udacity 108
Undergraduates 11, 40, 43, 77, 109, 191
United Nations Educational, Scientific and Cultural Organization (UNESCO) 37, 127, 154, 225, 227, 241, 242
United Nations High Commissioner for Refugees (UNHCR) 158, 241
university mission statements 5, 12, 13, 131, 133, 136, 152–3, 210
United Kingdom (UK) 4, 8, 9, 21, 40, 42, 45, 63, 148
United Nations Relief and Works Agency for Palestine Refugees in the Near East (UNWRA) 122

Value Creation Framework 133, 144, 162, 179, 180–1
video conferencing 41–2, 57, 62
vulnerable children 152, 157, 161, 176

Wenger, Etienne 140, 144, 162, 183, 242
WhatsApp 172–4
whiteboard 46, 52, 62, 73, 74
word cloud 28, 80, 114, 117, 118, 119, 121, 126, 161, 166–7, 181
workforce 5, 6, 24, 134
workload
   professionals 3
   teachers 83–7, 89–91, 93, 94–7, 101, 206
   learners 84
World Bank 137, 138, 149, 212, 237, 242

Zimmerman, Barry J. 70, 111

Printed in the USA
CPSIA information can be obtained
at www.ICGtesting.com
LVHW012123270224
772659LV00041B/298